THE LIFE AND DEATH OF KID CURRY

THE LIFE AND DEATH OF KID CURRY

Tiger of the Wild Bunch

Gary A. Wilson

TWODOT®

GUILFORD, CONNECTICUT
HELENA, MONTANA

A · TWODOT® · BOOK

An imprint and registered trademark of Rowman & Littlefield

Distributed by NATIONAL BOOK NETWORK

British Library Cataloguing-in-Publication Information available

Library of Congress Cataloging-in-Publication Data available

ISBN 978-1-4422-4739-0 (paperback)
ISBN 978-1-4422-4740-6 (e-book)

Contents

Dedication

To my grandchildren, Dallas, Kylie, and Jeren.

To Barney White, who died before we could do our Seattle book.

To Englishman Robyn Hode, a thirteenth-century Yorkshire bandit, who later became the sixteenth-century Robin Hood of Sherwood Forest, west of Nottingham. With this man began the tradition of outlaw legends and myths.

Tyger! Tyger! burning bright,
In the forests of the night,
What immortal hand or eye
Dare frame thy fearful symmetry?

William Blake (1757–1827),
English poet and painter

Foreword

The violence of Montana's gold rush of the 1860s has provided rich fodder for historians and writers. The deeds of the early vigilantes, still controversial today, have received more than their due. But later on in the 1880s, another period of lawlessness in Montana spawned cattle rustlers and gunmen with an equally violent history. Seasoned writer Gary Wilson, whose *Outlaw Tales* and *Long George Francis: Gentleman Outlaw of Montana* first brought this time period to an enthusiastic general readership, has once again proven that eastern Montana and its infamous bad guys are an equal match for the bad guys of the gold rush.

Set in Montana's rugged northern landscape, where rustling and brand altering were common livelihoods during the last decades of the nineteenth century, this book brings a little-celebrated area of the state to the forefront. Wilson writes vividly of the Little Rockies and the hidden places he knows so well. One-fourth of the book is set in Landusky, a little town with a large history.

For readers who loved Wilson's *Outlaw Tales of Montana*, here is the rest of the story that began with its final chapter, "The Outlaw Kid Curry and the Gentleman, Abe Gill." Researching the death of Pike Landusky for that story revealed how disparate was the information on Kid Curry, and Wilson determined to remedy it. That launched a ten-year search to gather all the available information into one place.

After a decade of meticulous research, Wilson's *The Life and Death of Kid Curry* finally brings the thrilling, complicated story of Harvey "Kid Curry" Logan to the reading public. Historical sleuthing brought bits and pieces of Logan's life together for the first time. Over the past century many contributed information to the pot, but the contents had never been mixed into that final delectable mélange. The facts were there but muddled with myth: a tidbit here, an episode there. Scattered information in unexpected places led Wilson across the United States in search of answers to his questions. Until now, the life of Kid Curry was a confusing picture of conflicting information, with the dots waiting to be connected. Years and years of collecting, comparing, documenting, and scrutinizing have made Wilson an authority on Kid Curry.

But Logan's life is not just an exciting story, filled with real characters who step out of the pages to draw the reader into the West of the late nineteenth and early twentieth centuries. *The Life and Death of Kid Curry* goes way beyond a good story and examines the life of this hard-bitten outlaw from an unbiased point of view. This is not an easy task. Wilson admits that Logan had very few, if any, good qualities. Still, he is one of those enigmatic characters that pique the curiosity, provoke discussion over the campfire, and prove without a doubt that history is not dead.

Wilson speculates that if Logan had survived, he would have been compelled to become honest. Instead, he served as executioner of the Wild Bunch, and had several killings under his belt to prove it. The Kid, a gunman with fine-tuned skill and uncanny precision, held a grudge for years until he could get even. He always got his man and never looked back.

Much that has been written about Harvey Logan is unsubstantiated and undocumented. It is not an easy task to sift through a century of legend and hearsay, sorting truth from fiction. *The Life and Death of Kid Curry*, however, gets the story right. In presenting a picture with all the parts, Wilson has made a major contribution to the history of the West. Here at last is the definitive study of the elusive Harvey Logan. And

Wilson not only gets the story right, he does so masterfully, producing an accurate history, a good story, and a good read at the same time. In so doing he has proven that the past is worth exploring, and history worth reading.

Ellen Baumler, Ph.D.
Montana Historical Society
Helena, Montana

Ellen Baumler is the interpretive historian for the Montana Historical Society and an award-winning author. She teaches history classes at the University of Montana-Helena, College of Technology.

Acknowledgments

Since this book is an expansion of a chapter of my previous book *Outlaw Tales of Montana,* many of the same people in its Acknowledgments need to be thanked again.

Others who contributed in an important way to this manuscript are: Daniel Buck of Washington, D.C., Earl Hofeldt of Montana, James O. Miller of Colorado, Russell Morehouse of Washington state (grand nephew of Arda Logan), Nate Murphy of Montana, Mollie O. Palmer of Florida, Jim Spangelo of Montana, and Colin Taylor of Wyoming. Taylor, over the years, has sent me a virtual encyclopedia on northern Wyoming history. Sharon Moran, grandniece of Lonie Logan, worked with me as we pieced together the scant but valuable materials and memories left behind by the Logan-Landusky-Moran family members.

And per usual, I am eternally grateful to the Havre-Hill County Library staff, who provided valuable research materials and enthusiasm, especially Francine Brady, the reference librarian. If there was any way at all of finding obscure reference materials, she could do it. I also appreciate the information sent to me by Holly Klingman, Parachute, Colorado, Library manager.

Also, since this book research covers an eleven-year period, many of the writings of Jim Dullenty have been helpful; Jim was the longtime editor and founder of the Western Outlaw Lawmen Association. And realistically, without the earlier publications by the likes of James Horan, Charles Kelley, Charles Siringo, Walt Coburn, Brown Waller, Larry

Pointer, Anne Meadows, Sylvia Lynch, Donna Ernst, Richard Patterson, Helen Duval-Arthur, and many others, this would have been a poor book indeed.

I am also grateful to the government, private, and public organizations—too many to mention here—who generously allowed me access to research materials.

Finally, thanks to God Almighty, who gave me this book in spite of it not being in my plans. Thy will be done!

While I have had many, many people to thank for their assistance, the ultimate responsibility for the facts and interpretations of history in this book rests with me. And that is always a heavy burden.

I hope I have played some small part in the preservation of western history.

Gary A. Wilson
Bull Hook Siding (Havre), Montana

It was the morning of December 27, 1894, in the Montana mining town of Landusky on the southern edge of the Little Rocky Mountains. Two days before, the community had celebrated Christmas with a lively dance and feast. It was the first Christmas since the community of twenty-some, false-fronted log cabins and crude clapboard houses had been officially organized, plotted, and named. The buildings sat near the banks of Rock Creek where it left the mountains to begin its southern journey to the Missouri River.

The snow-covered streets were empty except for a few men who had gone into the Jake Harris saloon and store. The clock on the wall showed it was about 10:30 a.m. Some of those who had enjoyed the wild and alcohol-soaked festivities had gathered in the saloon to escape the winter weather.

The proprietor, "Jew" Jake Harris, was tending bar as usual, using his sawed-off shotgun in place of one of his crutches. His leg had been amputated too close to his body to allow an artificial limb. Harris had lost his leg in a shoot-out with the Great Falls marshal, George Treat, and received a year in the state prison after some time in Helena's St. Peter's Hospital.

Tubercular Charles Hogan, a reputed gunman from Anaconda, Montana, was in the store part of the building, having placed his revolver under the counter. Others, including town founder Powell "Pike" Landusky, were either at the bar or playing a game of whist at a table. A young man named Mike Duke was cleaning wet ashes out of the potbelly stove so a welcome fire could be started.

Landusky, the first major discoverer of gold in the region, was pouring himself the first drink of the day when in walked Lorenzo "Lonie" (often erroneously spelled "Lonnie") Curry and ranching partner, Jim Thornhill. (Some inventive writers have claimed that Pike was already drunk the morning when he faced Harvey, but the facts do not support this story.) Lonie Curry and Thornhill continued on to the store section, ignoring Landusky and engaging Hogan in conversation. They bought a quarter's worth of apples just to keep Hogan busy.

Shortly, Harvey "Kid Curry" Logan came in through the front door. Johnny, brother of Harvey and Lonie, barred entry to the outside front door, rifle in hand. Harvey headed directly for Landusky, but "Pike" showed no outward acknowledgment of the Kid's presence. Thornhill and Lonie moved the disarmed Hogan forward and directed Harris to drop the scatter gun he was using as a cane.

Kid Curry reached Landusky, and without a word, slapped him hard on the back with his left hand, making Pike spill the whiskey and drop the bottle. As Landusky turned to meet his opponent, he received a hard, right-hand blow to the chin that dropped him to the crude wooden plank floor. In a battle silent but for grunts and groans and heavy breathing, the much bigger (but older) Landusky held his own at first—almost gouging out Curry's eyes until Curry twisted and rolled Landusky off. Now the cowboy, Kid Curry, was on top, pinning the miner's arms to his sides with his knees and hitting him in the face at will.

During the some five-minute fight, Thornhill and Lonie warned the others to stay out of it or they would be dealt with, although they pulled no weapons. Curry's weapon fell out of his coat pocket during the fierce battle, and Thornhill picked it up. He held it barrel first so he could not be convicted of assault.

Finally Landusky's friend and mining partner, Tom Carter, pleaded with Lonie and Jim to stop the Kid, but he was told to stay out of it. Pike, himself, finally pleaded for Curry to stop, and Thornhill told him to let Landusky up. The tough saloon brawler had finally met his match, or was he playing possum?

Curry got up with blood on his face and an eye that was nearly swollen shut. Landusky, once standing, got his shaky balance by spreading his legs and wiped some of the blood off his battered face on a coat sleeve. Landusky reached into his coat pocket—presumably for a handkerchief—but instead pulled out a new fangled semiautomatic 1893 7.62-mm Swedish Burchardt pistol.

Landusky pulled the trigger twice, aiming point blank at Curry, but apparently Landusky hadn't chambered a round. Either that, or the pistol was defective. Before Landusky could get the gun operational, Thornhill threw Curry his Colt .45 revolver, telling him to shoot Landusky. In the split-second interim, Curry had pushed the arm holding Landusky's pistol to one side and pointed his own pistol, firing three shots at his adversary and hitting him twice in the chest.

By then most of the saloon occupants had exited out the back door. Some had stayed until the shooting began. Harris, minus his shotgun crutch, hobbled out the back door, only to fall headfirst into a snow bank. He shouted, "Don't shoot, don't shoot!" Thornhill replied that Harris wasn't worth the powder to blow him to hell.

Thornhill, Lonie, and Harvey went out the back door behind a trampling herd of men, and then waited for Johnny to bring the spring wagon and saddle horses around from the livery barn across the street. Carter asked for a saddle horse so he could go for the doctor at Harlem. One Curry apparently said no, but he was overruled. They took off in the wagon to their Rock Creek ranch some five miles south of town, their rifles on display.

When the others returned to the saloon, they found that Landusky was having convulsions and had lapsed into a coma. A few minutes later, neither Harris nor Robert Ferguson was able to feel a pulse. The discoverer of the Little Rockies gold bonanza was dead. The pistol he had brought from St. Louis had failed him. Supposedly, at the Harlem railroad station he had shown it to people, saying he would kill Kid Curry with it.

The men who witnessed this gruesome spectacle in part or whole were a diverse group. There were cowboys, miners, laborers, a sawmill operator, a mine developer, plus the young man cleaning out the stove. Names mentioned include George Allis, Tom Carter, Ed Skelton, Albert Mathews, William MacKenzie, E. E. Riegle, Joe Contway, and Harris and Hogan. In years to come, this short list would swell to include almost everyone in the territory.

Pike was buried on a hill above his ranch about one mile south of town. Since no minister was available, John Ritch conducted the service. He was a miner and future historian for the Little Rockies mining country. The Currys and Thornhill supposedly discreetly watched the funeral service and burial from a nearby hill.

The story of self-defense was soon overwhelmed by those describing cold-blooded murder, scenarios in which Landusky was shot down just because he reached for a handkerchief. The best of these stories had Curry entering another saloon, covered in blood, and celebrating the murder by buying drinks for all.

On December 31, an inquest was held by Chouteau County Coroner R. S. Culbertson. A jury ruled that Harvey Curry was guilty of murder. Lonie and Jim Thornhill were named as accessories. Johnny's name was added later. Brother-in-law, Leander "Lee" Self, was also initially implicated, although he'd been out of state at the time of the killing, visiting Missouri.

Harvey Curry had no intention of being arrested for murder, so he waited at Thornhill Butte, approximately four miles southwest of Landusky until Thornhill could raise the money to buy out his share of the horse ranch. Once he had the money, Curry went south to north-central Wyoming where he joined the Hole-in-the-Wall gang.

George "Flatnose" Currie was reportedly the leader of the large gang of rustlers who frequented the red-walled valley from which branches of the Powder River and its tributaries flowed northeast.

Lonie Curry and Jim Thornhill went to trial at Fort Benton in March of 1895 for being accessories to the murder of Pike Landusky.

They were acquitted, however, when District Judge Dudley DeBose ruled that the killing had been done in self-defense. After two trials Johnny got off with a fine for simple assault.

These rulings didn't stop Harvey "Kid Curry" Logan from eventually becoming the most wanted criminal in the United States at the beginning of the twentieth century, a degree of notoriety that not even Butch Cassidy or the Sundance Kid or other members of the "Wild Bunch" would obtain. Yet Kid Curry's life of crime couldn't last long, as the Wild West was rapidly disappearing. Even Cassidy eventually saw the handwriting on the wall and headed for South America.

By 1912 the outlaw period of western history was essentially finished. The myths and legends, however, were just beginning. And Harvey Logan would come to be seen as one of the era's most notorious outlaws. Perhaps only Jesse James—a man Kid Curry idolized—exceeded his reputation. James Horan, however, biographer for the Pinkerton Detective Agency, considered Curry the worst of worst.

Here is his story . . .

The Kentucky Beginnings

Harvey "Kid Curry" Logan was arrested near Knoxville, Tennessee, in December of 1901, after a brawl and shoot-out in a Knoxville saloon in the bowery red-light district. Curry shot two policemen in the process, escaping out the back door by jumping into a creek bed. When arrested a few days later, he gave his name as Charles Johnson, even though he had used William Wilson a few days earlier. At the time, he was wanted for several murders and train robberies, as well as a variety of other crimes he had committed over the course of his seventeen-year career. Curry also said he was born in Chelsea, Iowa, and that his family had left there in 1877 when he was ten years old. Curry also claimed his family were all alive, but did not say where they were located.

However, Pinkerton Detective Agency agents were able to identify him as the notorious outlaw and killer Harvey Logan. In spite of their identification, he never gave any further information about himself. Curry also denied that he had ever been in jail before, and he definitely wasn't a cowboy or an outlaw. However, Curry did brag to the other inmates that he had killed at least three men.

This is much closer to reality than the twenty to forty deaths he had been credited with, although the Powell "Pike" Landusky killing was the only defensive shooting in a legal sense. Anyone who chased or crossed him for any reason was fair game.

If the authorities had checked his Iowa story, they would have found it wasn't far from the truth. His story about his family members all being alive wasn't true. Certainly his mother and four of five brothers were dead. And of course he had been in jail before in at least three towns. And he had been a cowboy since 1884, plus a farmhand before that.

Harvey Logan's immediate Welsh-Scotch family has been traced back to Lewis and Fleming Counties of Kentucky. There their father, William Henry Neville Logan, was born in 1834, and their mother, Eliza Jane Johnson, was born in 1838. The records show that except for eldest son, James, born in 1860, the rest of the family members—including daughter Arda—were born in Iowa. Six baby girls died in childbirth, as well as mother Eliza in Gentry County, Missouri. William's death date cannot be substantiated, but it was probably in the 1890s, possibly of natural causes in prison for having committed the act of murder.

The 1870 census for Tama County, Iowa, showed that the Logan family lived near Richland with the nearest post office at Helena. Interestingly, given the number of lies Harvey Logan otherwise told, there is indeed a Chelsea in Tama County on the Iowa River between Marshalltown and Cedar Rapids. With James W. in tow came Denver Henry "Hank" Logan in 1862, Harvey A. in 1867, Arda A. in 1868, John A. in 1870, and Lorenzo "Lonie" D. in 1872.

The Logan family next moved to Gentry County in northwestern Missouri, another farming area noted for hogs, poultry, cattle, corn, oats, and soybeans. Their farm was located between the Grand and Platte Rivers. The Logans may have lived near Gentryville, south of the county seat of Albany. It is not clear, however, whether the whole family moved there together, or if son James and father William moved first. Apparently William had a wanderlust that got the best of him at times, and he would go off, supporting himself by doing carpentry work. Some sources have suggested that he actually abandoned the family, taking James, before he found them again in Missouri; probably through his sisters-in-law in Dodson, Missouri, or Kansas. Hence Eliza may have sold the Iowa farm and moved the family to their new home by herself. Missouri state census records for 1880 show William and James in the Albany, Gentry County seat, jail, but it not known what crime they committed.

Thus the published accounts that Eliza died on the way to Dodson, and the children had to bury her; or that the move was made because of her husband's death; or that the family remained at Dodson with Eliza remarrying and dying shortly after the marriage are not true. It is possible that these stories were gathered by the Pinkertons from various informants given that James Horan, official biographer of the Pinkerton Detective Agency, used them in his books. The Logans' mother died in childbirth in about 1876. She would have been about thirty-five years old. After her death, the children had to find a new home. Young Arda Logan may have been the one to contact their aunt Elizabeth Lee in Dodson about moving there. The town was then a separate community located on the southern edge of Kansas City, Missouri. It consisted of little more than a few houses, a general store, school, and church.

Arda apparently managed either to obtain train fare for the family's trip to Kansas City or they rode for free, thanks to a sympathetic conductor. Aunt Lee already had seven children and grandchildren at home, plus an American Civil War–disabled husband to take care of. Thus she was only able to take in the two youngest children. Harvey and Johnny are believed to have stayed at another sister's home in Marian County, Kansas. William and Lucy Norris lived near the town of Peabody, and they may have had a store in town in addition to the farm. It isn't known what happened to Hank, but since, at the age of fourteen, he was old enough to work, he may have been taken in at another farm as a laborer. Lucy Ann died in 1885, a year before her sister Eliza.

The Logan boys were said to be quite different in temperament. Harvey was reserved and talked slowly. Lonie was outgoing and mischievous. The smaller Johnny was apparently the only brother with lighter eyes, and he was impulsive and quick-tempered. Their older brother, Hank, was the level-headed one, attempting to keep the others in line, at least later when they were adults in Montana. The oldest brother, James, and their father, William, apparently traveled together doing construction work, and perhaps came to work on the Oklahoma Territorial capital at Guthrie and/or the new prison at McAlester. James lived in the Oklahoma Territory before moving to California. Elfie Dessery-Landusky-Logan stayed briefly with him. The father, by this time, was perhaps either dead or in prison as alleged by the family. James became a successful merchant in California, dying in the San Jose, California, area in 1925 when he was sixty-five years old.

The Lee family house, where some of the Logan boys had resided, was a two-story frame house on a small hill about three hundred feet back from the northwest corner of Dodson Avenue, now 86th Street, and Troost Avenue in Kansas City. The father, Hiram Lee, was said to have been an invalid who spent the summer months in his rocking chair on the front porch. Reportedly his condition was due to wounds received in the War Between the States. Their son, Robert E. Lee, was named after the Confederate States of America general Robert E. Lee to whom the family was related. The family may have lived earlier at Lee's Summit to the southwest, and earlier yet at Shawnee, a few miles farther west across the border in Kansas. Lee's Summit was the home of the Younger boys, part of the James brothers' gang; also near that area was the Dalton gang. They were part of the violent seven-year war between Kansas and Missouri over slavery. Missouri was the "slave state," populated by Southerners especially from Virginia, Kentucky, and Tennessee. General Sterling Price's Missouri State Guards were the main line of defense in Missouri for the Confederacy, while guerrilla outfits under Charles W. Quantrill, "Bloody Bill" Anderson, and George Todd did further damage in both states. It would be fair to say that the area where the Lees resided was heavily Southern in sentiment, and the romantic tales that came down from these actions surely reached the ears of Harvey Logan and his brothers, especially the heroic acts of the Jameses and Youngers. They would have also been influenced by the fact that the Union forces made the residents of several counties, including Jackson, abandon their homes and live in designated areas while the soldiers plundered the countryside. As author James Horan put it, "The border war is unparallel in our history for brutality and savagery ... "

Harvey's violent tendencies showed themselves early. As a young man, he reportedly almost killed another boy after a baseball game collision in which some racial remarks ensued. Harvey and his brothers were always tagged as being part Indian or black because of their darker, Welsh complexions. Harvey also supposedly stole a vintage American Civil War U.S. Navy Colt .44 from the town drunk. Soon the brothers and cousin Robert E. "Bob" Lee were shooting up the nearby woods. Another story described Harvey backing up the town constable against a shed and threatening to kill him if he came to the Lee house with another complaint from the neighbors about the boys' bad behaviors. The 1880 census showed Bob Lee was about twelve and Harvey about thirteen.

But happily for the mistreated lawmen, Harvey got the "Go West Young Man" fever in late 1883 or early 1884, joining brother Hank on a westward journey. (Harvey would have been about seventeen and Hank twenty-two.) At this point it isn't known where James and their father were located, whether still in Missouri or perhaps Wyoming. A few years later they were in Oklahoma Territory, according to Logan family stories.

Perhaps the stories they heard of the West were the brothers' reason for leaving Missouri, but they would have read tales of the Wild West too. Aunt Lee remembered that the Logan boys were quite addicted to the dime store novels and weeklies about the action-packed West. These publications glorified outlaws as a Robin Hood class who lived a grand and romantic life.

According to author Frank R. Prassel, between 1901 and 1903, the Street and Smith Publishing House, alone, sold six million copies of 121 Jesse James novels. The outlaws were also the favorites in plays and even one production appearing on New York City's Broadway.

This desire to be good/bad guys would result in the violent deaths of two of the brothers and a disputed death of a third brother. However this wasn't true with brother Hank, who had his own reasons for leaving Kansas-Missouri. Unfortunately, Hank would die an early death and leave his brothers with no one to control them except Harvey's partner, Jim Thornhill, who was a former outlaw himself.

We can only imagine the many sights the boys took in during their trek west. They probably stopped at some of the old cow towns of Kansas that they had heard and read about, especially Dodge City on the Arkansas River. There they could have walked on the same rough boardwalks that had seen the likes of Wyatt Earp, Luke Short, William Barclay "Bat" Masterson, Wild Bill Hickok, and Bill Tilghman. They possibly traveled farther south to Caldwell, the border queen town, which would survive the banning of Texas longhorns in the now agrarian Kansas. Caldwell became the toughest town in the state with the most notorious saloon and dance hall, appropriately called the Red Light.

It is quite possible that the boys hooked up with a cattle herd being driven west and north, parallel to the Texas Panhandle from somewhere near Belton, Texas, on the Brazos River. This route was called the Goodnight-Loving Trail, and it followed the Pecos River to Fort Sumner, New Mexico, going to Las Vegas up the old Santa Fe Trail then through Raton Pass to Trinidad and finally Pueblo, Colorado. Another Texas trail went through the Oklahoma Territory and along the eastern portion of Colorado through Granada and Trail City, again terminating in Pueblo. It was not uncommon for herds to winter there on the Arkansas River and move to Denver for sale in the spring.

This is country that Harvey Logan would become more familiar with in later years as the outlaw safe lands began to dramatically shrink.

According to family history, when Hank and Harvey left the hay, grain, and cornfields behind, Hank left something else as well: a wife. (He might have been the one to change their name to Curry, in order to escape her.) Apparently she had given him a social disease, which he took as proof of her adultery. Where the name Curry came from, whether from a long-ago family member or neighbor, a county in New Mexico, or a currycomb, it's not known—though it is hardly the only fact about their lives that is a mystery. (Some sources claim it came from George "Flatnose" Currie, but this is almost certainly wrong.)

We don't hear from the Curry brothers again until they arrive in Pueblo, where they may have spent the winter with a cattle herd.

Either way, at some point, they got into trouble at a roadhouse or hog ranch on the outskirts of town. As one writer put it, "They left with a lot of lead flying." Former Pinkerton Detective Agency operative Charles Siringo first mentioned it in his 1919 book, *A Lone Star Cowboy*. Siringo spent several years tracking Logan and the Wild Bunch.

If the brothers did move on to Denver with a cattle herd in the spring, they saw one of the most substantial railroad, agricultural, and mining centers in the West. It was a city that Harvey came to like for its fine clothing shops, restaurants, hotels—and its large red-light district with several elegant parlor houses, according to Denver historian Mike Flanagan. The famed Holladay Street establishments covered a four-block area. Drinks and piano music were featured downstairs in plush surroundings of velvet and satin, and of course, the lighting was provided by crystal chandeliers. No swearing was allowed, and clients were only admitted who had been referred there. One such establishment, owned by Jennie Rogers, was a mansion three stories high with three parlors and fifteen bedrooms. Another famous resident madam was Martie Silks. Here on Holladay Street Harvey found high society, admiration, and servants to wait on him and serve apricot brandy.

From Denver, they could have gone north to Wyoming, picking up another cattle herd from Ogallala, Nebraska, the new queen of the cattle towns. Their final destination then would have been Miles City, Montana, along the Bozeman Trail, to the east of the Big Horn

Mountains and northeast along the Tongue River into Montana.

One leg of this journey, according to some inventive writers, included the future, legendary Hole-in-the-Wall outlaw valley where they supposedly first met George "Flatnose" Currie, the soon-to-be horse and cattle stealing king of Wyoming. Located some thirty miles west of the main north-south road (the old Bozeman Trail, now US 25) between Buffalo and Casper, the area consists of a north-south valley about thirty-five miles long with a colorful, rugged red-stone canyon wall on the east side, and the Big Horn Mountains to the west and part of the north. The Middle and Red Forks of the Powder River penetrate in several places, connecting with the Powder's tributary, Buffalo Creek, and its feeders, Blue, Beaver, Spring, and Willow Creeks.

The main entrance to the valley is roughly thirty miles west of the town of Kaycee. The trail parallels the Middle Fork and later the Red Fork, and passes through a canyon of black rock. Farther west, red rock is first encountered. Here is a supposedly narrow V-shaped notch in the wall, just wide enough for two horsemen or a wagon to pass through. (According to Wyoming historian, Colin Taylor, however, the "narrow" gap is actually about two hundred yards wide. Barnum Gap, as he calls it, has the waters of Beaver Creek running through it.) Just northwest of the confluence of Buffalo Creek and the Middle Fork stood the "town" of Barnum, consisting of a post office, store, and two cabins. This is probably the most famous entrance because it is identified with the old K-C ranch, a mile east of the town of Kaycee "on the south bank of the Middle Fork on a dry, barren rise" (according to a local Chamber of Commerce publication). This was a place used by the rustlers—especially horse thieves—who wintered stock in the valley before selling them in the spring. Cattle could be rustled from the Bighorn River Basin to the west and sold in the spring at railroad shipping points. The Union Pacific tracks were about a two-day ride from the valley, and Casper and Sheridan were both about sixty-five miles away.

South of this famous entrance was the way to a famous outlaw cave that likely offered security and protection to various gangs. And south again was what was probably the most used entrance, a narrow passage that led to the one-time outlaw ranch near where Spring Creek joins Buffalo Creek. Here were about six one-room cabins, a barn, and corrals. In outlaw mythology this was a complete town, made up of all outlaws and their women. And because Butch Cassidy had a cabin on Blue Creek south of old Barnum for a short period of time, this area is also mixed into a mythology that he shares with Harry "The Sundance Kid" Longabaugh and Etta Place.

The valley within a valley was once an inland prehistoric lake, and while the wall to the east acted as a protective barrier of sorts, the valley's real protection came from the threat of being killed if outsiders tried to enter. The area only became ranching country after the army drove the Indians out, culminating with a battle on the Red Fork north of what would become Barnum. In November of 1876, troops of the Fourth Cavalry and Twenty-third Infantry attacked a camp of Northern Cheyennes and Arapahos under Dull Knife and Little Wolf, driving the natives out of the valley and Big Horn Mountains.

Perhaps the now-named Curry brothers had heard of the valley on their way north to Montana, but it would have been basically empty at the time, except for perhaps a few legitimate ranchers who were eventually driven out by the outlaw element. However, they certainly would not have heard of George "Flatnose" Currie yet. It would be a few years before the young man, born in Canada and raised in both northwestern Wyoming near the town of Hulett and in Chadron, Nebraska, would return to the Rockies to begin his outlaw career.

The brothers' next stop was believed to be Miles City. They might have arrived with or without a northern cattle herd, but certainly not with a herd of stolen horses from Hole-in-the-Wall (as has elsewhere been written). Miles City was an important railroad stop for the Northern Pacific Railroad. There was a major army post, Fort Keogh, nearby. The south side of Main Street wasn't exactly a Holladay Street in Denver, but there was a solid block of primitive saloons, gambling dens, and brothels.

Perhaps the brothers could have found work in Custer County, but they were directed northwest toward the vicinity of newly established Fort Maginnis. Cattle were being moved from the overstocked Judith River basin into the Flatwillow Creek and Musselshell River country.

They arrived in 1884, not long before Fergus County was founded. The major gold strikes at Maiden and other strikes in the Judith Mountains had prompted the new county's establishment. The brothers were apparently directed to contact F. M. "Dad" Marsh at Rocky Point, a community perched on the cliffs above the south Missouri River. Originally the cabins were occupied by wolfers, trappers, buffalo hunters, and whiskey traders. There was one hotel, a restaurant, a general store, two saloons, a blacksmith, a feed stable, a warehouse, and ferry point across the river. Several rustlers made it their headquarters. Marsh furnished ranching supplies, and he was an unofficial employment agent for cowboys, besides supposedly being on the payroll of the ranchers as an informer on the activities of various rustlers.

The brothers apparently hit it off with Marsh, because he directed them to the Circle Bar cattle outfit of Hawes, Strevell, and Miles although it may have been late in the season. This was an English company with its brand registered in Miles City. Their round-up headquarters was on Crooked Creek, just south and east of Rocky Point. Foreman Johnny Lea, an ex-Texan, put them to work with his crew in the Judith Basin Cattle Pool, which in 1883 had over six hundred thousand cattle.

This pool allowed them to become acquainted with some major ranchers, including the famous Granville Stuart of the DHS, Robert Coburn of the future Circle C, James Fergus of the Fergus Cattle and Land Company, as well as future celebrity cowboys, Con Price, Charlie Russell, and Teddy "Blue" Abbott. In Abbott's classic biography, *We Pointed Them North: Recollections of a Cowpuncher* (written with Helena Huntington Smith), he says that he was an admirer of Hank Curry: "He was a fine fellow, always quiet, well-behaved and liked by his fellow cowboys."

Hank called his brother the "Kid" and the name stuck. As long as he was around, Hank exercised good control over his younger, more violence-prone brother. Harvey "Kid Curry" Logan had a tough man's reputation, and he was very strong for his build. He was about five feet seven and a half inches and 160 pounds, quick on his feet. Law officers later would say he had incredible strength and was very fast on the draw. Hank was the bigger of the two, but he was considered easy going. They were both admired for their horsemanship and roping abilities. Their features were dark, which again led to speculation about their race.

Near the time of the two brothers' arrival into Montana, local cattlemen were in the midst of cleaning up rustlers along the Yellowstone and Missouri Rivers. A group of outlaws lived in old cabins whose previous occupants had supplied wood for the steamboats plying the rivers. They stole horses on both sides of the international border and sold them in the opposite country. A group of vigilantes killed about fifteen of these men and ran many more off. Their work was concluded by the time the Currys arrived, but Harvey should have learned a lesson from it.

The brothers are believed to have returned home after the cattle were shipped. They surely had a lot to tell about the Wild West. They returned to Rocky Point, staying the winter, cutting and hauling forty cords of wood for the riverboats at eight dollars per cord. Thanks to Marsh, the boys—or at least, Hank—learned to read and write. Harvey and his younger brothers might have already had more schooling than Hank.

In the spring of 1885, the brothers returned to the Circle Bar ranch, ready for a full season of work. By 1886 the ranchers association had received permission to graze their thousands of cattle north of the Missouri River. One of the crew was a cowboy called Jim "Jimmer" Thornhill, who claimed to be from Jackson County, Missouri, (his descendents, however, have not found the name Thornhill in that part of Missouri) where the Lee family lived. A friendship with Harvey was apparently sealed when Thornhill, helping swim cattle across the cold, swift waters of the Missouri near Rocky Point, was knocked off his horse. Thornhill wasn't a swimmer, and he soon went under. Harvey had seen the accident, and grabbed Thornhill by the collar, pulling him up on his horse and likely saving his life.

Rancher Robert Coburn and his sons entered the lives of the brothers when Coburn bought the DHS ranch at Beaver Creek, on the east side of the Little Rocky Mountains and north along the boundary of the Fort Belknap Indian Reservation. Coburn had prospered in Helena's Last Chance Gulch and now went into the ranching business. During the famous, big die-up winter of 1887, he "only" lost 50 percent of his herd because of the shelter provided by the Little Rocky Mountains. To the southwest of the ranch were the two large timbered buttes that joined the south end of the mountain range. They were named for the Coburn family. To the north were the Milk River and the cow and railroad towns of Malta, Harlem, and Dodson. To the east were the Larb Hills and to the south, the Missouri River Breaks.

The ranch headquarters itself was quite vast, having a large number and variety of buildings. There was a residence for each Coburn (the family home was in Great Falls), a mess (kitchen) cabin, barns, a blacksmith shop, bunk houses, miscellaneous sheds, an icehouse, a meat-storage house, an office, and warehouses. On the east side of the Malta to Zortman trail were windmills, water tanks, a cow barn, and corrals. Across Beaver Creek were cattle sheds, feed bins, and a long, narrow reservoir from the dammed creek. They also had a post office and stage stop.

Thornhill and the Curry brothers both worked for the DHS and Circle C ranches. Harvey saved yet another life while working for the Coburns. Bob Coburn, while on a ride during a blizzard, had his horse stumble into a badger hole, breaking a foreleg. The horse had Bob trapped underneath, causing him a head injury and a broken jaw. When Harvey found Bob, he shot the injured horse and rolled it off him. He placed Coburn over his saddle and headed for the Circle C ranch house. From there he rode for a doctor, probably in Malta. He transported the inebriated physician in the ranch's buckboard, even though the doctor didn't want to go out in the storm. This act of bravery earned Harvey another friendship that would long endure.

The brothers also came to have reputations as top horsemen. The horse outfit part of the Broadwater and McNamara livestock outfit drove its animals from the Bear's Paw Mountains near Big Sandy to the Little Rockies, offering the brothers the opportunity to break the horses on a share basis. C. J. McNamara had built a ranch in the southwest corner of the Bear's Paw Mountains between the mountains and the river. He had over three hundred thousand fenced acres encompassing several creeks. The stable, fifteen hundred feet square, had thirty box stalls. He and "Colonel" Charles Broadwater supplied Fort Assinniboine and Fort Maginnis with goods, besides having a large warehouse in Big Sandy.

It was during this period of time, around 1886, that it is believed the brothers claimed land on Rock Creek, about five miles south of the future mining town of Landusky. The area had good grass, shelter from storms and numerous waterholes and flowing streams; plus the water possibly contained gold that had washed down from the mountains.

They also gained a touch more of civilization when the St. Paul, Minneapolis and Manitoba Railway came into Montana in 1887 along the Milk River. This meant the brothers no longer would have to cross the Missouri River to reach important services, like the doctor in Maiden. A stage line was also soon operating from both Harlem and Malta, brought on by the continuing gold discoveries in the Little Rockies. As the mining towns of Landusky and Zortman boomed, starting in about 1893, these stage lines hauled gold up and silver dollars back for payrolls.

The Curry boys' favorite watering hole seemed to be the saloon at Rocky Point. Marsh moved onto Big Sandy, on the Great Northern rail line, where the cattle business was booming and ran a hotel there. Life looked as if it was going to be good for the brothers, and their new partner, Jim Thornhill. The Curry clan prospered as more family members arrived. Johnny came from Missouri in the spring of 1888, going to work for the Fergus Land and Cattle Company. Lonie arrived about a year later to work for several ranches, including the Circle C and Circle Bar. Cousin Bob Lee also visited about two years later, but he apparently lived and worked in Cripple Creek, Colorado, as a miner and saloon employee during the winter. In 1889 Arda "Allie" came out from the Kansas City, Missouri, area with her husband, Leander "Lee" Self, and their two children. Allie had been twenty years old when she had married Self six years before. They brought twelve hundred dollars with them to invest in the new horse ranch (the money may have come from the sale of a farm they had just across the Kansas line near Stilwell in Johnson County), but Self was never happy in Montana, later saying that the brothers took his money and interfered with his marriage. Allie returned to Kansas City unhappy about everything. She soon divorced Self, and he never regained his status with his well-to-do family in Dodson.

In about 1889 a mystery uncle named Jefferson H. Curry appeared to file on mining water rights where the brothers's ranch was located near the conjunction of Warm Springs Creek and Rock Creek. He soon disappeared, leaving Harvey with access to more water in the same area. This alias could have been used by a variety of persons, including Harvey's oldest brother or even his father. Whomever Jefferson had really been, the boys now had fifteen hundred extra inches of legal water, complete with ditches to their property.

What more did they need?

As he was known to exclaim at least once, Powell Landusky came from "Pike County, Missouri, by God!"

In July of 1868 Pike set out from Missouri with a dozen or so friends to try and strike it rich in the Montana goldfields. But the wild Landusky got into trouble even before the riverboat had landed at Fort Benton, having terrorized the passengers and crew and challenged them to fistfights. Either his soon-to-be famous temper had gotten the best of him or he'd had too many drinks, or both. The aggressive, six foot, solidly built Polish-French Landusky and his rowdy friends must have made the trip quite uncomfortable for the other travelers.

Upon arriving at Fort Benton, the boat's captain complained to a vigilante group that happened to be in town on another mission. Pike must have calmed down, turned humble, and talked his way out of the tense situation in which he found himself. Hanging by the neck was not part of his plans.

Landusky hitched a ride south on the Mullan Road to the gold fields of the Helena area. Yet he hadn't learned his lesson and continued to fight anyone willing. But how could he learn a lesson when he kept winning?

Pike didn't find his bonanza in the Helena area, even if he was a bare-knuckle champion. He next moved on to another gold and silver strike in the Judith Mountains at Maiden(ville)—an area that once had six thousand inhabitants before the precious metals gave out. Sometime around 1878, Landusky became a trader in the Flatwillow Creek area. Pike and his partner Joe Hamilton (he went through a number of different partners) had three log cabins and a picket corral about seven feet high to protect the houses from Indian raids. They also had a cook and a young man to watch the horses to prevent rustling by Indians.

Cattle king Granville Stuart visited the area in 1880. Stuart was impressed with the variety of vegetables grown there and the deep, rich soil, but after surveying the county, he picked a ranch site to the north, closer to the Judith Mountains. An unwelcome soon-to-be neighbor was Fort Maginnis, but with the number of hostile Lakota Sioux and Blackfoot Confederacy warriors in the area and with a new source of supplies and mail, maybe it would be worthwhile putting up with the soldiers' antics.

Gardening and trapping beaver were probably better occupations for Pike than trading. He had scrape after scrape with the Indian parties, who also came to believe that he was at the least, an evil spirit. In his last confrontation, Pike had a portion of his jaw broken, leaving a large facial scar and some of his teeth missing. After ten days on a whiskey diet, he had the wound dressed by the doctor at Fort Maginnis but later had to have it rebroken and reset by another doctor at Maiden. None of this helped his disposition, either.

He had acquired this and other wounds at his trading post on Flatwillow Creek. Pike had been drunk and had decided to shoot into a Blackfoot camp, aiming to kill a leading warrior named White Calf. Instead, Pike killed a woman, and the returning fire shattered part of his jaw and inflicted other bodily wounds. Partners Johnny Healey and Joe Hamilton tried to stop him, but he wouldn't listen. This happened after Pike had knocked an Indian man down and thrown firewood at him, claiming the man had tried to stab him. He also attacked White Calf and Chief Running Rabbit. Though badly injured, Pike continued to fire until the Indian band was driven off.

Thanks to Pike, their lucrative trade had been destroyed, and the traders lost most of their horses to boot.

In an earlier episode, however, Pike had come out the winner. This happened on the Judith River where he had a confrontation with some Lakota Sioux. After he took them on with a frying pan, they hastily left his camp, leaving two ponies behind to appease the evil spirit that possessed him. He may have been provoked by something as simple as not wanting to share breakfast.

On another occasion, a trio of Lakota Sioux visited a camp he had in the same general area. Pike recognized two of them as being the ones who had stolen his trapping gear, pelts, and furs the winter before. Pike killed two of them with his axe, and chased the third across the frozen river before catching and killing him. He scalped all three men and placed their chopped-up body parts in a hole in the river. His partner, "Flopping" Bill Campbell, wisely decided to find a new partner and location.

In yet another episode, Pike had some Lakota Sioux visitors at his campsite during mealtime. One in the party made the mistake of reaching into his frying pan for a steak. Landusky threw him into the fire, then beat and kicked the others until they, too, escaped from the crazy one. So did his then-partner, John Wirt.

But the severe wounds he had acquired from the Blackfeet finally ended his trading career, and, around 1881, he returned to the mining town of Maiden to nurse his wounds. Apparently this recuperation didn't take long, as he was soon in the saloon, livery stable, and passenger/freight business, running a line between Maiden and the county seat of White Sulphur Springs. A former trading post partner, Joe Hamilton, joined the business.

By this time Pike had a reputation for violence. If he was drinking, even the smallest things could provoke a reaction. One curious man, after asking Landusky where he was from, was knocked to the floor, receiving the loud, boasting answer, "From Pike County, Missouri, by God!" On the other hand, Landusky's generosity to friends was also well known, as was his respect for women. The big social event in his life came when he married Canadian-born Julia St. Denis-Dessery in

Maiden's first wedding ceremony. The service was presided over by Justice of the Peace "Pony" McFarland. With Julia came an instant family of four daughters and a son.

Julia's family had come west from Lansing, Michigan, when she was about seven years old. She claimed to have walked barefoot most of the way with her older sister. Their destination was the goldfields on Cherry Creek near the new towns of Denver City and Aurora. Julia said in her memoirs that they were forced to leave because of problems with the Cheyenne. After briefly returning to Michigan, the family went west again in 1864, arriving first in Virginia City, Montana Territory, before moving on to the Gallatin River Valley to claim a homestead. Julia said that the valley was full of snow and game was scarce. Their livestock suffered from the lack of food because of the deep snowdrifts. In the spring St. Denis decided it was time to move again, and they headed for the gold fields in Virginia City and then Last Chance Gulch at Helena.

Unhappy with both places, they next operated a hotel in the vicinity of new gold strikes south of Deer Lodge, Montana, near the Continental Divide. They charged a dollar per meal. When the beds were full, they charged for floor space. Julia said she was working as a barmaid at the ripe old age of twelve. She weighed out gold dust for the drinks. Reportedly the miners liked young "Curley" and gave her generous tips.

But the St. Denis family had had enough of the West by 1867, and headed east again. At a place called Tonganoxie, near Kansas City, she was married off by her father to a man named Victor Dessery. Her new husband was a railroader, and he soon found a job in Shreveport, Louisiana. This first stop in Louisiana apparently accounts for some writers claiming that Julia came from that state. The couple next went to Leadville, Colorado. By then Dessery was working as a locomotive engineer, presumably with the Denver and Rio Grande Western Railroad. The next stop in his career took them to Denver, a place Julia had visited much earlier. A daughter was born to them in the Mile High City. Her legal name was Cindinilla Athanissa Dessery, but her pet name was "Elfie."

There were other children as well, and after their fifth baby, Laura or "Lollie," was born, Julia's St. Denis grandfather had died, so she and the children moved to his ranch near Lewistown, Montana, where their widowed grandmother still lived. Victor Dessery stayed in Denver to work but provided his family with railroad passes. Julia now had five children, Dora, Elfie, Lollie, Mary Alice, and Victor. She had apparently separated from her husband for good. In Montana she somehow became acquainted with Pike Landusky, perhaps while visiting Maiden.

Elfie had many memories of her early life in the Maiden, Missouri River, and Landusky areas. The only negative memory she had of the ranch was of oldest sister Alice carrying her while climbing up a tree above a steep cliff. Alice somehow broke her arm, and Elfie walked along the top of the cliff crying until help came. Her next memories are of her family living in Maiden with Pike after the marriage. Pike would come home from work and take Dora and Elfie on his knee, singing to them. She recalled visiting Grandma's ranch and being fed bowls of cream and riding on a hay wagon with her uncles. Daughter Julia was born before they left Maiden, making six children.

At one point Pike disappeared "for a long time." When he returned, he brought a buffalo for food. This would have likely been when his partners first discovered placer gold in the Little Rockies. His partners, Dutch Louie—Louis Myers—and Frank Aldrich, were sluicing for gold and each taking out about twenty dollars per day. Dutch Louie found the first gold in June of 1884. Supposedly Pike's partners had found inspiration to prospect after leaving the Missouri River Breaks just ahead of the vigilantes, who were hanging livestock thieves. This was about the time Harvey and Hank arrived in the Little Rockies, so they were on the scene for the first miners stampede.

Their gold find in the Little Rockies brought several hundred prospectors to the area. Landusky went to Maiden with the news, and Aldrich went to the post trader's store at Fort Assinniboine for supplies, further spreading the news. A mining district was formed, but it was short lived. The surface gold was soon gone and with it the two thousand or so men who had come to mine it. (Southwest of that mining activity, Pike and his partners had found a shallow mining pit near the mouth of Beauchamp Creek.)

Elfie remembered the move to Little Alder Gulch where the first strikes had been made. Pike and his partners had built a log cabin for his family so they wouldn't have to live in his bachelor's dugout quarters. The children played in the creek where the sluice boxes were located. Sometimes the children picked up nuggets, throwing them back to make a splash. Another experience with water wasn't as much fun: A cloud burst created a flash flood, filling the cabin and washing off the sod roof. They next moved to a ranch house out of the gulch, probably near the head of Rock Creek to the southwest where the future town of Landusky would be built. Pike had had problems with a claim jumper at the old location, even mistakenly pointing his revolver at the wrong bunch, which included his future son-in-law, Bob Orman.

Pike was prospecting on Indian land, but for the next three years he continued his search for the mother lode without interference from local soldiers. Another child, Charlie, was born in 1885. Julia said every fall they took a thirty-five-mile trip to Rocky Point for groceries at Marsh's store. Later when the road came west along the Milk River, paralleling the railroad, they shopped at Harlem, Malta, Chinook, and Havre.

Landusky had to do something to support his family during his gold searches, and he spent the cattle-killing winter of 1886–1887 between the Missouri and Milk Rivers, working for Granville Stuart's DHS Cattle Company. Meanwhile Julia had to persevere at the cabin with her children and new baby.

Working with Pike was the celebrated cowboy, Teddy "Blue" Abbott, who recalled in his autobiography that he got along fine with Pike, and didn't see much of his famous temper. (Abbott did describe Pike suffering that winter from his old jaw injury. It often left him with frozen slobber on his face.) But during one visit to Pike's cabin, where Abbott was also staying, Julia told Pike that she had thought some local Gros Ventre Indians camped near the cabin had insulted her. Pike went crazy, hitting, cussing, and threatening the Indians with death. Abbott said he just sat quietly on his horse, not knowing what else to do.

Abbott praised Pike for knowing the survival tricks of the trade and sharing them with Abbott. For example, for use as a fire starter, Pike carved pine splinters and soaked them in kerosene. He also wore layers of clothes that he could add or subtract from, depending on the weather. When Abbott ignored him about wearing something around his eyes to prevent snow-blindness, he suffered for it with a temporary vision loss. During a Christmas Eve snowstorm, the temperature dropped to minus sixty degrees. They were forever digging the poor pack mule out of the drifting snow. The pair tried to get home for Christmas but only made it to Johnny Healey's ranch near Lodge Pole Creek. Unfortunately the storm only grew worse, and they ate a Christmas of deer meat and plum duff.

Landusky and Abbott barely made it home with their worn-out animals. Their fingers were so numb and the ropes so frozen that it took a great effort to unload the packs. Julia stormed out of the cabin when she saw them approach and tore into Pike for not coming home for Christmas. He wisely kept silent until she finished, when he said she sure was in the lead when tongues were handed out. Abbott said that she was easily a match for Pike's temper.

After the belated Christmas celebration, Teddy Blue and Pike traveled north to the Milk River country, looking for rustlers that might be in the area. They found no one and, finally out of supplies, traveled to Rocky Point to take a break from the record winter. By spring more than 50 to 90 percent of several cattle herds were dead. The rivers, creeks, and coulees were full of carcasses.

Abbott thought well of Pike, finding him to be a good provider and someone who was kind to his family. He also thought that Julia was a good housekeeper and "a real nice little woman when she wasn't stirred up about something."

At one point Landusky went to the Black Hills, leaving his family in Montana. Luckily, he returned with some gold because Julia was quite upset with him for being gone so long. In his absence she had moved to a shack on Rock Creek near the future town of Landusky. Julia and Alice had built an addition onto the shack with the help of some miners, including Bob Orman, who eventually married the daughter.

The Landuskys' lives changed dramatically in August of 1893 when Orman and Landusky hit pay dirt. With his stake from the Black Hills, Pike had been able to mine full time. Having paused in their prospecting to go down the mountain to drink from a stream, Orman and Landusky were heading back up the mountain when they stopped to inspect an odd rock specimen. They took it home, crushed and washed it, and found a sliver of gold three inches long in the pan. They began vigorously working the site, mostly at night, taking the rock home so as not to alert the soldiers from Fort Assinniboine who half-heartedly patrolled the area. (The Indians of Fort Belknap later surrendered the mineral belt of the Little Rockies for $360,000. It amounted to $10 per acre. No land with grass or water was supposed to have been sold.)

The thread of gold eventually turned into a claim that produced as much as thirteen thousand dollars a ton on picked ore. It was rumored that they had obtained one hundred thousand dollars from a hole less than one hundred feet deep. Hence a more substantial miners stampede came to the area for the hard rock mining. By then Landusky had filed several claims throughout the mountains. Tom Carter of Helena became a partner at this point. Even Harvey Curry and his brother Lonie had filed mining claims.

Before the big hard-rock strikes, Elfie remembered Hank Curry riding about the county and stopping at their house. According to mother Julia, the Curry boys visited often, enjoying her cooking. For the first few years, the brothers were on good terms with the Landuskys. Hank and Lonie were apparently the main visitors, according to Elfie's memoirs. Harvey would come by and talk without getting off his horse, being rather quiet and reserved. Jim Thornhill must have had a good relationship, too, because he's in a picture with the family.

During a barn dance on the Currys' horse ranch, Elfie met Lonie for the first time. She found him to be young but was impressed with his fiddle playing.

Lonie and Johnny were running a saloon at Rocky Point but returned to Landusky after the big strike. Johnny built a livery barn in town, and Lonie ran a saloon near the mining gulch. This left Hank and Harvey to do most of the horse breaking for their horse ranch. Allie, her husband, Lee, and their two children showed up to claim some land between the brothers' place and Pike Landusky.

The bad blood between Landusky and Harvey seems to have begun in 1892 when Pike borrowed a plow from the brothers, returning it much later with a broken handle. The Currys returned the now useless plow to Pike's property, which Pike took as an insult. An increasing friction between cowboys and miners added to the problem. The miners and townspeople were justifiably upset because the cowboys liked to cause a ruckus in town, guns blazing.

But according to Elfie, things worsened when Hank began seeing the Landuskys' live-in schoolteacher, Mary Everett. By then the old home had become the milk house and a larger house had been built to include room for a teacher and visiting children and families. Pike even offered to pay Mary five hundred dollars not to go out with Hank one night. Mary refused the money, although she didn't see Hank again, either. In fact she had her sister finish out her contract so she could leave. When the brothers shot up some of Pike's outbuildings, that didn't really help calm the situation, either.

Meanwhile Kid Curry was gaining a reputation for being a tough man. Historian Gene Barnard related in the *History of Phillips County* that a neighbor's father, William Spenser, had had a run-in with him. Spenser had come to the Little Rockies in 1894, making his money from logging and building cabins. He lived to the east of Larb Hills, roughly south of Saco and Hinsdale. Spenser acquired a mare that was a fast racer. He entered it in several races, including a local Fourth of July race that also included Harvey Curry as a participant. Spenser won the pot, but Harvey was a sore loser. He roped Spenser around the arm, intending to drag him behind his horse. But then he stopped, took off the rope, and departed. Spenser turned around and saw his partner Ole Veseth with a rifle. Curry had known he would use it.

The longer the Currys were there, the more trouble they caused.

By the summer of 1889, Harvey and Hank were running their own ranching operation. The two younger brothers, Lonie and Johnny, were helping with the ranch as well as working in the saloon business. None of the Curry boys could have been called model citizens, except maybe for the older Hank. And Thornhill's outlaw background didn't lend itself to a good reputation, either. Neighbors said they never seemed to hurt for beef at their meals, although they were running a horse ranch.

At one point Johnny, the smaller brother with a lighter complexion (and one who also liked to call himself the "Kid"), got into a shooting match, coming out second best. His opponent was "a well-seasoned German ex-cowboy" who was described as a sheepherder and/or a prospector, perhaps named Olson. There are two versions as to their meeting. In the first version, Johnny shot up a flock of sheep while the unarmed Olson was hugging the ground. In the second version, Johnny made the man dance to the tune of his Colt .45 in the Rocky Point saloon. Either way, when they met up again on the Rocky Point–Zortman trail, Johnny's adversary had a rifle at the ready. Both fired, and Curry's horse was shot out from under him. Another rifle round struck him in the right arm as he was struggling to get to out from under the horse. Then a third round hit him in the right elbow, causing Johnny to pass out from the pain. The victor departed with only a bullet hole in his hat.

Somehow Johnny made it to his feet and either walked back to the brothers' ranch or, more likely, found his way to another ranch. The other brothers (or just Lonie) took him either to the Fort Belknap Indian agency or St. Paul's Mission where his wounds were dressed, and then he was taken to Harlem and loaded on a GNR train for a trip to the St. Clare Hospital in Fort Benton, the nearest medical facility. The doctors did their best to save the arm, but they had to amputate because the lower arm and joint were so badly shattered. Supposedly, the shooter disappeared before Harvey could get to him. But according to some, the Kid may have committed his first unrecorded killing. (Walt Coburn, however, biographer of the Coburn Circle C Ranch, maintains that Pike Landusky was Harvey's first killing.)

There is another unverifiable story that Harvey killed a miner because he called the Kid's mother a "quadroon" (mixed black-white racial makeup). However, this was probably the same fight that Harvey had with Pike Landusky, since no evidence exists of such a killing. Another story has Curry robbing the bank at Roy, Montana, and then hiding in the nearby town of Giltedge after his horse gave out. However, Roy didn't have a real population until the 1900s, after the homestead boom. By then Harvey was long gone and reportedly dead.

Johnny Ritch, then a miner at Landusky and later the area's historian, wrote that the Currys "would have never been successful at ranching because they wanted more to be gunfighters." Ritch said that the boys kept their ranch house as neat as a pin and that a table was kept on the porch for their guns. He further stated that they never went outside without being armed.

Since they liked to emulate the gunfighters of the eastern Montana region—and there were several—the brothers probably paid close attention to an attempted train robbery that took place west of Malta in November of 1892. (Actually they would have learned how *not* to rob a train.) The trio of bandits was led by Harry Alonzo "Sundance Kid" Longabaugh, who had gained his moniker for doing jail time in Sundance, Wyoming, for stealing a saddle, bridle, chaps, pistol, spurs, and a horse.

After climbing up on the front baggage car (it was a "blind" car, which meant it had no window) and then onto the engine tender and cab, Longabaugh, William Madden, and Harry Bass ordered the engineer to stop in approximately the same area where a later robbery committed by Harvey Logan would take place. They all proceeded to the express car and commanded the express messenger to open the door. Two of them entered while the third watched the train crew. The "local" safe contained only $19.02 in cash and a check for $6.05. Not having done their homework, they then ordered him to open the "through" safe, but he explained he did not have the combination, which was true. (A through safe could typically only be opened at the train's final destination.) Since the bandits had neither black powder nor dynamite, the caper was over. Longabaugh fled the area, but the two hapless, unemployed cowboys returned to town, where they were arrested. During the robbery, they hadn't even kept their masks on, so the lawmen had a good description of them.

The Great Northern Express Company offered a reward of five hundred dollars for Longabaugh's capture. The company's circular described him as being five feet eleven inches tall, with a dark complexion and a short dark mustache. He was about twenty-five years old, slender, with a slight stoop in head and shoulders. He had a short upper lip and exposed his teeth when talking. His teeth were white and clean with a small dark spot on the upper tooth to the right of center. Furthermore, during the robbery he had worn a medium-sized soft black hat, a dark double-breasted sack coat, dark, close-fitting pants, and blue overalls. The train crew had also described his horse as being a bay with a Half Circle Cross brand on the shoulder.

This was the most accurate description anyone would have of a future Wild Bunch member until about 1901, when the famous "Fort Worth Five" photo was taken. There would also be a photo taken of Etta Place and Longabaugh in New York City, before they left for South America.

From this experience we can assume that Harvey, along with the others, would have learned the right way to plan and execute a train robbery.

Meanwhile, back in the Little Rockies, people continued to take sides on whether the Curry boys were tarnished angels or part demons. Sheriff Sid Willis of Valley County said that the Curry boys were well thought of, and they had as good a start as any young men in the country. Marian T. Burke, a Little Rockies miner, thought highly of Lonie Curry. In the winter of 1893, Lonie had been a visitor to a miner's camp that included Burke. Out of their meager supplies, they had fed him dried venison and oatmeal porridge. Lonie told them to go to town and charge supplies under his name and come out to their ranch for a meal. Burke said there wasn't a woman on the premises, but the house was neat and clean for four bachelors. Burke also mentioned the guns on the table next to the washstand and their prowess with them. They showed him the best shooting Burke had seen in his forty-two years.

Some said that the Currys were okay until they started drinking heavily. But the drinking would increase with Hank's soon-to-be absence and subsequent death. Johnny tried in vain to be a tough guy and exhibited a tendency to be gun-happy. This led to not only the loss of his arm but also his early death.

Floyd Hardin, whose family settled in on the big bend of the Milk River in 1896, related some Curry brothers stories of his own in his 1972 history book, *Campfires and Cowchips*. Hardin knew a Joe Legg who had owned a horse ranch on the Tongue River and, in the winter, operated a blacksmith shop in the mining town of Maiden. Legg found a place on the Missouri River bottoms that he liked as a ranch site. At the same time another ranching operation had decided they wanted the same spot, because the Currys had laid claim to their first choice. Then the brothers tried to grab Legg's claim, too, so either way they could sell the ranch owners a piece of property. However, Legg was determined to hold the land, and he built a log cabin on the disputed property with gun ports on all sides. In the end the Currys lost both pieces of property and hence didn't make any money from their shenanigans.

Apparently there wasn't any lasting animosity over the affair, and Harvey visited the ranch frequently. However, it did annoy Legg that Curry would jump his horse over a board gate that was located close to the ranch buildings. This stunt resulted in damage to his gate every time. Finally Legg got out his old Sharps rifle and let fly with a few rounds. Since the range was beyond Curry's pistol's capabilities, he retreated— never to return.

Bill "Milk River" Harmon, a Little Rockies miner and former "bullwhacker" for the Diamond B Transportation Company, related in a 1935 newspaper article that it was a common occurrence for one or all three of the Currys to beat up some poor devil with their six-guns. Harmon described them as "mean, bull-dogging cusses."

Some of these encounters showed up in Chouteau County court records at Fort Benton. There were several assault charges leveled against the Currys (including a complaint filed by Jake Harris, Pike's bartender), but no jury would convict them, either out of fear or loyalty. The boys loved to ride into the saloon and shoot up at the ceiling. According to legend one of the Curry brothers once went through the floor and cellar of a saloon, horse and all. Another time the brothers reportedly broke up a Christmas saloon dance, smashing a guitar and breaking a piano. Apparently they either didn't like the music or Lonie wasn't invited to play!

In later years former Chouteau County District Judge Dudley Dubose had some insight into the brothers' behavior. Dubose said they did well in the livestock business, building up a cattle herd worth fifteen thousand dollars (actually, they had a herd of horses), but they were more interested in making it as bad men. This echoed Johnny Ritch's comments. Dubose saw them in his court many times for assault, but no jury would convict them.

An anonymous Lewistown-area rancher, probably cattle king James Fergus, said that Kid Curry was a little wild and somewhat restless but could be a true friend and would give a man his last dollar. He also added that the Kid always had his nose in pulp novels, reading about the likes of Jesse and Frank James and the Younger brothers of Missouri.

Judge Dubose considered Harvey Curry the best of the brothers and thought that the Kid might have turned out okay had he been separated from the bad men who infected that section of the country. Dubose didn't elaborate as to who these bad men were, but most likely they were part of those who had fled northcentral Wyoming during the rustler's war in the early 1890s. On the other hand Dubose had no use for Johnny or Lonie, calling them bad eggs.

Johnny had a falling out with F. M. "Dad" Marsh, and Marsh filed a civil suit against him. Johnny had not repaid a loan of $933.70 that he had used to build a livery stable in Landusky. Marsh apparently didn't hold a grudge against Lonie, however, joining C. J. McNamara in providing bail for Lonie after Landusky's killing. In Marsh's only written comments about Johnny, he said, "Johnny was a little fella who soon learned to pack a gun and wanted to be bad."

The feud between Landusky and the brothers soon escalated beyond the school teacher and plow incidents. The Lonie and Elfie relationship reportedly became more serious, the two meeting after dark. This did not suit Pike at all, since Lonie had a reputation as a ladies man. According to Walt Coburn, Pike "began to call Lonie a whore master and said that Kid Curry was a brand artist." Of course Pike didn't say this in a quiet manner, either. This escalating feud also tended to divide the population into two opposing camps: the miners versus the cowboys.

Hank's hold on the boys began to diminish because of illness. He reportedly had a bad cough and was spitting up blood. A Fort Benton doctor said he had consumption (tuberculosis) and walking pneumonia. Hank aggravated these conditions by pulling a cow out of a bog several miles south of the ranch during wet weather. The doctor told him that unless he moved to a dryer climate, he would die within the year. Hence Hank, at the age of thirty-one, entrusted his brothers to their twenty-eight-year-old ranching partner, James "Jimmer" Thornhill, a reputed past outlaw himself. From there, according to some sources, Hank set out for either Steamboat Springs or Glenwood Springs, later dying either on the trip or after he reached Colorado.

Older brother Jim moved on to Needles, California, after his wife left him. There, on the Arizona-California border, between the Colorado River and the Sacramento Mountains, James had apparently operated a store. Hank may have moved there to be with his older brother before dying. He is reportedly buried there. James eventually moved on to San Jose County where he died in 1925 at the age of sixty-five. He had been in the wholesale grocery business, peddling coffee, tea, and spices. He dropped dead while feeding his horses at a barn in the rear of his home. The obituary only mentioned a son in Los Angeles, but it was actually a daughter called "Lou." He also had a daughter named Cala, according to researcher Colin Taylor.

Hank's leaving the Little Rockies and his subsequent death permanently finished any chance the remaining brothers had of not following the outlaw life. And Hank's advice to be leery of Pike proved to be sound.

The brothers had surely heard the stories of Landusky's violent temper and how he would resort to any tactics to win. In 1885, for instance, Pike got into an argument with one of his mining partners, "Dutch Louie" Myers. Pike went back to his tent, stewed about it, and returned to Myers's tent, shooting him in the chest. Myers and another partner struggled with Pike, finally disarming him. Myers survived to file a complaint in federal court in Helena, and Pike was arrested by a deputy United States marshal. Pike was taken to Helena to post bond. There was no subsequent trial, so perhaps Pike and Myers patched up their differences, or Pike bought Myers out.

In Rocky Point, Pike had earlier fought with a man named Gallagher, who had challenged Pike's prowess. Landusky was losing the fight until he grabbed a revolver and pounded his opponent into submission—and then threw him into the Missouri River. When bartender Jake Harris tried to stop a fight in Pike's saloon, Pike objected, striking Harris with his cane, breaking two fingers.

The only person who stood up to Pike and suffered no injuries, besides his wife, was Warren Berry. Berry contracted to construct a log building for Pike. Berry had it six or seven logs high on blocks when Pike came to inspect it. Pike asked why it didn't have a foundation. Berry replied that he wasn't contracted to build a foundation. They argued until Berry lost his temper and tore the partial structure down. Pike finally agreed to do the foundation himself, but Berry said he was through with the project. Pike threatened him, saying he wouldn't get any more work in the area and might as well leave. "The hell you say," retorted Berry. "I'll be around here when you're in hell." (Pike died in 1894; Berry was still alive in 1935.)

The summer of 1894 was busy for the miners and businessmen of Landusky and Zortman, pushing the feud temporarily into the background. The *Helena Independent* and *Havre Advertiser* both proclaimed the goldfields of the Little Rockies as the next Last Chance Gulch. The town had four saloons, including one owned by a R. Curry, perhaps the first cousin, Robert E. Lee of Dodson, Missouri.

In June a town site was legally formed, although much of the gold being mined was on Indian lands (these lands were removed from the reservation in 1906 for a pittance). Landusky became the town's official name, even though the cowboys voted for Rock Creek. Pike established a post office at the saloon. Landusky became postmaster; and Harris, the assistant. Harris got in trouble with a postal inspector when the inspector saw Harris throw the mail in a pile on a pool table. Harris kicked him out. Landusky smoothed things over with the man and built a regulation post office.

Pike continued to tell anyone who would listen what he planned to do to Harvey and Lonie, such as killing them with his bare hands. That fall, he finally got to do something about it when Harvey and Lonie were arrested for assaulting one James Ross in Harris's saloon on October 5, 1894. Ross claimed that Harvey had held a shotgun on him while he was badly beaten.

The Currys disputed this, claiming Pike and Ross had made up the charges to frame them. Sheriff Jack Buckley came to Landusky and arrested the pair.

33

Apparently the brothers had been in town at the time because none of their friends knew of their arrest. Some historians claim that Buckley temporarily deputized Pike, putting Harvey and John in his custody until Buckley could execute other arrest warrants. However, Jack Buckley's brother, Phil, who worked both as a deputy and jailer, said in a 1960 *Great Falls Tribune* article that his brother had deputized a friend to watch over them for a few hours and that the unidentified man had then turned them over to Landusky. Buckley said his brother would never have allowed Landusky to guard them and that he also never forgave himself for what later happened.

But regardless of how it happened, they were now in Pike's custody, and he had a lot of hate to disperse. Landusky chained them in his milk house. Julia was not aware of this, and she sent Elfie in to get some milk. Elfie was surprised and embarrassed to see the brothers, although Harvey kidded her about watching out that a cat didn't get her milk. With the boys confined, Pike could afford to take his time and have a few drinks of whiskey before dispensing his justice. Landusky worked them over with his fists, then stomped and kicked them until he got tired. He spat tobacco in their faces, calling them all the vile names he could think of, including insults to their mother. Then Pike relieved himself on them. Bored with all that, he took out his knife and threatened to make eunuchs of them. Harvey told Pike that if he used the knife, he would be the first man the town ever lynched. Harvey demanded to be let go for a fair fight, but Landusky refused, believing that they were on their way to jail and so would finally be out of his hair. The Kid promised that they would meet again and that he would return the favor, only worse.

The boys survived the beating and, to Pike's chagrin, the assault charges as well. "Dad" Marsh said that Landusky felt remorse (or fear) after he calmed down. He even tried to regain the Currys' friendship but, of course, to no avail.

A big celebration was planned for the Christmas of 1894, although the pending showdown between Pike and Harvey was at the back of everyone's minds. There was a truce of sorts—if you don't count some of Pike's outbuildings being shot up—as the new community of Landusky celebrated its future as the gold capital of Montana. Johnny lent his new livery barn for a supper and dance, and Lonie agreed to play the fiddle with Al Wise on piano and banjo and another fiddler, Dan Moran. A rancher ten miles out of town volunteered the use of his wife's Mason and Hamlin organ that had previously only been used to play religious music. It arrived on an old ox cart.

John Ritch volunteered the use of his newly built Landusky cabin and cook stove for the preparing and serving of the meal. "Tie-up" George, the best round-up cook in the country, was hired to oversee the preparation but was under strict orders not to get drunk until the food was ready. Warren Berry, who had built most of the structures in the area—and survived an argument with Pike—insisted that they needed a meal more elegant than turkey and suggested an oyster banquet. The celebration committee commissioned the stage driver, "Lousy," to tele-graph the order. Lousy apparently thought oysters grew in Minneapolis, and he sent a telegram to the railroad agent there to order them. There are two versions of what the town received. First, they may have actu-ally received big, fresh, juicy Baltimore oysters packed in ice with a freight bill that exceeded the cost of oysters. Or they may have just received canned "Cove" variety oysters from a food-store shelf in Minneapolis. Whichever, they ended up with two wash boilers of oys-ter stew. The rest of the food and drink was provided by the participants and saloons.

Over one hundred people gathered for the two-day and two-night celebration. It was a big hit with those who attended. A no-guns regulation was enforced, and men left their weapons in the saloons with the barkeeps. Walt Coburn described people arriving on horseback, buckboard, dead X wagons, spring wagons, and top/buggies from as far away as Rocky Point and the old Fort Musselshell crossing. Coburn dis-agreed with the writer/researchers who claimed that some celebrants stayed on after the festival was over. Instead, he said, they departed right after the party, because people knew what was going to happen between Harvey and Pike.

Elfie danced with Harvey at the celebration, and she remembered that he was eating an apple, giving her a bite. Harvey said that "if it wasn't for that young brother of mine I might have a chance." Pike and Harvey had a quiet war of words at the dance, which according to Thornhill, Pike initiated. Pike again reiterated his threat to kill Harvey with his bare hands, and Harvey said he would give him the same treatment.

Before the celebration Pike had gone back to St. Louis to bring back several relatives and possibly friends to relocate in the mining area. He also brought back a new-fangled semiautomatic pistol—a 7.62 mm Swedish Burchardt—that he told people he would use to kill Kid Curry (apparently the bare-hands killing was out). Pike probably felt somewhat secure around Curry with Hogan and Harris to back him up, plus some friends. However, he hadn't figured on Thornhill and the other brothers planning on a confrontation as well.

Some writers continue to say that Harvey killed Landusky in a murderous rage, but it was Landusky who first went for his gun. Harvey had apparently been satisfied when Landusky had said he had enough.

Thornhill claimed he did his best to talk Harvey out of the fight but to no avail. The use of the law, the cowardly beatings, and disgraceful insults about his mother could not be ignored.

And so in Jake Harris's saloon, the bad blood between Harvey "Kid Curry" Logan and Powell "Pike" Landusky finally found its resolution. Harvey rose from the floor, bloodied and half-blind but victorious. Pike pointed a pistol at him, and Logan fired in retaliation.

Elfie would remember Pike's final days well. That evening she had seen Pike and wished him a Merry Christmas. She said Pike's face had lit up, and he had smiled.

The morning of his death, the family, including Pike, ate breakfast together. After Pike left for the saloon, the children went sledding on a nearby hill. When someone brought the news that Pike had been killed, they all gathered back in the house, sitting in stunned silence. Soon Pike's friends brought the body home and put him on the bed in the parents' bedroom. Elfie wrote that she slipped in every so often to look at him. The body stayed in the bedroom for a while because they were having a hard time digging a grave in the frozen earth. Elfie said there were lots of people at the gravesite service. They sang "Rock of Ages" and, in the absence of an ordained minister, Johnny Ritch read from a bible. There is a story that Harvey, Jim and the others watched the proceedings from a nearby butte, then returned to the ranch to figure out their future.

Harvey decided the best thing to do was sell his share of the ranch to Thornhill and head for Hole-in-the-Wall, Wyoming. The Coburns came to the rescue, buying horses from the ranch and providing the funds for Thornhill to buy out Harvey. Thornhill would have to start over again, establishing a new horse herd from scratch. He eventually became quite successful and respectable, buying more land and even serving on the local school board.

Harvey is believed to have stayed at Thornhill Butte until the deal with the Coburn family was complete. Perhaps if the local coroner's jury hadn't decided it was murder, Harvey might have stayed. Certainly, Harvey's move out of Landusky cannot be blamed entirely on his killing of Pike, since Harvey saw the outlaw life as more exciting and romantic than the tedious job of raising horses and mining for gold.

The trials of his brothers and Thornhill for their part in the killing of Pike occurred the following summer. Judge Dubose threw out the charges of accessories to murder filed against Thornhill and the two brothers. Only Johnny had to pay a fine for having a weapon displayed outside the saloon's front entrance. It's possible that Harvey might have actually remained until the trial, or at least returned at some point, because the following May, Valley County Sheriff Sid Willis claimed he ran into the Kid while looking for escaped prisoners along the Missouri River Breaks near the Musselshell River. Harvey had the sheriff cornered but put his revolver away when he saw it was Willis. Willis had been looking for some escaped prisoners from his Glasgow jail. Harvey told Willis to extend an invitation to Sheriff George McLaughlin of Chouteau County to come and get him. It is likely, though, that Willis kept to his own county's problems.

The loss of Landusky and the escape of Harvey Curry didn't affect the economy of either Landusky or Zortman. Stage driver Ruel Harner hauled twelve hundred pounds of gold bullion a month from the mines and brought back ten thousand dollars in cash for the miners' payroll. The Little Rockies mining district was in second place among the gold-producing districts in Montana.

But for Harvey "Kid Curry" Logan, the mining life was of little interest now. He had decided to turn outlaw in Wyoming's Powder River country. Wasn't stealing gold easier than mining it?

Twenty–seven-year-old Harvey Logan now found himself drifting into a world vastly different from what he'd known in the Little Rockies. Actually, the fabled Hole-in-the-Wall valley wasn't the only area in which the rustlers had been operating. In fact, large-scale rustling was occurring in several counties, running from Casper to the south to Buffalo on the north, and the Lost Cabin country and Wind River country around Thermopolis and the Owl Creek Mountains to the southwest. To the west rose the Big Horn Mountains and the streams of the Powder River. At one point, the cattle barons of the Cheyenne-based Wyoming Stock Growers Association proclaimed Buffalo the rustler capital of Wyoming.

Initially the area had only a military post, Fort McKinney. It was just west of the junction of the Bozeman Trail and the trail through Powder River Pass into the Big Horn Mountains. Supplies were brought from the nearest Union Pacific Railway supply point at the Rock Creek Station, 250 miles to the south. The establishment of the fort, the town's regional supply and agricultural base, plus the arrival of thousands of cattle, turned Buffalo into a prospering town of one thousand citizens by 1890. It boasted two banks, a sawmill, a flour mill, and even an Episcopal church (on the southern hill just past the red-light district).

Back in the 1880s—and as far as the outlaws were concerned—Buffalo's main attribute was that its courts had never convicted a rustler.

Both the city and county were "corrupt," at least according to the large cattle barons. The general store gave rustlers credit, just as they would anyone else. The cattlemen's association said that all Johnson County ranchers were rustlers and even seized their cattle if they tried to ship them. Of course anyone who tried to settle a legal homestead on "their" grasslands was automatically a rustler, and some died mysterious deaths.

Relations between the cattlemen and the cowboys didn't really turn rocky until about 1884, when most of the big, foreign-owned cattle companies began arriving. At that time the Powder River country contained some 181,000 cattle. Profits, wages, and employment were all at their peaks. Originally, cowboys had been paid five dollars for every motherless calf they could find for the owners. This practice was soon stopped, however, as was the custom of allowing cowboys to buy mavericks or even have cattle of their own. In fact a cowboy was fired if he owned his own animals. Cowboys next experienced both a wage cut and the loss of grub-line privileges during the winter layoff.

The overstocking of the range, the severe drought of 1886, and the devastating winter of 1886–87, all added to the large ranchers' problems. Putting the smaller ranchers and farmers off the range soon became an even higher priority. First came the random killings and then the 1892 attempted invasion by a group of killers organized in Cheyenne with a hit list of Johnson County and Buffalo officials and key "rustlers." This was necessary because the Johnson County "rustlers" were forming their own farmer and stockgrower associations. The intended hired-gun murder spree was a miserable failure and only added to the strength of the small, but organized, group of professional rustlers, who were fast becoming heroes.

To the south of Buffalo, where several branches of the Powder River come together, is the small ranching community of Kaycee. Here Moreton Frewen, under his 76 brand, brought in the first of the area's large cattle herds. Frewen only personally stayed until 1885, finally leaving his castle on the Powder River to be carted away by the same homesteaders he had fought, its lumber being used to build their shacks. At the junction of the Powder River branches, Johnny Nolan, a former wagon boss of Horace Plunkett's EK ranch, homesteaded a Frewen line camp. His cattle had the K-C brand. In 1892 his cabin was destroyed by the cattlemen's hired guns. Later this became a rendezvous site for Harvey Logan and his compatriots. It was conveniently located at the center of their illegal activities.

The K-C ranch was mainly made up of men who had been black-listed from the cattle range. The same was true of the Hat Ranch on the Red Fork of the Powder River where Jack Flagg was one of the leaders of the cattle-baron opposition. Nate Champion was made out to be the leader of an outlaw band called the Red Sash Gang. There apparently was such a gang, but it was led by a Charles Taylor.

Logan would not meet Champion, the man it took fifty-some hired guns to kill, but he would help to form the kind of gang that the cattlemen's association should have concentrated on wiping out.

According to the Pinkerton National Detective Agency, which did investigative work for cattlemen, railroads, and bankers, the number of outlaws in the valley swelled after the Johnson County war peaked in 1892. At the time most called Hole-in-the-Wall the red-walled valley of Buffalo Creek. Here it was said lived a community of homeless cowhands, drifters, killers, and wanted men.

Later, imaginative writers added a false-fronted town within the walls, complete with saloons and dance halls, presided over by Butch Cassidy, the Sundance Kid, Etta Place, and the rest of the Wild Bunch. Actually the nearest community was Kaycee, a few miles east of the valley. It had grown up in the same area where Nolan had established his K-C ranch. It began in 1896 with a blacksmith shop, followed by a general store and saloon.

The newer, hardcore outlaws didn't just steal livestock, they also robbed sheep camps, travelers, stores, post offices, ranchers, and more. They may also have been involved in several stagecoach robberies.

Sometime during this lawless era, George Sutherland "Flatnose" Currie returned to Wyoming from Chadron, Nebraska, to be a cowboy.

Author Pearl Baker said that he worked for H. F. Whitcomb's Bar FS on the Belle Fourche River. Since this was near his boyhood home of Hulett, Wyoming, in Crook County, it's quite possible. But in the end he, too, drifted into the Powder River country. Right or wrong, researchers have decided that, after Nate Champion's death, Flatnose George became the leader of the Powder River/Hole-in-the-Wall Gang. In reality there seemed to be several loose-knit gangs or groups of cowboys operating in the area. There were also cowboys stealing part time while they worked for large ranchers or had their own small places.

George Currie apparently operated at times in the Lost Cabin country, on the southern edge of the Big Horn Mountains. This was about sixty miles to the southwest of Hole-in-the-Wall along Badwater and Alkali Creeks.

It seems that Harvey Logan enjoyed anonymity for his first few years in northern Wyoming, apparently not being involved in any major criminal actions nor being put in jail for them. However, back in Montana, his brother Johnny couldn't say the same thing, and this time it would result in his death.

The trouble started over a parcel of land approximately six miles south of Landusky and about a mile south of the original Curry-Thornhill ranch. This ground was owned by "Uncle" Dan Tressler and his family. Tressler's wife, Lucy (or Lulu Belle), was described as "a striking look-ing blonde." They had six children to watch over, plus one on the way. The couple had married in Tennessee in 1882. Lately, however, she had been hooking up with Johnny Curry, so perhaps number seven was his child. Tressler took his teenage son and five young daughters to a ranch near Harlem. He had sold his ranch on Rock Creek to Abe Gill and John Winters for six hundred dollars. The unsurveyed land included a house, water rights, dams, and ditches. This would put Gill and Winters in a possible dispute of water rights with the Curry-Thornhill ranch.

Lucy thought Dan had vacated the ranch, so she and Johnny went to reclaim it but found Winters living there. Winters's partner and step-brother, Abraham "Abe" Ditmars Gill, had returned to the East for naval-reserve training. The college-educated Gill had come from a prominent New York State family. Winters had been adopted by Dr. Charles Gill after his father had been killed in the American Civil War. Before coming to the Little Rockies, Winters had owned a saddle-making and tack shop in Malta. Apparently he was well liked and respected by the noncriminal element. The same was true of Tressler.

Lucy found Dan, and she asked for half the money he had made from the sale, but he refused her since he had to raise the children. They could hardly argue about that, so Johnny went after Winters to vacate the Tressler place and leave the country. But Winters was no novice cowboy. He had begun his career by working for some of those famous ranching outfits that had brought cattle north from Texas, and he was considered good with a gun. He may have also worked earlier at the Coburn ranch with the Currys.

On another occasion, a visitor to the Winters-Gill ranch had had a close call when he was shot at while taking a ride. Apparently, Winters recognized the horse as one of his own. Luckily the bullet only went through the crown of the visitor's hat. Winters was later quoted as saying, "If they want me, they know where I am."

It was unfortunate for Winters that his partner and stepbrother, Abe Gill, had gone back east to do his duty with the Atlantic Coast Naval Coastal Artillery—especially since Winters didn't know who else would back Johnny's play for the property.

Since Johnny's verbal threats hadn't made Winters move out, he resorted to nightly rides, threatening him with death and causing Winters to either keep his shades down or cover them with a double gunny sack. When he heard Johnny's horse, he would blow out the lamp and crouch behind his locked door with his double-barreled shotgun at the ready. One night he heard the usual hoofbeats of Johnny's horse and waited for the threats. This time Johnny gave him ten days to leave the country, or else. Ten days later, true to his word, Johnny appeared at

10:00 p.m., riding a partially broken range animal. One-armed Johnny kept his bridle reins tied to the saddle horn so he could drop them when going for his six-gun.

Curry commanded that Winters come outside. Winters complied, placing his shotgun just inside the door. After repeating his original command to leave or else, Johnny drew and fired on what he thought was an unarmed man. Luckily for Winters, though, the horse spooked, and Johnny's bullet missed him by inches. Johnny desperately tried to regain control of his horse, which was going in circles with its head down. Johnny couldn't grab the reins without dropping his revolver. Winters took the opportunity to grab his shotgun. He fired one barrel. The buckshot hit Johnny in the chest and belly. Johnny still hadn't gained control of his frightened, wounded animal, but he fired again—and so did Winters. Winters's buckshot struck Johnny on his left side and chest. Johnny was able to fire wildly one more time before he fell to the ground, dead. Winters was unharmed.

Walt Coburn commented that Johnny had "died as he lived, with his boots on and a smoking six-shooter in his hand." If Johnny had lived a few minutes, he might have said that this was not the way it was supposed to end, at least according to all the Wild West books and magazines he had read.

Now Winters decided he was in big trouble. Lonie and Thornhill were still around, so were the Coburns, and would Harvey come back? Winters decided the best thing to do was turn himself into the law for protection. Winters hurriedly saddled his horse, possibly with the help of Lampkin, who apparently worked at the ranch and had witnessed the shooting.

Winters headed out at a good clip, rifle across the saddle. Winters didn't make it to Harlem because his horse gave out at the John Brown place on the Fort Belknap Reservation. In fact a rumor quickly spread that Winters was surrounded by the "Curry gang" at a cabin on the Brown place. Winters wrote a note about his situation, and it was delivered to R. W. Garland, a Malta merchant, a nearby rancher and sometime lawman. The Chouteau County sheriff's department in turn received Garland's telegram, and a party went out to collect Winters and take him into protective custody.

A sheriff's posse looked for Lonie and Harvey around the Little Rockies. Finding nothing, Winters returned to his ranch, knowing the boys had hiding places the law either didn't know about or wouldn't approach.

A coroner's inquest was held at Fort Benton, and Winters was pronounced not guilty, having shot in self-defense. There was little sympathy for Johnny, while Winters had several friends in both Valley and Chouteau Counties. Also, at the time of the shooting, a deputy had been looking for Johnny with an arrest warrant for assault. Winters probably relaxed somewhat when he heard that Lonie had joined Harvey in Wyoming, perhaps in part to escape an arrest warrant issued for his assault upon someone named Shorty Parker, who at the time had been working at Charley Perry's store on the Fort Belknap Reservation. Lonie and W. W. "Wash" Lampkin had been returning by stage from Harlem and had stopped at the store. Lonie would say that he went behind the counter at the store to get a match, and Parker came out of the backroom with his gun in hand. Both played hide and seek, using the counter as protection. Apparently several shots were fired, and Parker was wounded in the arm. Lonie then clubbed the man with his revolver. Apparently each filed charges against the other. Lampkin also got into an altercation with Perry at some point.

Lonie occasionally secretly returned to the Landusky area to visit Elfie. Two children resulted from these visits, Lonie Junior and Mayme or "Mamie." Elfie was described as "a well-built woman, good looking with long black hair, fair skin with blue eyes." Another beauty, Lucy Tressler, took up with Jim Thornhill after Johnny's death. They reportedly had a good relationship, which resulted in marriage in March of 1904 before the justice of the peace in Landusky. Lucy and Jim were both about forty years old. Lucy gave birth to a daughter, Sarah, who was supposed to be Dan's, not Johnny's, daughter.

A major event that would have a major affect on the "Roberts brothers" occurred the month prior to Johnny's death. Robert LeRoy "Butch Cassidy" Parker had been released from the Wyoming State Prison after serving a sentence for horse stealing. He would soon move to the Powder Springs area of northwestern Colorado to start a major outlaw organization. The Currie and Curry gang would eventually become a major part of it.

In the interim, Abe Gill had returned to the ranch for a short time before the Spanish-American War. He was appointed a U.S. land commissioner and also served in that capacity with the Department of Agriculture. Gill's involvement with the disputed Tressler ranch, especially when combined with the fact that he was now handling homestead applications for former ranch lands, earned him animosity in some quarters. Being part Spanish and from a wealthy New York family didn't help either. He also had a strict law-and-order stance, allowing lawmen to headquarter at his ranch when they were in the Little Rockies. Gill and his stepbrother were aware of the animosity and were cautious, often traveling at night to avoid ambushes. They had a few close calls.

And so did Jake Harris. The Pike Landusky ally was continually being harassed by Curry brothers' sympathizers and friends, his saloon sometimes peppered with rifle fire. He even filed charges, but there were no lawmen to protect him in Landusky. Harris finally left in 1897. His saloon was soon burned down, the fire taking a mining office with it. There was a shooting carnival as it burned.

It was quietly said that Winters and possibly Gill were marked for death. Surely it would be just a matter of time before Harvey killed Winters and maybe threw in Gill as a bonus. The stepbrothers received a daily reminder of this thinking given that Johnny's grave was to the north across the creek.

The locals followed the brothers' outlaw career in Wyoming. Once they became major outlaws, their exploits were covered in the newspapers of the Hi-Line railroad towns. "Jew" Jake Harris was soon forgotten as he traveled to the mining town of Giltedge and later disappeared in Alaska.

The attention of those with an interest in the activities of outlaws was now focused on northern Wyoming and on Harvey and Lonie in particular.

Thanks to Harvey and Lonie Curry (who were now going by the alias of Roberts), George Currie, and other rustlers, Johnson County was at the height of its rustling activities. (The Currys' use of the Roberts name added to the lawmen's confusion since there were actual Roberts brothers—Will and Sterling—in the area. Will even rode with the gang, according to author James Horan.)

Since the large ranching operations were gradually becoming accustomed to not controlling the range, the hardcore rustlers were losing their support. By 1897 certain small ranchers had won a foothold as legitimate operators. Perhaps because the larger corporations were no longer being controlled by foreign interests but by Omaha and Chicago, they were easier to deal with. A new interest in enforcing the law found its focus in crime-laden Buffalo. Besides, the rustlers had been threatened with armed attacks by the Cheyenne cattlemen's association as well as military martial law if order wasn't restored.

The new Johnson County sheriff, Al Sproul, was under intense pressure to do something about the rustlers. He hired a young Texas cowboy named Billy Deane, who soon showed an ambition to become a famous lawman by capturing the entire Curry-Currie gang by himself. Perhaps he was bold and fearless but more likely just foolhardy.

One of his first stops in his anticrime campaign was the Alfred Grigg home and post office, west of Kaycee. It was a regular mail stop for various outlaws and may have been a small general store, also. The mail was routed through Buffalo, south near the main fork of the Powder River, to Mayoworth, down Kallenbaugh Draw to the Griggs' place. Deane was talking with Mr. Grigg when Grigg's wife noticed two men approaching the building. She recognized them as two of the men that Deane was seeking. She immediately sent the children to the cellar. Once inside, one of the two outlaws tried to shoot Deane, but Mrs. Grigg grabbed his gun and it went off, firing a shot into the ceiling. After Grigg got his gun and Deane drew his, the two retreated, joining two other men waiting outside. Deane said he better leave and not put the family in anymore danger, even though the family begged him not to go. Apparently the family didn't suffer for their actions since the outlaws needed their mail and didn't need bad publicity. One of the men was thought to have been Harvey Logan.

Deane's next and last encounter with the gang occurred on April 13, at the shearing pens of the Kaltenbach sheep camp south of the K-C ranch. Twenty shearers watched Deane tangle with members of the rustler gang. Deane was apparently observing the shearing operation when he noticed four men approaching over the hill and down the creek. With his field glasses he apparently saw that they were the same four men involved in the post-office incident. Deane advanced, dismounted near the corral gate, and began to fire at them. The gunfire was immediately returned, and Deane's horse broke loose. When he attempted to catch it, he took several bullets in the back—killing him instantly. According to newspaper accounts of the day, the killers then roped Deane's body, dragging it through the sagebrush until he was unrecognizable. After his death, his rifle stock was found to have been shattered, allowing only one round or so to be fired. According to author Charles Kelly, it was well known that George Currie and Harvey and Lonie Curry (now going by Roberts) had done the killing. Who the fourth man might have been isn't known, but there was talk of someone called "Dusty Jim." Wyoming researcher Colin Taylor believes that this Dusty Jim's last name was McCloud.

The group continued its exploits in the Lost Cabin country, robbing

Bader's road ranch, stealing from sheep camps, and rustling twenty-five head of saddle horses and mules from the Swift Company sheep camp. There was also a store robbery, an isolated ranch robbed, and a traveler relieved of $480. Author Brown Waller even lays a robbery of a Powderville, Montana, post office at their feet, an incident in which the postmaster was also killed.

They next decided to rob a bank, moving up to the big time. Researcher and author Larry Pointer stated that they looked over the countryside as far north as Dickinson, North Dakota. In the end, however, they picked Belle Fourche's South Dakota Bank. Since ranchers and lawmen were threatening to enter the outlaw valley to retrieve their stolen cattle and horses, and the killing of Deane hadn't won them any popularity contests, they may have been after traveling money. Also, they may have been wanting to impress Butch Cassidy.

Their choice of banks might have been influenced by the fact that Wyoming cattle baron John Clay was an owner. Besides, the town was just across the state line in country that Currie probably knew well since he had spent his childhood in the area. There was also a convenient escape route back home through the Bear Lodge Mountains, Black Hills, or north into Montana following the Little Missouri River. Or they just could follow the Belle Fourche River either way.

The town had been swept by fire in 1895, but it had recovered, and it was hosting a reunion of American Civil War veterans. The unintentional highlight of the week was the burning down of the jail by a one-legged drunk veteran, who used this method to escape. The boys expected the bank to be full of the merchants' money on Monday morning. Plus it was already a wealthy town, being a center for the Black Hill mineral belt and a central railhead for shipping cattle.

Reportedly six men were involved in the robbery, although only five could be identified. They were George "Flatnose" Currie, the king of the rustlers (according to the Pinkertons), the Roberts brothers (Harvey and Lonie), Walt Punteney, and Tom O'Day. The sixth mystery man was identified as "Harvey Ray." According to Larry Pointer, an 1896 Wyoming census showed such a man living near Ten Sleep, Wyoming. Ten Sleep is just northwest of the Hole-in-the-Wall at the beginnings of the Bighorn River basin. (Colin Taylor also found evidence of this man. Ray had been arrested in Natrona County in the winter of 1896 for cattle rustling. He made bail and never returned.) "Indian" Will Roberts also was mentioned by some; and at one point, Harry Longabaugh was suspected, but he neither matched the description nor had the opportunity since he had a legitimate ranching job in the Little Snake River Valley with a Bert Charter. The two were working at the Al Reader ranch.

On Saturday, June 26, Tom O'Day was assigned the task of scouting the town and bank layout while the others set up camp in the nearby hills. O'Day should have done the job, since he was a veteran rustler. Unfortunately, he scouted out the drinking establishments instead, and passed out in a chair in Sebastion's Saloon. O'Day didn't return until Sunday morning, hence the robbery was rescheduled for Monday morning.

O'Day and Punteney were sent ahead to fade into the shadows across from the bank, but O'Day faded into the nearest saloon, again Sebastion's. About thirty minutes later, the others arrived. Perhaps three entered the bank while Lonie tended the horses. Meanwhile O'Day had left the saloon with two bottles of whiskey and a pint stuffed in his clothing. He put the quarts in his saddlebags and rode back to his lookout post in front of Giles Hardware store. A few minutes later O'Day returned to the saloon. Thus O'Day failed to signal to Punteney who in turn was supposed to signal to the three on the side of the bank that all was well. Hence the would-be robbers walked into the bank without intelligence and with one of the other members of their party drunk, again.

As reconstructed later, the three walked into the two-story stone building with guns drawn. Inside were head cashier Arthur H. Marble, board director Reverend E. C. Clough, an accountant or teller, and four customers: A. A. Dana, Dave Arnold, Ernest Mitchell, and J. H.

Chapman of Deadwood. George Currie ordered those who were making deposits to put their money into a bag he held. Harvey Logan ordered the teller to collect the money from under the counter and put it in his sack. Marble then apparently grabbed a revolver from under the counter and pointed it at Logan, pulling the trigger. It didn't fire, however, and he dropped it. Marble must have forgotten that the town marshal had temporarily switched guns with the bank because his had malfunctioned.

Meanwhile, outside the bank, Alanson Giles of the hardware store had noticed that the people inside the bank appeared to have their hands in the air. Giles went across the street and looked in the window, confirming that the bank was being robbed. Giles raised an alarm, and Currie fired his gun, possibly aiming at Giles through the glass front door. The robbers rushed out with the meager morning receipts, losing a chance at the big money in a tray beneath the counter as well as the vault's contents.

Punteney and Lonie Logan fired into the air to create an impression that it was just cowboy's raising a ruckus. O'Day came out of the saloon, shooting up and down the street instead of up in the air. One round went through a door and grazed a man's cheek. The panicked O'Day tried to fade in the gathering crowd. Meanwhile his horse, whiskey still in the saddle bags, bolted and joined the fleeing riders. O'Day next jumped on a nearby white mule, yelling, "I'll get them!" However, the mule went its own way—as mules do—and then returned to where it had started.

The others rode southwest past the Scatney Building and down Sixth Street. They briefly stopped near an artesian well two hundred yards up Sundance Hill on the road out of town to see what had happened to the hapless O'Day. Apparently they weren't too bothered by the old American Civil War veteran, John McClure, who was firing his trusty old cap and ball .44 at them, nor by Marble firing a rifle down the street where, in any case, only townspeople now were. Joe Miller, the local blacksmith, pursued them, but his horse was shot out from under him by another local citizen, Frank C. Bennett, who mistook him for one of the robbers.

Meanwhile O'Day was ordered off the mule by a someone named "Fatty." When he couldn't find another horse, O'Day headed for a nearby outhouse where he disposed of his pistol. Upon exiting, he was apprehended as the man who had tried to steal the mule by the butcher, Russell Bauman, Walt Simpson, and others. The outhouse was upended by three men and raked out to reveal O'Day's pistol, holster, and some cartridges. A search of his person revealed the pint of whiskey, some more cartridges, and a check for $392.50 from cattle sales. This was more than the robbery netted!

The town had no jail, so O'Day was held in a room near the county attorney's office. A large crowd had gathered, wishing to do him bodily harm, so he was moved to the Lawrence County jail at Deadwood, twenty-two miles to the south. After O'Day was taken care of, a posse under Sheriff George Fuller was organized, largely made up of cowboys who believed the bandits to also be prominent rustlers.

The posse caught up with the bandits at a small track of timber near the Clay ranch, twelve miles from town. Even though a message was sent back to town, bringing even more assistance on horseback and in buggies, during the night the robbers managed to slip through the picket lines. They were last heard of on the Little Missouri River below Camp Crook, an old pioneer town in the northwest corner of Harding County near the Montana line. A $625 reward was offered for each.

Once back in the Powder River country, the Curry brothers and their cohorts heard more bad news. The robbery attempt had produced a major reaction from the large ranchers, who were now determined to clean the Hole-in-the-Wall valley of its outlaw activity. The first attempt in this regard occurred on July 18, ten days after the bank robbery. Three days after setting out, on July 21, a group led by lawman Joe LeFors and CY ranch foreman Bob Divine entered the valley through the southern gap that led to the outlaw ranch. (The CY was owned by Judge Joseph M. Carey and his son, Robert D. Carey, both important members of the Wyoming Stock Growers Association who had served as state governors and representatives in Congress. Their land holdings had originally included the town of Casper and a fifteen thousand-acre holding at Box Elder Valley near Glenrock, as well as more land in South Dakota.)

The LeFors and Divine party encountered a group of men near the top of a hill about one mile from the outlaw ranch. The two parties passed each other in single file, almost within arm's reach. But the lawmen encountered no conflict until they arrived at the outlaw ranch buildings. At this point they saw Bob Taylor and the Smiths on the Lander-to-Buffalo stage road. Taylor was wanted for murder in Missouri, and he was believed to be one of the leaders of the rustlers. Bob Smith, an alleged outlaw, got off his horse, which Divine claimed was a hostile act. Divine fired. And while Divine later said he had shot Smith with his revolver, it was actually found that Smith was shot in the back with what was probably a .30-40 rifle bullet. He also had a bullet in the right lung. Several of the posse members headed for cover, leaving Divine, his son Lee, and Joe LeFors to fight it out with the outlaws. After the smoke cleared, Divine and his son were slightly wounded, Divine's horse was dead, and Bob Smith was dying. Bob's brother-in-law, Al Smith, escaped during the altercation, but he had also been shot.

Taylor stayed with Smith until some other outlaws came out of the cabin and carried him inside. Divine refused to allow Smith to have water, but valley resident Tom Gardner went to the creek and brought him water in his hat. Gardner also declined to give up his pistol, and no one argued the point. The 170 or so cattle the invading party had collected were abandoned, and the posse made a speedy retreat.

Smith's wife was sent for in Buffalo; Smith died the next day. They took Taylor to Casper and then to Buffalo for trial, but he was released because the county authorities said they couldn't get a conviction in Johnson County. (Taylor had been held in Natrona County for about three weeks until a land survey concluded that the shootings had occurred in Johnson County.) On being released, Taylor said he was leaving the area for good.

But the ranchers and lawmen now had more of an idea about what they were up against. Even while the Smith brothers and their father were operating their own ranch, they were allegedly rustling on the side. Along with Kaycee rancher John Nolan, the Smith family was considered the main culprits. As historian Helena Huntington Smith put it in an article for *Montana: The Magazine of Western History*, "The gang followed the CY roundups like wolves prowling around a buffalo herd. They worked ahead, throwing small bunches of cattle to one side, then driving them into the Wall country to burn over the brands at their leisure." Many of the cattle found in the outlaw valley had reportedly been rebranded by George Currie, with Walt Punteney's help. However the full-time, hardcore outlaws (such as Harvey Logan) weren't in evidence.

A few weeks later, another foray into the valley was organized. And when Johnson County's sheriff, Al Sproal, heard how many stolen animals the group had observed, he decided to join. Sheriff Patten of Natrona County also joined the group, as did the sheriff and a deputy from Butte County, South Dakota, with warrants for the Belle Fourche bank robbers. After the addition of some cattle company foremen and stock inspectors from Montana, the group, under W. D. "Billy" Smith, totaled fifty-four men.

Divine published a letter in the local paper, the *Natrona County Tribune*, explaining their plans. He wrote that they weren't looking for trouble; they were just working cowboys looking for their cattle. He explained that he was bringing the law along so everyone was treated right. In closing, he wrote, "The time has come for all honest working men to declare themselves in favor of law and justice. And if those men want to fight us when we know we are right, I say fight." Divine received a letter in reply from the "Revenge Gange" *[sic]*, a group of twelve men who claimed they were appointed to kill Divine if he stuck his "damned old gray head" into the valley.

The party went forward in spite of the "Revenge Gange" letter and notices telling them to stay out. As they traveled, they were being watched from a distance. Divine's crew rounded up about 550 head of cattle. Nothing occurred until they tried to leave. A group of about twenty men with rifles briefly blocked their way. But they then allowed them to pass after Sheriff Sproal rode up, saying their mission was peaceful. He also bawled them out for being rustlers and not good cowboys. No sign was seen of the major players of the Hole-in-the-Wall gang. (Divine estimated that the main rustlers in the gang, including Currie and the Currys, numbered at least twenty men. He claimed he knew the identity of eleven of them.) In fact Divine returned several more times to gather cattle and was never bothered. Divine gave any Hole-in-the-Wall "ranchers" the chance to check his animals for any that might be legitimate, but they declined.

The year 1897 saw the start of a peace process between the small, legitimate ranchers and formerly blacklisted cowboys with the big outfits such as the Carey CY, the Ogallala, the Pugsleys, and the Half Circle L. And the incursions into the valley by lawmen had made some of the Wyoming newspaper editors braver. Some ran editorials; others just mentioned the efforts.

Before exiting the Powder River country, the Currys may have been involved in another robbery. In years past, a Lander-to-Rawlins stagecoach had typically been robbed on an almost annual basis, and it was getting to be that time again. The stage changed horses at the Lost Soldier Pass, which skirted the Great Divide Basin. Two masked men, each wearing a black handkerchief over his face, put station manager Dave Bell under guard in the stage barn and waited for the southbound Rawlins stage. There were no passengers, and an expected shipment of gold dust from the Atlantic City mines was not aboard. Instead, the stagecoach driver was only relieved of his mailbags. After opening the bags in the livery barn, the robbers took their loot and headed west toward the desert on the Lander Road. The driver was so frightened that he couldn't give an accurate description, but Harvey Curry (who had so far used at least three different surnames, including Roberts, Howard, and Jones) was mentioned as one possible robber. There's no record of the amount that was taken from the stagecoach.

After their valley had been invaded and warrants for the Belle Fourche bank robbery issued, Harvey Curry and George Currie (with some other men) decided to head south and join Butch Cassidy at Powder Springs-Browns Park. Harvey and George perhaps didn't have to feel too inferior after their failed Belle Fourche, South Dakota, bank robbery given that Cassidy had failed at not only robbing a bank in Evanston, Wyoming, but also a mine payroll in Rock Springs and a Union Pacific train. Apparently all of Cassidy's potential victims had been warned in advance. (The outlaw's security improved after that when Cassidy decided to include fewer people in the planning loop and use an informal message drop system rather than the postal service.)

Harvey and George's trip south to Powder Springs, which began on August 19, was hardly a quiet one, as their outlaw group (supposedly numbering, in at least one account, as many as seventy-five men) robbed sheep camps as they went, often demanding supplies from their victims. They were seen crossing Lost Soldier Pass and the Union Pacific Railroad tracks at the Fillmore railroad station in Albany County.

The newspapers in Colorado, Wyoming, Utah, and Idaho covered their activities, calling them everything from a "Big Band of Outlaws" to the "Great American Crime League." They were credited with having some four hundred members and were said to keep their stolen livestock in isolated corrals until it was market time. The rustling was reportedly done at night, with the days being spent drinking and gambling away their ill-gained money. A man named Jeff Dunbar was credited with having led the gang for the last ten years, as well as with having killed twelve men. His brother, William "Mike" Dunbar had migrated west from Illinois in 1892 to operate a saloon in Casper, Wyoming. After his brother, Jeff, shot a man to death, they both relocated to Dixon in July of 1893, where Mike ran a saloon. Jeff was the real outlaw of the two and was killed in an 1898 shootout in a Dixon saloon. Mike later gave assistance to the Butch Cassidy gang, serving as a contact man between the members. Mike, his wife, and children moved to Encampment, Wyoming, in about 1900.

Powder Springs is a tributary of the Little Snake River. Located northeast of Brown's Park (also called Brown's Hole or Brown's Valley), according to outlaw historian Donna B. Ernst it consisted of two springs that ran into the Little Snake River just above the Wyoming border. To the northeast were the communities of Baggs, Dixon, and Savery. The upper springs was located a mile north of the Wyoming-Colorado line among rocks and crevices in a bowl-shaped valley, slightly west of Powder Mountain. The lower springs was about two miles farther south in flatter, more rolling terrain, a tiny oasis in a bleak, sage-covered wasteland.

Author Brown Waller, in *The Last of the Great Train Robbers,* described how the gang made its headquarters at the old Crittenden horse ranch, having driven the owner out after rustling all his livestock. The immediate area could furnish enough water for about 150 head of cattle, but, at least according to one article, the greater Little Snake River Valley could hold up to one thousand head of cattle and horses. Stories vary as to who was the real rustler leader. Dick Bender (or Benda) is sometimes given that title. And he was encamped there in the spring of 1897 when Butch Cassidy arrived. This could have been the same bunch that Butch Cassidy and Elzy Lay had been involved with earlier, when they were distributing counterfeit money in northwest Utah.

Currie and Logan missed the big July celebration that Cassidy had sponsored in the border towns of Baggs and Dixon by about three weeks. After a robbery in Utah in which Butch Cassidy and the boys had robbed the Castle Gate-Pleasant Valley Coal Company's payroll of over eight thousand dollars in gold coins and currency, they had spent the early spring hiding out at Robber's Roost in southeast Utah. Besides Cassidy, the others thought to be involved were Elzy Lay, Wilbur "Bub"

Meeks, and Joe Walker. This was after the successful bank robbery in southeastern Idaho at the Montpelier bank when, again, Lay and Meeks had been along. The money was to be used in the legal defense of former gang member and friend, Matt Warner. Warner, Butch Cassidy, and Tom McCarty had earlier operated together.

During the celebration, Jack Ryan's Bulldog Saloon had been shot up by the cowboys. The rest of Baggs had closed itself up after hearing about the party in nearby Dixon. (Ryan was later so well compensated in gold that he was able to start a new saloon in Rawlins and become a trusted compatriot of the Wild Bunch.) According to author Charles Kelly, these and similar wild town celebrations resulted in the name the Wild Bunch.

Robert LeRoy "Butch Cassidy" Parker had been serving time in the Wyoming State Penitentiary at Laramie for horse theft about the same time as Harvey Logan was joining the cattle rustlers in Wyoming. Up until prison, Cassidy had been a small-time rustler and erstwhile robber (with Tom McCarty and Matt Warner) after holding up a Telluride (and possibly a Denver) bank. Once he was released from prison, he returned to Brown's Park where he had previously spent time at Matt Warner's ranch on Diamond Mountain. His first recruits into his gang were Wilbur "Bub" Meeks and Elsworth "Elzy" or "Elza" Lay.

Butch Cassidy's family was Mormon and came from southern Utah. Butch met his first outlaw, Mike Cassidy, while helping with a dairy business at a nearby ranch. The association with Mike Cassidy led the young Robert Leroy Parker to work with the notorious outlaw, Cap Brown. In addition to working legitimate jobs (between robberies) as a cowboy, miner-packer, and butcher, Parker would also eventually spend a short time in the Hole-in-the-Wall country before going to prison.

After prison he returned to Brown's Park. In addition to starting his own gang, he also worked as a legitimate cowboy for the Bassett family ranch.

Brown's Park, in the rugged, isolated and secluded valley of Colorado's Green River, was a good temporary home for him. Herb

Bassett had worked both as a schoolteacher and bookkeeper before moving into the valley, where he now acted not only as a postmaster and Moffat County commissioner but also as a justice of the peace. His wife, Elizabeth, and their children were the ones in the cattle business. Because of the location, the ranch also acted as a travelers' inn and social center.

Butch divided his time between the ranch of Charley Crouse and the Bassett place. According to Larry Pointer, "Cassidy became the main attraction with his open friendliness and keen sense of humor." Pointer also said that Cassidy divided his attention there between the Bassetts' library and their oldest daughter, Josie.

The small ranchers of the valley, including the Bassetts, were constantly being crowded by larger ranches, such as Ora Haley's Two Bar and the Middlesex Land and Cattle Company. One of these larger ranchers, J. S. Hoy, wrote an unpublished manuscript in which he called his neighbors thieves and rustlers. He thought that Elizabeth Bassett, the head of the "Bassett gang," was the worst. In reality she was managing a ranch of legitimately acquired cattle. Her neighbors had great respect for her abilities. The "gang" Hoy referred to were her partners in their unofficial small cattlemen's association, some of whom did have checkered pasts.

In any case, the easy life of the Powder Springs-Brown's Hole gang(s) was nearing the end. Although Butch may have been the new leader of the Hole-in-the-Wall and Bender gangs, it wouldn't last because they had stolen so much livestock within a radius of two hundred miles that ranchers were either quitting the country or selling out. For all their bravado, Butch and his boys were still just common rustlers.

Currie and Logan had decided to rob another bank. They had their eyes on a Red Lodge, Montana, bank owned by Bighorn Basin rancher John Chapman, the man who had helped deputy sheriff Bob Caverly arrest Butch Cassidy in 1892. Besides Currie and Logan, there was Walt

Punteney and a mystery man, perhaps Harry "the Sundance Kid" Longabaugh.

The Pennsylvania-born Longabaugh had come west in 1882 at the age of fourteen, following a cousin's family. He may have worked for several cattle ranches, including one near Springer, New Mexico; the L–C Ranch near Monticello, Utah; and the Suffolk ranch in Wyoming on the Cheyenne River. The historical record also mentions the Pittsburgh Land and Cattle Company near Monticello, Utah. He also supposedly had an arrest warrant for larceny issued for him in Lusk, Wyoming. After bringing an N–Bar–N herd up from Texas, Longabaugh ended up working for several eastern Montana ranchers. The Valley County Ranch employed several outlaws who had left Wyoming in a hurry during the cattlemen's war. Longabaugh then went to Canada, perhaps prompted by problems in Sundance, Wyoming, plus a subsequent charge for threatening a deputy sheriff. In present-day Alberta he worked as a horse breaker, as a railroad construction worker, and in a saloon. After leaving Canada, he returned to Miles City and attempted a train robbery at Malta with two unemployed cowboys.

Longabaugh eventually turned up in the Little Snake River Valley, working for various ranchers. In 1896 or 1897, he hooked up with Bert Charter, who was on the fringe of the Wild Bunch. It's not known for certain whether he met Butch for the first time at this point or if they had met earlier. (According to Donna B. Ernst, Longabaugh had been working for the Reader Ranch near Savery, Wyoming, before leaving the area in August of 1897, just after the wild celebration at Baggs. He reportedly returned in 1898 to work at the Kelsey Ranch.)

Thus Longabaugh may have accompanied George Currie, Harvey Logan and Walt Puteny on the ride to Red Lodge, Montana, a town of about six thousand people on the eastern edge of the Beartooth Mountains. It was (and is) the county seat of Carbon County, which meant it had both a town marshal and sheriff's department. From town it was about thirty miles north to the Yellowstone River at Columbus and about the same to northern Wyoming.

The boys might have known ahead of time that the town marshal was Byron St. Clair, formerly of Fort Washakie, Wyoming, southeast of Hole-in-the-Wall. They suggested it would be a good time for him to go out of town for an overdue fishing trip because they planned on robbing the bank. Instead St. Clair informed Sheriff John Dunn of their plans. Meanwhile, the gang had left town by early Monday morning, becoming suspicious of St. Clair's loyalty. They were seen buying camping supplies in town and later riding north toward the Yellowstone River. If Currie was accompanying them, it is believed that he left them at that point, returning to Wyoming, perhaps in disgust.

On Monday, Sheriff John Dunn led a small posse north, following their trail. Riding with them was Billy Smith, a Miles City-Custer County stock detective, as well as two other lawmen. Smith had earlier helped capture Longabaugh when he was on a train for Sundance, Wyoming, but he had escaped from his escort. Smith also was investigating the recent report of a doctor in Billings, Montana, about treating a man for a broken leg. If they had paid him for their services, he wouldn't have filed a report and given the law descriptions that matched the Belle Fourche robbers. Since then, Smith had been on the outlook for them. The injured man might have been Currie, which would explain why he quit the bunch.

The posse followed them north to Absarokee, just skirting the Beartooth Mountains, then following the Stillwater River to its junction with the Yellowstone River at Columbus. From there, they continued on the trail to Lavina, located about forty-five miles north on the Musselshell. If Longabaugh was along, this was country he knew. (According to author Edward M. Kirby, Longabaugh had worked for the John T. Murphy Cattle Company near Lavina.) What seems strange now is that the outlaws' flight was so leisurely. Stopping to drink at Jolley's Saloon in Lavina wasn't smart, unless they really believed no one was following them (since they hadn't robbed anybody). And were they too poor to use money other than a check stolen from the bank at Belle Fourche? At this point the posse was about an hour behind. Donna B.

Ernst wrote that the outlaws had intended to return to Red Lodge, but that wouldn't have been a smart move, either. They camped about twenty miles north, perhaps near the stage road to Lewistown. In fact they had the convenience of several stage trails out of Lavina, including Lewistown, Fort Benton, Roundup, and Billings.

The posse caught up with them about 5:00 p.m. on Wednesday, September 22. At the time Punteney and perhaps Longabaugh were getting water from nearby, and Logan was picketing his horse. When Dunn called for them to surrender, Punteney and perhaps Longabaugh jumped behind a cut bank but then surrendered without firing a shot, since there was no hope of escape. Logan, on the other hand, jumped behind his horse, drawing his Colt .45. Dunn immediately fired a shot that went through the horse's neck and hit Logan in the wrist, making him drop his weapon. A second version has Dunn firing two shots, one hitting Logan's wrist, the other his horse. Logan ran behind a sand dune, but the attempt at escape was useless.

The lawmen took the captured outlaws to Billings, as Sheriff Dunn correctly believed that at least two of them had been involved in the Belle Fourche bank robbery. In Billings, two of them were identified by the bank teller. On Tuesday, the three men, using the aliases of Charlie Frost, Frank Jones, and Thomas Jones, agreed to return to South Dakota without extradition papers. Sheriff Butts, Smith, and Hicks took them on the Burlington Route Railroad to Deadwood in the Black Hills. Here they joined Tom O'Day at the Lawrence County jail. The Belle Fourche jail was old and in poor condition as the result of a fire. They were represented at the preliminary hearing by local attorneys Frank McLoughlin and W. O. Temple; bail was set at ten thousand dollars for each suspect. This time all three of them were identified. On October 2 Logan, Punteney, and O'Day (and the fourth, unknown man) went to H. R. Locke's photography studio. Mr. Unknown, however, refused to have his picture taken. The images that resulted are very professional with full body shots and elegant backgrounds. Logan's new picture and wrist scar would hereafter take him off the list of invisible outlaws.

Their lawyers filed an affidavit on October 13, asking the court for an extension so material witnesses could be brought from Wyoming. Apparently that didn't work, because they were indicted by the state on October 15 for first-degree robbery. Harvey Ray and George Currie were indicted in absentia. The extension for the probably bogus witnesses wasn't necessary, though, because they escaped from the Lawrence County jail the night of October 31.

How did they escape? As usual, the accounts vary slightly. It was 8:45 p.m. and time to remove the prisoners from the corridor area and return them to their individual cells. Mansfield could throw a switch and lock the individual cells without entering the corridor. However, the prisoners somehow convinced the jailer that the cells were already locked. Mansfield entered the corridor to release and relock the cells. As he entered, his wife was supposed to relock the door behind him, but prisoner "Frank Roberts" put his foot in the door and local murder suspect William Moore struck the jailer a hard blow to the face. The others also pounced on the jailer and dragged his wife in, too. The boys left them there after slapping Mrs. Mansfield around to keep her quiet, exiting through the kitchen to the back door. William Moore went over the fence while the others left by the courtyard gate. They split again, with Punteney ending up with the poison O'Day, as Harvey Logan and their unidentified accessory struck out in their own. There was a report that the two escaped on horses provided by Lonie Logan. Or five horses may have been picketed in Spearfish Canyon, about ten miles to the northwest.

Meanwhile the Mansfields either found a way to release themselves through the outer door or they yelled loud enough that help arrived. Sheriff Plunket lived just across the street and quickly organized a search party of the immediate neighborhood, finding no trace of the escapees. A posse was organized and Sheriff Butts in Belle Fourche was notified to do the same. Perhaps the two posses could corral the outlaws before they turned west into either Wyoming of Montana. The sheriff also contacted Lincoln, Nebraska, about obtaining bloodhounds.

Reportedly, Punteney with the out-of-shape (but at least sober) O'Day in tow followed Deadwood's Carney Street, heading to the Chicago and Northwestern's railroad tracks by way of Whitewood Creek. At the top of McGovern Hill, O'Day lost a handkerchief, apparently obtained from another prisoner in trade. From a hilltop near the Chautauqua grounds and a water ditch, the two observed the lanterns of men searching for them. Hence they went in another direction west toward Blacktail Gulch and Flat Bottom Creek. (Perhaps present-day Deadwood Creek Road toward Central City, and then Maitland, connecting with the Spearfish Road.)

Still there was confusion as to if the fugitives had really separated. Four men were seen on the Carbonate Road about 11:00 p.m. This would have been in the direction of Spearfish Canyon where the horses had supposedly been picketed. Plus early Monday night it was reported that four men tried to take a farmer's horse away from him at the False Bottom Creek crossing on Spearfish Road. But the man had successfully eluded them and headed for the town of Spearfish to give the alarm. Posses quickly converged on the area, searching all sheds, barns, tree groves, and clumps of brush along the False Bottom Creek near the Gunsooly ranch on the Spearfish Road.

About midnight two members of a posse, James Terry and Matt McDonaugh, observed a faint campfire in a thicket. They crawled toward the light and recognized Punteney and O'Day. Since they only had one shotgun between them, they decided to wait until morning to summon reinforcements. Unfortunately one of their horses made a noise loud enough for the fugitives to hear, causing them to flee to another secluded location. But the unlucky pair were scared from the new location the next morning by a young hunter shooting at rabbits near the creek. The shots brought all the posse members, thinking a fight had begun. However, O'Day and Punteney were able to outflank them, bypassing the John Thomas ranch to go on their way. Three miles southwest of Spearfish, however, the law finally caught up with them, and they were captured without a fight by Spearfish town marshal Craig.

Punteney probably could have escaped on his own if he had not elected to stay with O'Day, who was in poor physical condition from his jail time. The captives were returned to Deadwood and placed back in their cells, now wearing ankle bracelets. They were exhausted and had eaten nothing since Sunday except some rutabaga from a farmer's field.

But while these two had been the center of attention, the other two had escaped. A report on Logan and his mystery companion had them stealing a horse and saddle from a farmer's field near Giesler's sawmill on Crow Creek. They were last seen headed for the Bear Lodge Mountains, north of Sundance, Wyoming. The posses did try to check the area where the fabled horses were supposedly picketed in the canyon but found nothing. This might have been a clever diversion, whether there were actual horses present or not.

Deputy Sheriff Ricks picked up a trail that led toward the Little Powder River, which flows north into Montana, joining the Powder River at Broadus. They could have either continued southwest toward Kaycee or gone north into Montana.

Nothing more was heard about the fugitives, except Logan and another unknown man who may have gone to Montana. Wherever it was that he went, Logan wasn't seen between December and the spring of 1898 when he began robbing again.

But the county officials did have Punteney and O'Day in custody. In April of 1898 Punteney was put on trial for the Belle Fourche bank robbery—and acquitted. Two different witnesses from the Bighorn River Basin, Bob McCoy and Sam Brown, testified that Punteney had had dinner at Brown's ranch near Thermopolis the day before the robbery, nearly three hundred miles away. McCoy was allegedly the bagman for Cassidy's payments to the defense attorneys. The county officials, ranchers, and bank officers were so frustrated by the injustice that the charges were dropped against O'Day.

After this experience Punteney apparently went straight, moving to the Lost Cabin country on Bridger Creek until 1912. Author Larry Pointer wrote that Punteney moved to the Camp Stool ranch near

THE ROBERTS BROTHERS, WYOMING OUTLAWS

Crowheart Butte and then to Pinedale in 1923 where he bought a saloon, dying there in 1949. He reportedly rode in the Wild Bill Cody's Wild West Show. He does, however, play a part in a later drama that may have included Logan after his jailbreak from the Knox County, Tennessee, jail in 1903.

O'Day continued rustling back and forth across the Wyoming and Montana border. He was arrested in November of 1903 for stealing horses and was sentenced to six years in prison. Apparently, after he was captured at the 2B Ranch on Bridger Creek, there was to have been a rescue attempt in the Lost Cabin country while he was on the way to Casper with Sheriff Webb. But the sheriff detoured off the road and through some hills. O'Day had several friends or gang members at his trial, but they caused no trouble. O'Day behaved himself in prison and was released after four years. He married and forsook the rustling game as the judge had advised him to do. The couple moved to a ranch in Nebraska, left to him by an uncle. One story had O'Day dying in Texas soon after his release, but perhaps he circulated it himself to be left alone.

This ended the major outlaw activities for 1897, with the ranchers even more determined to wipe out those rustlers who had once more eluded the law. Even though the Wild Bunch had yet to commit their major robberies, the year 1897 was still considered the peak for the major outlaws in the Southwest, such as the "Black Jack" Ketchum and the High Five "Black Jack" Christian gangs.

Harvey and Lonie were still unknown to the law by name, but George Currie was dead center in its sights. After all, hadn't the Pinkertons called Currie the king of Wyoming's rustlers? Harvey Ray was a mystery man and Longabaugh was still unknown, except for his Sundance, Wyoming, jail time.

The outlaws would continue stealing livestock as well as committing petty crimes. What perhaps they didn't know was that the Pinkerton Detective Agency was investigating them on behalf of the Union Pacific Railroad, which was concerned about Powder Springs becoming a base of operations for future train robberies. At least one special agent was sent to investigate. He returned with the report that the area had many fine stolen horses, which were being fattened on grain stolen from adjacent sheep camps.

Great horses for great train robberies?

February and early March came in to the Powder River and Powder Springs areas with a bang.

First, the death of a young boy, William Strang, put an end to the days when Powder Springs could be an outlaw sanctuary. Strang was murdered by a fugitive killer, Patrick "Swede" Johnson, who was neither Swedish nor Irish, but a native Missourian and wanted for murder in Thompson, Utah (then called Thompson Springs). Author Richard Patterson described Johnson as "a hard-drinking cowpuncher and part-time rustler." The boy died at one of the Hoy brothers' ranches near Pine Mountain, north across the Wyoming border on Rock Creek, a tributary of the Green River. Strang was the son of a prospector, who was working abandoned claims in Ewing Canyon of Brown's Hole. The boy was under the temporary care of Albert "Speck" Williams, a former slave, coachman, soldier, and miner. For several years Williams had operated a ferry on the Green River, and he knew every outlaw, including Butch Cassidy. While watching Strang, he was operating a ferry at the mouth of Red Creek. Swede Johnson rode by and invited the boy to the ranch to learn to rope steers.

Strang's only crime was pouring water on Johnson while Johnson was taking a nap. Johnson started shooting at Strang's feet when Strang was going to the barn for horses (versions vary in details). One of these "playful" shots ended up in Strang's spine, and he died within the hour.

Johnson fled with fellow rustler, Jack "The Judge" Bennett, to

Powder Springs. They shared a camp with outlaw-fugitives Harry Tracy and David Lant, escapees from Utah State Penitentiary. Both men had been hiding in Uintah County, southwest of Vernal, Utah, near the town of Naples. When Tracy and Lant stole two horses, Sheriff William Preece of that county sent a posse after them, and they fled to Powder Springs. The two sent Bennett, who wasn't wanted by the law, for supplies and they in turn headed for Cold Springs Mountain. Another posse, under a sheriff from Routt County, was closing in from the east. At the Herb and Elizabeth Bassett ranch, located near the mouth of Vermillion Creek on the Green River, this posse learned of Strang's death and joined the Wyoming posse already looking for Strang's killer and friends. The fugitives then doubled back to Douglas Mountain, hoping to cross the river in Lodore Canyon to Diamond Mountain and on to Vernal.

Valentine Hoy, brother to J. S. Hoy, decided to form his own posse of local ranchers. He was soon followed by the Routt County sheriff. These posses ran into the outlaws on a steep trail after the wanted men had reversed their course (the trail was still blocked by deep winter snow). The three outlaws dove behind some large boulders for cover. Hoy, thinking that Johnson was alone, charged up the hill. Even after discovering there were three men, he still went after them, not knowing that Tracy was a killer. Hoy was about six feet from the fugitives when Tracy shot him in the heart. The posse made no further efforts to capture the outlaws, but later nabbed Bennett when he showed up with the supplies. Tracy and Lant were captured a few days later, only to soon escape, leaving the Brown's Park area behind.

Eventually several tri-state posses rendezvoused at the Bassetts' ranch, finally catching the three near Lookout Mountain. Bennett was nabbed bringing the supplies and ended his days swinging from the connecting upper pole of two tall gate posts. Seven vigilantes witnessed Bennett's execution, but the large number of lawmen and their posses were later vague about the circumstances of the death, as was Bennett's guard, Deputy Sheriff Farnham.

In March of 1898, J. S. Hoy demanded that action be taken against the outlaw gangs. As examples, he cited Tracy and Lant as the kind of men who were being allowed to stay in Brown's Park without intervention from law enforcement. He wanted an effort organized between law enforcement agencies from Canada to Mexico, including large rewards for the capture of criminals. He advocated extermination, hunting the outlaws down like dogs. The gang members took offense, but kept to their code of not bothering neighbors, instead going after a cattle camp of Hoy's in Colorado. They stole everything in sight, including cattle, horses, wagons, grub, and camp equipment. What they couldn't carry off, they destroyed.

This action may have intimidated ranchers, but not the four area governors (from Colorado, Wyoming, Utah, and Idaho). These men met in Denver to come up with a plan as Hoy had suggested. One idea was to circle Brown's Hole with state militia and arrest or kill any man who could not give an account of himself. Another governor thought it better to use a small force of men to eliminate the outlaws one by one. This force would be made up of five experienced officers from each of the three states around Brown's Park. The experienced lawmen would receive a hundred dollars a month and have the authority to kill on sight. Former army scout and Pinkerton agent Tom Horn had already killed several supposed outlaws and rustlers, but he had been working for cattlemen's associations, which often meant that the supposed "outlaws" he killed were likely innocent homesteaders. Horn, of course, ended up at the end of rope. Even his influential rancher friends couldn't save him.

The governors' plans were shelved when the Spanish-American War broke out on April 25, 1898. The war probably helped the outlaws in that some of the more experienced lawmen were joining state volunteer units. However, because of the Hoy and Strang killings, all law-enforcement agencies were now welcome in Brown's Hole, and so the Wild Bunch had to move on to the Southwest. They were basically on the run, and they would stay that way until their demise or capture.

Even the isolated Robber's Roost was receiving attention from the Utah governor, Heber Wells. He made up a list of the twelve most well-known rustlers who were using it as a headquarters and offered a reward of five hundred dollars for each man.

The Robber's Roost in southwestern Utah, at the summit of the San Rafael Swell, was the most remote and rugged of outlaw hideouts. A treeless and arid elevated plateau, it was cut with a complicated tangle of cliffs, canyons, and buttes. The outlaws' hiding place was on the northwest side of the plateau, on top of a mesa at the end of a steep, crooked trail. It had water, grass, and shade. Three trails led into the Roost: One ran forty-five miles from Hanksville, located to the west; another came from Bluff City to the southwest; and the third was sixty-five miles from the Green River community on the Green River to the north. The Green River provided the eastern boundary of the Roost; to the west were the Orange Cliffs. About fifty miles south were the Henry Mountains.

The incentives provided by Governor Wells brought fast action. With an eye on the reward money, Sheriff Jack Tyler of Moab entered Roost Canyon, and while the men he was after escaped, he proved that the law could enter the canyon and survive. Next Deputy U.S. Marshal Joe Bush took a try at it and captured an outlaw called "Silver Tip" on the Paria River, located to the south near the Arizona line. Previously in March of 1897, Sheriff Ebenezer's posse from Price, Utah, followed outlaw Joe Walker and his stolen horses to Robber's Roost. They found his camp at the mouth of a small blind canyon at Mexican Bend. The wounding of one posse member in a shoot-out ended that expedition. In April of 1898, after Walker and friends roughed up two young cowboys and took their horses and cattle, an expedition under Sheriff C. W. Allred of Price joined with Deputy U.S. Marshall Joe Bush to pursue Walker again. They followed the Price River and found a trail that led toward the Book Cliffs and Range Valley. The trail then led toward the Green River. Near Florence Creek, they found four men. Walker and John Herron were killed in the gunfight. There was quite the excitement when Herron (or Herring) was thought to be Butch Cassidy. The posse brought them back to civilization via the train from Thompson.

The point was being driven home to the outlaws that all three supply and rest-and-relaxation stations—Hole-in-the-Wall, Powder Springs, and now Robber's Roost—were no longer available for any extended period of time.

Harvey Logan was apparently quite busy during the spring and summer of 1898, if you believe the reports. In a book by Frank Lamb, *The Wild Bunch,* and in another book by Lamb's son, F. Bruce Lamb, *Kid Curry: The Life and Time of Harvey Logan,* Harvey is said to have robbed a bank in Arizona with the help of Ben Kilpatrick. The robbery supposedly happened in the mining town of Clifton, on the main north-south trail through southeast Arizona and southwest New Mexico. Kilpatrick, along with Will Carver (an outlaw from Texas), were former members of the Ketchum brothers' gang, which had consisted of "Black Jack" Tom Ketchum, Sam Ketchum, Carver, Kilpatrick, Dave Atkins, and others. The gang had killed several men, and they had robbed about seven trains throughout Texas, New Mexico, and Arizona.

The bank robbery supposedly happened about February of 1898. By then Logan had dropped the "Kid" moniker, and was at times calling himself Tom Caphart (or Kephart), the name of an actual, small-time outlaw operating in the same areas. The robbery, both Lambs claimed, had netted about twelve thousand dollars. But there are problems with this story. First no record of this robbery exists, either in newspapers or in the archives of the local historical society. The only local major outlaw event known to the residents of Green Lee County occurred in a canyon sixteen miles south of Clifton, now known as Black Jack Canyon, formerly Cole Creek Canyon. Christian was the leader of the High Five gang, and the supposed original "Black Jack." (The "Logan bank robbery" took an even more bizarre turn in 1898 when, as certain authors have claimed, Logan used his ill-gotten gain to travel to France. This is unlikely, although he may, at some point, have visited Paris.)

The next part of Harvey Logan's story begins in the town of Big Piney in western Wyoming. This was roaming country for the Currie and Logan outlaws when they were at the Hole-in-the-Wall and Kaycee areas. A combination country store and post office was opened by town founder Daniel B. Budd in March of 1897. In August of 1898 he was robbed of over two hundred dollars by three men, one of whom was believed to be Harvey Logan. The three men, strangers to Budd, had previously ordered fifty dollars in merchandise. They packed the goods on their horses, then returned to rob the store. The thieves were kind enough to return Budd's watch when he told them it was a keepsake. They were last seen heading north toward Wells.

Two townsmen followed the robbers to the timber by a tie camp near the Wells ranch. This was probably near Horse Creek, where railroad ties for the western railroads were made. The following day a posse from Pinedale, including U.S. Postal Inspector Waterbury and a Sheriff Ward, picked up the trail again, following the robbers to the high country above the Green River lakes. They found the outlaws camped in the timber. A firefight soon started with the sheriff and at least one posse member being wounded. The posse wisely did not try to follow the outlaws into the thick timber.

The outlaws moved east at a leisurely pace, traveling only about one hundred miles in eight days. The chase continued with only Waterbury and Deputy Sheriff Huston riding across the Big Horn Mountains and through the Powder River country. One version of the story says they lost the trail there, with the lawmen being convinced that it was Currie and the Roberts brothers in front of them. Another version says the posse was reinforced, and followed the gang to the Preston ranch near Gillette where the criminals stole thirty head of horses only to release them near the Montana line to cover their tracks. Next they might have picked up another herd of horses from the Northern Cattle Company, driving them north into Montana. Supposedly this posse stopped at the state line, and a Billings and Miles City posse took over the chase.

After their escape from the posse in Montana, the historical record doesn't find Logan, Currie, and Longabaugh again until we see them involved a train robbery in northern Nevada. Perhaps the flood of negative publicity (and its accompanying effect on the local lawmen) compelled the boys to stage a robbery elsewhere. It's quite possible they picked northern Nevada in the Humboldt River country because the area had a good market for stolen horses. They may have just been delivering a herd when they found a promising train to rob. The Spanish-American War had brought quite a demand for horses.

They are suspected of having robbed the Southern Pacific Railroad train number one, which was traveling northeast from Humboldt early on the morning of July 14, 1898. About 1:10 a.m., the train pulled out of the Humboldt station with two bandits on the blind front baggage car. About one mile out they climbed over the tender into the locomotive cab. They had the engineer pull ahead to milepost number 3,784 where horses were picketed. Once stopped, the bandits marched the engineer and fireman back to the express car. The express men refused to open the car—until the thieves threatened to blow it up.

Meanwhile the rear brakeman was suspecting a hold-up because of the unexpected stop. He jumped off the train, running back to the Humboldt Station to telephone ahead to Winnemucca. The sheriff organized a posse and requisitioned a special train.

While the two outlaws worked on the express car, the third bandit shot along the sides of the train to keep other trainmen and passengers inside. The blowing of the through safe revealed $20,000 to $26,000 in cash, and some jewelry. The gunmen politely shook hands with the trainmen and mounted their horses. They were last seen riding off to the north. The engineer would describe the bandits as being "two [white] men and a negro." Given Logan's darker complexion, this was a fairly common description of him.

After organizing at Winnemucca and traveling to Humboldt, inspecting the robbery scene then picking up the trail, the posse was about two hours behind the escaping gang. At the scene they found more dynamite, even though the charges that had been used had almost destroyed the safe's contents. Some discarded silver watches were also found on the trail. The posse gave up the chase because of a lack of supplies and worn-out horses. Humboldt County Sheriff McDeid and a Wells, Fargo agent continued to search, finding two possible suspects, Leslie Bowie and James Shaw, who were later exonerated at their trial. According to author Donna B. Ernst, the Pinkerton Detective Agency said that the trio of Longabaugh, Curry, and Currie had been seen together in the Humboldt River area around this period of time. This might have also been an opportunity for them to gather intelligence on a bank at Winnemucca for their later use.

Meanwhile another Robber's Roost outlaw met his end in Price, Utah. C. D. "Gunplay" Maxwell, alias John Carter, was also on Governor Wells's wanted list. Maxwell had been on a posse that had gone after Joe Walker in the Book Cliffs region northeast of Thompson. Maxwell wanted Walker dead because he considered him a rival—and there was only enough "glory" for one. Maxwell probably would have survived as a rustler, but he had to try bank robbery as well. His influential outlaw and stolen cattle-buying friends couldn't keep him out of the law's way. A Springville, Utah, bank job got Maxwell $3,020 in gold and a lot of trouble. He was captured by a posse at Hobble Creek just four miles outside of town. On September 20, 1898, he was sentenced to fourteen years in prison. His influential friends were able to get his sentence reduced, but he later became a liability to the same people, and his death may have come as the result of an assassination on the streets of Price in 1903.

While Harvey Logan was on the loose, being blamed for almost every major robbery in the area, Butch Cassidy was living in relative quiet, working with Elzy Lay at the WS ranch near Alma, New Mexico. Many large cattle ranches weren't fussy about whom they hired, as long as the men were good cowboys. In fact some companies specifically wanted men to work at their remote camps away from civilization and lawmen, in case they had had some trouble with the law. Remote Alma was on the end of the stage line from Silver City. The ranch was located on old Apache Indian hunting grounds near the San Francisco River. The San Francisco Mountains were on the west, the Mogollon range stood to the east and the Blues to the north.

The English-owned ranch was managed by Captain William French of Stokestown, county of Roscommon, Ireland. French, formerly of the British Army, had originally come to the ranch from California to manage some cattle he and some friends had purchased. He had started from the ground up in the ranching business, gaining the respect of cowhands and townspeople alike.

But French was experiencing some of the same problems as other ranchers throughout the West. The higher prices for beef were producing more thieves, and his foreman and crew couldn't (or wouldn't) stop the rustling. Cattle were being shipped by train from Magdalena near Socorro to a new range near Springer in Colfax County. This became part of Black Jack Ketchum's outlaw turf. French already knew about Ketchum as he had stolen two of French's personal horses.

French and his current ranch foreman agreed that Perry Tucker, who had previously worked at the ranch, was the right man for the foreman's job. To locate Tucker, French sent a letter to either Deming, New Mexico (where the Diamond A was located), or to Douglas, Arizona. In any case, Tucker came to French's ranch accompanied by Cassidy, who was now calling himself Jim Lowe (after an actual small-time outlaw, according to author James Horan). Lay was calling himself William McGinnis, an old friend of "Lowe's." Lowe became Tucker's assistant, and "Mac" became the bronc buster and horse wrangler on the cattle drive to the Magdalena railroad siding. Lowe ran the cattle drives, doing the best job French had ever seen.

French noticed almost immediately that better cowhands were showing up, and as they did, the theft of his livestock was decreasing. At this point, French couldn't have imagined that his ranch was becoming a major retreat for wanted men. And he didn't understand why some of the men acted as strangers to each other one minute, and then the next were sitting "under a fence in close contact like long lost brothers."

It was the first time that probably either French or the Wild Bunch had a sense of relief. French's ranch was operating well and the outlaws had peace and quiet from the law, although it would be of short duration.

The boys either finished their work in the fall or stayed on through the winter as part of a skeleton crew. In any case there appears to be no further notice of them until 1899. By then Butch may have been keeping busy with his saloon in Alma.

In March and April of 1899, Currie, Logan, and Longabaugh apparently returned to northern Nevada, perhaps again delivering a herd of horses. This time they shook off the trail dust further east of Humboldt on the Humboldt River at Elko. If they were indeed the same men who had robbed the Southern Pacific train at the Humboldt railroad station, they wouldn't have wanted to spend time in either Winnemucca or Humboldt. They settled in a rooming house to enjoy the pleasures of the town, especially gambling. The card playing was handled by Harry in his dress-up clothes. But his appearance didn't seem to help him with the cards, and he eventually lost all their money.

On either April 3 or 6, the trio entered the Club Saloon after midnight just when owner James Gutridge and the bartender, C. B. Nichols, were counting the receipts at the open safe behind the bar. One bandit moved the two around to the bar front and the third cleaned out the safe of between $550 and $3,000. The sheriff arrested three locals, but they proved to be innocent. Suspicion now focused on the three strangers, who it was now thought also might have been the train robbers at Humboldt. The names they had used were Joe Stewart, John Hunter, and Frank Bozeman. Since the saloon robbery occurred late at night, a posse probably wasn't raised until morning, if at all.

Far from Nevada, in the San Rafael, and Green River and Dirty Devil-Robber's Roost country, the crusade against rustlers was continuing to take its toll. The Roost gang was now down to Bill "Silver Tip" Wall, Blue John Griffith, Tom Dilly, and "Indian" Ed Newcomb. Sheriff Jesse Tyler of Moab continued to patrol the area, bringing back stolen horses. In the early spring of 1899, the gang returned to the Roost Ranch north of the Dirty Devil River. After being attacked there by a posse, Wall and Griffith split up. As mentioned earlier, Silver Tip was captured by Deputy U.S. Marshal Joe Bush, but he eventually escaped, never to be seen again.

The law was fast closing up the outlaws' old haunts, but the Wild Bunch had some life in it yet.

The Train Robbers' Syndicate

Newspapers all over the country covered the June 1899 incident, creating a huge amount of publicity for what would come to be called the Wilcox Train Robbery. The *Cheyenne Tribune* published a long headline, "Six masked men flag the train near Rock Creek—use dynamite to open express company safe. Escape north through Casper—pursued by sheriff and posses—ambush and kill Sheriff Hazen." The paper went on to call it "one of the most daring holdups in the western country." It occurred on the main line of the Union Pacific Railroad about 113 miles west of Cheyenne on Friday morning, June 2.

At about 2:15 a.m., engineer William "Grindstone" Jones in the first of two separate sections of the Overland Flyer (each with its own engine), which was carrying mail and express, observed a danger signal through the heavy downpour—two flashing lanterns, one red and the other white—just east of a bridge over a dry gulch. The train was between Wilcox and LeRoy, nine miles west of the Rock Creek station. Jones stopped the train per the signal, and two or three masked men climbed aboard the cab. After detaching a tourist sleeper and a private car from the mail and express cars, the two men ordered Jones to ease the train forward past the bridge. Jones didn't move fast enough and was slugged with a revolver by one of the bandits. The leader, believed to be George Currie, told the bandit (perhaps Harvey Logan) not to kill Jones.

The rear brakeman jumped off and flagged the second section (the passenger section) only five minutes behind where they had stopped.

The conductor came forward to see several men with guns, and he in turn headed back to warn the second section. After the bridge was thought to have been blown, the bandits ordered engineer Jones to move forward to Como Ridge where other bandits were waiting.

Once there and after the bridge had been dynamited, a fireman named Dietrick (whose job it was to shovel coal from the tender into the boiler) and the injured engineer Jones were marched back to the mail car. One clerk looked out the window to see why the train had stopped, and he thought the crewmen were chasing off some hoboes. The bandits started pounding on the mail-car door, calling for someone named Sherman, who was absent but whom they had apparently been expecting to be on the trip. The senior mail clerk, Burt Bruce, refused to open the door, ordering clerk Robert Lawson to extinguish the lights. For about fifteen minutes they threatened to blow up the car but then only fired rifle shots into it. The bandits could see the approaching lights of the second section, and the crew told them it was carrying soldiers. The five mail clerks were told they were only after the express car, but the bandits had with them enough dynamite to blow up the whole train. Fireman Dietrick tried to lift a robber's mask. The bandit didn't hit him, but he told Dietrick that if he tried it again, he would be struck. Dietrick did get booted in the rear end when ordered to the engine cab.

The bandits now had the mail clerks in tow. They next moved to the express car where their objective, the through safe, was located. In a scene that was portrayed in the movie, *Butch Cassidy and the Sundance Kid,* the bandits ordered the express messenger, C. E. Woodcock, to open up. He refused. Out of patience and time, the bandits blew the door. The charge threw Woodcock against the iron safe and left him dazed or unconscious. Both the local and through safes were blown. Soon bank-notes were floating in the air. There had also been a shipment of raspberries that was turned to jelly. The men collected their booty of cash, banknotes, and a few packages of jewelry and headed in a northerly direction.

The second section of the train was able to cross the damaged bridge and proceed to the robbery scene. Behind a snow fence that ran alongside the tracks, the crew found blankets, grain sacks, quilts, and more dynamite. The two sacks of dynamite had reportedly been stolen from Mahoney's railroad grading works in Cheyenne. Meanwhile the first section of the train had gone ahead to Aurora where there was a telegraph station.

The money take, as recounted by author Brown Waller, was $34,000, with $3,500 of it being unsigned currency of the First National Bank of Portland, Oregon. According to the *Cheyenne Ledger,* quoting a Union Pacific Railroad representative, the loss was about $700 in "good" money and $34,000 in unsigned national currency. (Local banks could issue currency if they bought an equal amount of federal bonds.) The bandits apparently missed another package with $10,000. Some of the currency also had the lower right corner torn away by the blast, as well as raspberry stains. Wild Bunch attorney Douglas Preston was also aboard the train, and he was seen by mining operator Finley P. Gridley. Judging from Preston's guilty reaction upon being recognized, Gridley didn't think it was an accident that Preston was aboard.

After the robbery, the outlaws mounted their horses and ceremoniously fired into the air before galloping away. Three went north, and three perhaps went toward Lander and the Shoshone reservation to the northwest. Although six men were reported by the engineer and fireman, only three were seen by the rest of the crew, and it is still a matter of debate just how many men made up the gang. The outlaws wore long masks reaching below their necks. They treated the crew well, except for the profane bandit, presumably Harvey Logan, who clubbed Jones. One man was described as being about six feet tall, another as about five feet seven inches. The taller one—the leader—was said to have been about fifty years old with a flattened nose and a squeaky voice. Two others were described as being dark skinned, one slightly larger than the other. They were possibly brothers.

The robbery was well timed, given that the isolated rail line was going to soon be moved northward to proceed through Rock River, Medicine Bow, and Hanna, making any future robberies much more difficult. At first, some of the crew that was working on the new section were under suspicion, but they were quickly eliminated from consideration as accomplices.

When the chase began, so did the local and national press coverage. George Currie and the Roberts brothers were credited with the robbery, but Butch Cassidy was mentioned as standing by in case of trouble. In fact, he was probably not involved, although he may have been involved in the planning. His prison photo was even shown in national newspapers. According to author Richard Patterson, the Pinkerton Agency's fliers privately listed Harvey Logan as the gang's leader. The posse split into two groups, one group following the bandits to the north and the other going northwest toward Lander. The outlook for the capture of the bandits was considered good since the North Platte River was at flood stage and all the bridges were supposedly guarded. But the weather conditions (heavy rain) weren't good for quickly following a trail or using blockades.

Early Saturday morning the chase began. Posses had been organized at Rawlins, Laramie, Dana, Medicine Bow, Casper, Rock Springs, Douglas, and Cheyenne. Union Pacific Railroad detectives were arriving on a special express train and car. The rewards being offered totaled up to two thousand dollars per robber. The Rawlins posse of Carbon County was apparently the first to arrive at the scene and start the northward trek, sometimes in knee-deep mud, keeping on the trail because one of the three outlaws' horse had a peculiarly shaped horseshoe. The trail led across the Laramie River plains, through La Bonte Creek Canyon, toward Douglas, then abruptly turned northwest, across the Laramie Mountains through Hat Six Canyon, and then followed the foothills to a marshy depression between Casper and Muddy Mountain. In almost forty-eight hours, the outlaws had covered about 110 miles.

It was now about 12:00 a.m. on Sunday, June 4, and Casper's rainy streets were empty. The outlaws passed by cowboys in the saloons who thought the gang members were either cowboys on their way home or patrolling lawmen. The trio continued on to Bucknum's livery stable, but he wouldn't answer the door, thinking they were just some drunks he didn't want to deal with. They did apparently get supplies and fresh horses from somewhere, perhaps from relatives of Currie.

Four different posses were out trying to prevent the robbers from crossing the North Platte River. All bridges were being watched except, unbelievably, the main one. The gang rode across the unguarded river bridge, despite the fact that several lawmen and Union Pacific Railroad detectives had arrived in Casper Saturday afternoon, making it their headquarters. The Rawlins posse and the posse under Union Pacific Railroad special agent Frank Wheeler hadn't yet arrived at Casper. They apparently were waiting for news of the outlaws' location.

Local rancher Al Hudspeth reported Sunday morning to the Natrona sheriff's office that while searching for stray horses six miles northwest of Casper on Casper Creek, he had run into three suspicious men near the new oil well shacks by the creek. One was cooking breakfast. The other two had come out of a shack at his approach, carrying rifles. They told him to "hit the road and hit it quick." He left the area and reported the incident. The three seemed to fit the description of the bandits, and a nine-man posse was formed under Sheriffs Oscar Hiestand of Natrona County and Joe Hazen of Converse County and Union Pacific Railroad Detective Frank Wheeler. A telegram was also sent to stock detective Joe LeFors of New Castle that he should join them.

The three were gone when the posse arrived, but muddy ground had made the trail easy to follow. It led north across high sandy hills toward the Powder River. The posse caught up with the men near a ranch on the Salt Creek Road about fifteen miles north of Casper. The three fired at the posse from behind a hill using bullets propelled by the newer, more powerful smokeless powder. One of the posse's horse was hit, and Sheriff Hiestand's horse bolted when a round hit the ground in front of it. The posse never saw the shooters. The sheriff walked back fifteen miles to secure a horse. Since it was apparently of poor quality, he went back to

Casper, finding another horse as well as supplies for the his men.

Meanwhile Hazen, Dr. J. F. Leeper, E. T. Payton, Al Hudspeth, J. F. Crawford, Sam Fish, J. B. Bradley, Lee Devine (of the CY Ranch), Tom McDonald, and Charles Heagney stayed on the trail. They dogged the outlaws all day Sunday and into Monday.

The outlaws set up a camp at Teapot Rock about twenty-five miles north of Casper, near East Teapot Creek. (The rock, seventy-five feet high and three hundred feet around, then resembled a teapot, but erosion has since made it look more like a disfigured hand.) The outlaws had been keeping to the low, pine-crested hills, yet now apparently abandoned caution and ate on an open treeless sandy flat. They felt some confidence because of their superior, high-powered rifles (using smokeless powder) that they'd be able to keep the posse members at a distance. They soon headed down a draw to the head of Teapot Creek, riding in the creek for about six miles to avoid leaving a trail. The posse rode a trail along the Pine Bluffs, spotting the three in a valley about a mile ahead. The posse had gained several members, and the leaders decided to try and surround the outlaws near the Jumbo waterhole or spring. They were now about forty miles north of Casper. The posse covered all valley entrances except for a dry creek bed in a narrow ravine surrounded by steep cliffs. They decided to wait until morning to attack, camping near the head of Jumbo watering hole. In the meantime the outlaws escaped.

The posse found the outlaws' saddled horses on the ridge after the horses had grazed away from camp. The day before the posse had also found a Pacific Express Winchester shotgun. Plus the outlaws had abandoned certain food supplies. They also learned that some of the posse members had passed within thirty feet of where the outlaws had been hiding in the sagebrush. The saddlebags on the horses contained rifle ammunition and some of the jewelry from the robbery. Now the fugitives were on foot and low on ammunition. The horses were found to be owned by Tom O'Day, Bob Taylor, and a Manual Manetta of Hole-in-the-Wall.

On foot now, the outlaws hoofed it ten miles to where they planned to make another stand in a deep coulee behind a rock formation. By 10:00 a.m. the posse had lost their trail, so Sheriff Hazen and Dr. Leeper continued to backtrack the loose outlaw horses to the head of a draw near the Jumbo waterhole, although the rest of the posse had wanted to look in a different direction. Hazen found the trail and called for Dr. Leeper. Leeper rode to within about six feet of Hazen when a rifle bullet struck Hazen in the stomach from seventy-five yards away. The round's impact was said to have lifted Hazen several inches off the ground. Hazen pulled himself up and ran back ten yards before falling. Leeper hit the ground as bullets flew about him, hoping the shooters would think he was dead. After the shooting stopped, Leeper did what he could for Hazen while the bandits headed down the Sullivan Fork of Castle Creek to the north of Castle Creek drainage. Author James Horan has written that CY cowboy Tom McDonald had been killed, but he had brought the news of Hazen's death to Casper.

Sheriff Hazen didn't reach Casper until the following morning because the posse had trouble finding a wagon for him. From Casper he was returned to Douglas on a special train. He was attended to by both a local doctor and a Union Pacific Railroad surgeon brought in from Cheyenne. But the rough ride to Casper and the significant loss of blood had both taken their tolls, and Hazen did not survive. The well-liked and well-respected forty-five-year-old Hazen had been in his second term as sheriff and had served a term in the state legislature. Although there weren't any death benefits for his wife and two children, Hazen had made money in the mining business at Hazenville as well as running a livery stable in Douglas. Plus he had an insurance policy through the Fraternal Order of Woodman.

Meanwhile, the posse had surrounded the coulee where the ambush had taken place, but found nothing, losing a lot of time in the process. They then struck a trail on a high ridge that led back to Kaycee and the Hole-in-the-Wall. By this time the posse had been joined by U.S. Marshal Hadsell's posse. Hadsell had requested Joe LeFors, but unfortunately LeFors and the Union Pacific Railroad and the new operative got into a personality clash, which harmed the pursuit efforts. Previously Hadsell's posse had been searching for the other three "ghost" outlaws in the Wind River country. At this point it wasn't clear if the other three robbers even existed.

On Tuesday morning, after traveling sixteen miles, the outlaws stopped at Kid's sheep camp at Sullivan Springs, but did not stay long. Wednesday morning, they had breakfast at Nelson's sheep camp near the "French oil wells," a reference to wells sunk by the Franco-Wyoming Oil Company, which also put down the first pipeline to the Casper refineries. John C. DeVore and herder Melia fed them. DeVore recognized Currie and the Curry-Roberts brothers, but he wasn't aware of the train robbery. Currie was apparently in a good mood. After breakfast the gang plodded on, following the South Fork of the Powder River to the Bar C ranch of Robert Tisdale. The Tisdale brothers, J. N. and Robert, were substantial ranchers, backed by midwestern money. They were not friendly to the small ranchers. Hence it gave the outlaws great pleasure to force Robert to feed them on Thursday morning. In spite of the high rivers, they then waded the river because the bridges were all guarded.

The posse reached Tisdale's ranch the following morning, still a day behind the gang. The fugitives, meanwhile, were being welcomed at John Nolan's ranch at Kaycee. The accepted story is that they stopped there for one day before moving on to the Red Fork where they obtained horses and supplies at the Billy Hill's ranch. Not true, says Wyoming historian Colin Taylor. They in fact stayed several nights at Nolen's ranch until he could find them saddles for the mounts. But Billy Hill never lived the story down and eventually moved to Canada.

Early on Friday June 9, a Union Pacific Railroad special agent named Tobin and posse member A. E. Minium arrived at the KC Ranch with a load of tarps for the posse to use. They mistakenly knocked on the door of Nolan's ranch house, but no one answered. They asked the blacksmith and cowboys about a posse staying there, but no one knew anything about it, and Nolan was out on a horse roundup. They finally went to Tisdale's, and there found the rest of the posse. It certainly would have been interesting to have the pursued and pursuers at the same ranch!

Lawman Hadsell and LeFors were perplexed that their sixty-five men couldn't prevent the trio from reaching the Powder River. (Including the unorganized men scouting the country, there were actually over two hundred men pursuing the trio.) The foul-ups were laid at the feet of Frank Wheeler, the Union Pacific Railroad special agent in charge of the search (a man who would supposedly listen to no one). It even seemed to them that Wheeler really didn't want to catch the gang, especially after Hazen's death. However, others have said that LeFors was overrated in his trailing prowess and always criticized others to make himself look better. In the meantime, however, and unknown to the lawmen, the outlaws were only a few miles away. At the Nolan place, a young girl, Cecil Ritter, was visiting Nolan's daughter and saw three men nervously looking out shaded windows to see if anyone was coming for them. John Nolan and a brother-in-law eventually found mounts and saddles for the three men. When leaving Nolan's, they were warned that Joe LeFors had joined the posse. Currie supposedly replied, "Joe LeFors would not get within rifle range of us." They left behind watches from the robbery as payment. A relative of Nolan's, Joe Gant, was supposedly arrested in Des Moines, Iowa, in possession of one of the watches.

The posse of Hadsell, LeFors, and Wheeler searched the area between Kaycee and Buffalo with no luck. Some felt that the outlaws had by now reached Montana. LeFors spent five days, traveling almost two hundred miles, following a possible trail that started near Hole-in-the-Wall, making only short stops at night in dry camps with little food. The trail led to the north end of EK Mountain through Dull Knife Pass, past the Billy Hill ranch in the Big Horn Mountains, west over the Big Horns and then down into the Bighorn Basin on No Water Creek, northeast of Thermopolis. In the meanwhile they were on Norwood

Creek, north of No Water and Kirby Creeks. From there they went west on Kirby Creek, eventually picking up the road to Thermopolis.

The posse, reinvigorated with dogs, thought they had picked up a trail, but they claimed that a local deputy sheriff persuaded the posse to detour west off the trail instead of staying on the south trail, taking the Lander lawmen away from those they pursued. LeFors thought the deputy had deliberately sent them on the wrong trail, but he had no proof. On top of this, the dogs gave up forty miles from Thermopolis. The pursuit was over, although LeFors followed several dead-end trails.

The boys crossed the Owl Creek Mountains from the Wind River by climbing a well-hidden trail up a side canyon on the west side of the Wind River Canyon. They went through Mexican Pass to return to the Wind River Basin.

They rendezvoused at the Muddy Creek Road ranch southwest of Thermopolis where Emery Burnaugh had recently located. Burnaugh was a friend of Cassidy's, and had recently moved to the area after a marriage. According to the Burnaughs, and as related primarily by author Larry Pointer, at least five outlaws—including Butch Cassidy—met in a cave behind the ranch buildings. It is not clear whether George Currie participated in this reunion or if he had already taken his cut. Currie had decided he'd had enough of train and bank robbing. He would stick to the mundane life of rustling livestock. Alice Burnaugh made sandwiches for the outlaws, and her two boys, Carl and Claude, took the food out to them in a lard pail. Bud, the youngest son, understood that one of the men had been badly wounded. He apparently died at the ranch a short time after arriving. Larry Pointer believed the dead man to be Harvey Ray, since he was never heard of again, and the others could be accounted for in future activities.

If Ray had been involved in the train heist, the two Curry brothers made three, Elzy Lay made four, and George Currie made five. Lay was implicated because, according to Anne Bassett of Brown's Park, Lay had given her a map showing the location where he had hid his part of the robbery money. Lay instructed her to send the money to his mother if he was killed. Longabaugh was likely the sixth participant in the robbery. (Although the famous Paul Newman film portrayed Cassidy as participating in the robbery, he, at most, took part in the planning.)

As related by Richard Patterson, shortly after meeting at Burnaugh's, Butch Cassidy was seen south of Thermopolis by attorney William L. Simpson. Simpson had previously put Cassidy behind bars for horse thievery. Simpson asked Butch if he had violated his oath to him, to District Judge Jesse Knight, and to Governor Richards not to commit any more crime in Wyoming. Cassidy told Simpson that he had helped in the escape but not the robbery.

According to author Charles Kelly, the outlaws all headed for Brown's Hole and then, via the Green River, proceeded to Robber's Roost where Cassidy paid his bill to a Hanksville merchant and his former employer, Charles Gibbons. Gibbons used the money for a trip with his wife to Salt Lake City, where he was arrested for having the stolen money. (The currency was identified by its serial numbers, and possibly by the torn corners.) He was able to convince the authorities that he wasn't part of Butch Cassidy's gang. Gibbons no doubt was initially angry at Butch, but later must have had a laugh over it as none of Butch's friends could stay mad at him very long.

As for Hadsell and LeFors, they might have taken some solace in the words of professional man hunter, Fred Hans, quoted in the *New York Times* as saying that the escape of the Wilcox outlaws was "the most remarkable flight in the criminal history of the West."

Enter the Pinkertons

Until the Wilcox train robbery, the Wild Bunch had been living a peaceful life in the Southwest, not pursued by the Pinkerton Agency (or any other law enforcement agency). They had been on good behavior, not committing any train or bank robberies in the area.

However, after the train heist, the outlaws were back in the spotlight as they apparently desired. They now had the full attention of the Pinkerton Detective Agency. According to James Horan, the official biographer of the agency, the Pinkertons "were the nineteenth century prototype of the present-day Federal Bureau of Investigation, and a forerunner of [Europe's] Interpol." Besides conducting their own direct investigations, they had a large number of police officers, sheriffs, public officials, businesspeople, private citizens, and even outlaws working both sides of the law, helping the agency lift the veil of secrecy that had protected the western outlaws. The Pinkertons did this by offering rewards, distributing wanted posters, and compiling information about the wanted men. The nerve center of the western operation was the office in Denver, Colorado.

Two weeks after the Wilcox train robbery and the killing of a sheriff, two veteran Pinkerton Agency operatives joined in the chase, Charlie Siringo and W. O. Sayles. From the Denver office they traveled to Salt Lake City where they obtained saddles, horses, a pack animal, and camping gear. Their first stop was Brown's Park. They had heard from lawman C. W. "Doc" Shores that two of the Wilcox robbers had just passed through Hanksville, Utah, on their way south. The two detectives arrived there ten days later, delayed due to heavy rains. At Hanksville, they learned that two men had come through, driving thirteen extra horses. The outlaws had crossed the Colorado River at the Dandy Crossing ferry where the Dirty Devil River joined the Colorado and continued southeast through White Canyon to Bluff City then south to Alma, New Mexico. The detectives also learned that a lone man with five more horses had crossed the river five days later. The man had told the ferry operator that he was going to "where the grass was good, and camp until he heard from his friends." The description of this man matched that of Harvey Logan.

The two Pinkertons picked up Logan's trail in White Canyon where he had taken his horses up onto a high rocky bluff. Evening set in and Sayles returned to Dandy's Crossing to obtain grain for their horses. Siringo meanwhile had climbed to the top of the level mesa where he lost the trail in a rocky arroyo. He searched the canyon for two miles and until dark, finding nothing. Siringo had missed the outlaw's camp by a half mile, according to a prospector who was watching the whole scene. Apparently Logan had been camped there for two weeks. When Sayles returned, they decided to follow the tracks of the other two outlaws. They never really found a trail after that, even though they searched in Colorado and New Mexico. It appears they were wrongly steered, either accidentally or intentionally. Sayles was ordered north to Harlem, Montana, where Wilcox robbery money was showing up. Siringo went all over the country, going as far as the Mississippi River, before receiving instructions to meet Sayles in Helena, Montana. There Siringo learned that the Currys were really the Logan family of Landusky, and that Lonie and his "brother" Bob had sold their saloon after being visited by a stranger. Some researchers claim Sayles and Siringo visited the saloon, or at least the town. James Horan, however, says that Lonie and cousin Bob Lee left before Sayles arrived a second time to apprehend them. Sayles had also been in the Giltedge and Lewistown areas with the Fergus County sheriff.

Siringo was given the job of going to Landusky and trying to learn more about the Currys, knowledge that both hoped would help in their capture.

About that time members of the Wild Bunch committed another train robbery, bringing the gang added attention and contributing to Harvey Logan's growing infamy, even though he was not involved. In fact Donna Ernst's research shows he was visiting family in the Kansas City and Dodson areas at the time.

On July 11, 1899, at about 11:00 p.m., a southbound Colorado and Southern "Texas Flyer" was robbed near Folsom, New Mexico, on an S-curve at Twin Mountain, just over the line from Trinidad, Colorado. Apparently a bandit had boarded when the train stopped to take on water at Folsom. The planning of the robbery had taken place in Lambert's Saloon next door to the James Hotel in Cimarron. The robbers included Elzy Lay, Sam Ketchum, and Will "Cowboy" Carver. They followed their usual procedure, taking members of the crew with them to the combination baggage and mail car, the door of which was quickly opened after a few shots were fired into it. But they used too much dynamite and blew up both the safe and the car. After all their work, they found the through safe was empty of all but a few packages; apparently the money had been taken off at the last stop. So they settled for eating some of a shipment of peaches and pears found in the express car, downed with whiskey.

There may have been a fourth bandit, a "Red" Weaver who might have ridden double with another man as they fled west. If so, he left the group near Springer where the WS ranch had property. The others continued on to a hideout cave in Turkey Creek Canyon, twenty miles farther west. A posse was organized at Trinidad, Colorado, consisting of Sheriff Edward Farr of Huerfano County, special railroad agent Will Reno of Denver, deputies F. H. Smith and Henry Love, Perfecto Cordova, Miguel Lopez, special express agents Captain Thatcher and James H. Morgan, U.S. Marshal Foraker, Wilson Elliot of Wells, Fargo, and Deputy Sheriff George Titsworth of Los Animos County. They found the robbers in an isolated canyon off Canadian Canyon on July 16, 1899.

The gun battle began before the posse was fully in position behind protective cover. Lay, known as William McGinnis, was shot while filling the coffee pot at a spring outside the hideout cave. There was a corral nearby. Ketchum came out to drag Lay behind a rock barrier but, in the process, became seriously wounded himself. Carver, known as G. W. Franks, was now left to fight the posse alone. And indeed, he was able to drive the posse back, killing Sheriff Farr and wounding several others. Elliot said that Carver "fought like a wildcat." Lying prone behind the barricade, he fired at the smoke of their weapons. They were using more modern weapons with cleaner, more powerful smokeless powder. The posse withdrew at dusk, and Carver had the task of getting the two wounded men on their horses. Lay was able to ride, but accounts differ with regard to Ketchum. He was either supported on his horse between the two, or rested and left later by himself. Either way, he ended up at the Lambert ranch, located at the confluence of Cimarron and Ute Creeks. The ranch crew dressed his wounds, but when the owner returned, Ketchum was turned over to the law.

WS manager William French was in the area on business for the ranch. On the way from Springer to Cimarron, he ran into C and S railroad detective William Reno, who had fled the shooting scene at Turkey Canyon. French heard that one of the outlaws was his old hand McGinnis, and that Sam Ketchum had been captured. French gave Reno a ride back to Springer where French learned more about the robbery.

Carver and Lay, meanwhile, had fled south to an unknown ranch where Carver dropped Lay off. A couple from Mexico apparently cared for him night and day, saving his life. About five weeks later, Carver and Lay met up again near the Lusk ranch near Carlsbad, camping east of the Pecos River. Carver had left camp for supplies when Sheriff McStewart and his men captured Lay. With Lay's capture, Carver temporarily scratched the outlaws' plans to escape to Texas, returning instead to the WS ranch. Logan also returned about that time. It is not clear whether Logan had planned to meet the two at their camp and join in the robbing of a bank in Carlsbad. French was asked to go Lay's bail, but he knew it wouldn't be granted in a capital case. He did appear as a character witness, however. A newspaper in Raton, New Mexico (where the trial was held), said that the "cowboys of northern New Mexico" paid for his expert defense attorney's fees. Lay received a life sentence for second-degree murder, but he was released after ten years due to good behavior. He was the only original Wild Bunch member to officially live a long life and die a natural death.

After Lay's capture and conviction, times were quiet at the WS ranch, even though French was apprehensive about having suspected outlaws on his ranch. About a month later his worst fears were confirmed when a Pinkerton Agency detective came to visit. The agent's mission was to find out who was passing bills from the Wilcox train robbery. Some of the currency—easy to trace with its blown-off corners—had turned up at the Silver City bank. It had then been traced back to the Alma general store, where a storekeeper told the detectives that the banknotes had come from an employee of the WS ranch, Johnny Ward. French had two Johnny Wards working for him, "Big" and "Little." It turned out that Little Johnny had allegedly received the notes from another WS cowboy who had called himself, "McDonigal," a man who had since left the area. The money had supposedly come from the sale of a horse to McDonigal. The Pinkerton man copied the serial numbers of the bills Ward had left in his possession, then let him keep the remainder. He also showed French a group photo, hoping he might recognize a face or two. French picked out his trail boss, Jim Lowe, whom the Pinkerton Agency then identified as Butch Cassidy, a man he would describe as the leader of the best organized gang that had ever existed in the West. The Pinkerton man was apparently Frank Murray (future Pinkerton assistant superintendent in the Denver office), and he had spotted Cassidy in Cassidy's Alma saloon that very morning, deciding not to try and arrest him by himself. Instead, he would try and track down this McDonigal.

When Cassidy returned to the ranch, French told him of his visit from the Pinkerton agent, and that he now knew he was Butch Cassidy. Butch then related to French that it hadn't taken long for Butch and his gang to figure out the stranger was a Pinkerton man, and they had even bought him drinks. The other gang members wanted to kill him, but Butch intervened, apparently based on Murray's promise to keep Cassidy's presence there a secret. Murray must have kept that promise because Butch stayed at Alma and the WS ranch until the end of 1899 without further trouble from any law enforcement agency.

Ranch foreman Perry Tucker decided it was time for him to move on back to Arizona and his ranch interests. Butch and French discussed the possibility of Butch becoming foreman, but they both came to the conclusion that it was best if he left. It is really quite believable that Butch was tired of the outlaw life and really wished he could stay on the ranch. A later action of his would prove it.

As a final favor to French and without French's knowledge, Butch and his traveling companion, "Red" Weaver, took with them all the horses from a neighboring ranch, an outfit that had built up its herd from French's. The rancher even had to walk several miles to a neighbor's place to borrow a horse to report the theft. The neighbor soon sold out, and French had no more problems with its herd. This gesture, though, brought Butch and Red trouble when the Apache County sheriff arrested them in St. Johns when they were unable to prove ownership of the horses they were herding. They appeared for arraignment back at Socorro, New Mexico, on April 25, 1900. They pled not guilty and posted a small bail, but the charges were eventually dismissed, probably thanks to French.

After leaving Alma, Butch went north to Utah to discuss a pardon or amnesty for his crimes, through attorneys Douglas Preston of Rock Springs and Orlando Powers of Salt Lake City. Apparently, had it not been for a missed meeting, the amnesty deal almost worked out. Another attempt was later made, but the train robbery in Tipton, Wyoming, finished that effort.

Cassidy was now in limbo and thinking seriously about South America. Harvey was hiding in Texas, and Lonie Logan and cousin Bob Lee were left to meet their own fates.

As reported by Sayles to Siringo, Lonie and Bob were operating a saloon in Harlem, Montana, on a Great Northern Railroad line. This was the shipping and receiving point for the town of Landusky where at least Lonie had resided.

Lonie, Harvey, and George Currie had all been identified as the three known northward-fleeing bandits of the Wilcox Station holdup. They were also associated with the killing of Sheriff Josiah Hazen, although only Harvey was directly blamed.

Chouteau County District Judge Dudley Dubose saw Lonie in Helena, when he helped him cash a check for fifty dollars, later learning that Lonie had needed the money to ride the train to a point near the robbery, perhaps Kemmerer, Wyoming. According to author Wayne Kindred, three of the bandits were in that town on April 10, buying a weapon and team, a wagon, camping outfit, and two saddle horses. Besides being wanted for the Wilcox robbery, Lonie was still wanted in connection with the 1897 Belle Fourche bank robbery. He was also known as a probable accessory to the killing of a Johnson County deputy, William Deane.

Lonie apparently arrived in Helena soon after the Wilcox robbery, along with Bob Lee, who, along with a new partner, had secured a job in Washington Gulch as timekeepers for the Hickler and Sudden Mining Company. The gulch was located in the Gold Creek area west of Helena. Lee and his partner started mining on their own in September. They also prospected in the French Bar on the Missouri River.

Meanwhile Lonie took a wide circuit to get to Harlem, apparently trying to build up alibis for the time of the train robbery. He visited friends in Lewistown, Giltedge, Rocky Point, and finally Landusky, where he saw both his family and Jim Thornhill, their former partner in the Landusky ranch. Lonie escorted a Hattie Nichols of Lewistown— who was apparently related to Thornhill through marriage—on the trip, returning her to Lewistown. Supposedly Lonie planned to buy mining equipment so he could develop his Landusky properties. Apparently, his share of the Wilcox money was intended to finance this venture as well as the saloon in Harlem. On July 5 he purchased a half interest in George Bowle's Club Saloon. Lonie paid five hundred dollars down and signed a note for the balance. It was now the Bowle's and Curry saloon. Lonie also rented a house in Harlem for his family on September 30, just before he returned to Helena. Before leaving, he spruced up the saloon with a new bar.

Lonie next took the train to Helena on October 22, renting a livery rig to go the seventy miles from there to Washington Gulch. On the way Lonie got drunk and offered a large sum of money to be driven to the claim of Bob Lee and his partner. A former employer, W. H. Sudden, agreed to take Lonie in the morning.

Lee and Lonie were reunited the following day and left after a couple of days in Great Falls to be meet former Valley County Sheriff Sid Willis at his Mint Saloon, a bar where soon-to-be famous painter Charlie Russell would eventually hang his hat. According to author Brown Waller, the visit went well, and they "were together everyday and had a hilarious time." However, Lonie apparently spent at least one of the stolen bills.

Once back in Harlem on Sunday, November 5, Lonie and Lee (who now called themselves "the Curry brothers") bought out the other interest in the saloon, redecorating it in early December. Things were going well, and the town was impressed with Lonie, a young man who had matured since the days when he'd shot up Landusky with his brothers. He made friends with the merchants and town's citizens, especially Bill Hart, who had a saloon in a local hotel, and J. D. B. Griegg, the newspaper editor. In fact Lonie was photographed helping to ink Griegg's first edition. Lonie also played fiddle and banjo for local dances, to which Bob escorted Elfie. A holiday turkey shoot was also planned to take place behind their saloon, with thirty turkeys to be awarded.

This situation probably felt great to Lonie, just as Butch Cassidy had thought or hoped the same thing about Alma. But one thing was going wrong—they were spending lots of money and had to dip into the stolen bills. They had kept the Wilcox money in a safe at the Cecil Hotel, and now they gave some of it to the local post office for change. In order to break the bills, however, the post office had to send five of the one hundred dollar notes to the Stockman's National Bank of Fort Benton. The Pinkerton Agency was notified, and the money was identified as part of the Wilcox money. Pinkerton sent Sayles to investigate since Siringo was on the trail of the other bandits. Sayles made his headquarters in Helena, taking at least one trip to Harlem on December 27, 1899. In the interim, the bank kept stalling, saying that the money had not yet been deposited. (Lee's correspondence with the bank was later used as evidence against him when he went to trial for his involvement in the robbery.)

Sayles's plan was to identify the brothers with help from the postmaster and return with reinforcements to apprehend them. But Sayles had apparently asked too many questions around the small town, and Lonie and Lee were tipped off. They left the area while Sayles waited for Siringo to come north to join him. They sold the saloon to George J. Ringwold of Great Falls, who had a small store south of town near the Milk River. They received three hundred dollars in cash, plus a note for the remainder, payable to Jim Thornhill of Landusky.

They also stole money raised in a raffle by Miss Clara Hirdler. She had been ill, and the money may have been meant to help her with medical bills. Some authors have said Lonie and Lee rode off to Landusky to say good-bye to Elfie and the kids, although this seems unlikely. The ride from Harlem would have taken too much time since so many lawmen had already been notified of their whereabouts.

They rode to the Zurich Great Northern train depot, sixteen miles west of Harlem, and boarded a train to Havre. Their trip south continued to Great Falls, then to Helena, Butte, and finally to Colorado. Conductor Louis Bayrell collected the fare from Bob out of a five-dollar bill. He didn't recognize Lonie, who was partly disguised by a drawn-down hat, a muffler over the bottom of his face (his mustache had been shaved off), and the collar up on his overcoat. Their trip ended at Cripple Creek, Colorado, west of Colorado Springs. Bob got a job dealing stud poker at the Antler Club. Lonie, now calling himself Frank Miller, went to the post office every day until a registered letter came from Jim Thornhill. Perhaps deciding that Bob had a better chance of disappearing into the woodwork if he wasn't around, Lonie departed for Dodson, Missouri. The postmaster had been suspicious of "Miller," however, and had notified the Pinkertons.

The two Pinkerton agents in Helena split up, with Sayles going after the pair in Colorado. Sayles went to Cripple Creek, missing Lonie by two weeks. Now calling himself Charles L. Carter, Siringo went undercover as an outlaw (something he did very well) to see what he could learn about Logan in Landusky. Siringo boarded a train for Great Falls, where he outfitted himself for a trip. From Great Falls he went to Lewistown. When he left Lewistown for Rocky Point, it was quite cold and snowing heavily. He had to turn back, seeking shelter at Giltedge. He tried a different route via "the red barn" ranch where he was held up again until the warm, chinook winds arrived. There he learned that Lonie had stopped at the same ranch both before and after the Wilcox robbery.

The Pinkertons continued their pursuit of Lonie and Bob Lee while Siringo traveled toward Landusky in a sea of prairie mud. The detective agency got a break when a letter from Lonie, in Dodson, to Elfie was intercepted. Lonie had been there since February 21. A posse was formed with three Kansas City, Missouri, police detectives and three Pinkerton men. They planned to raid the Lee farmhouse on Tuesday, February 27, but the party was stymied by a heavy snowstorm as well as a lack of rental horses and buggies. They remained in Kansas City until they could leave for Dodson the next morning in two four-horse carriages. The sixteen-mile journey took two hours, and they arrived about 8:00 a.m.

The Lee farm was located a mile west of Dodson. The house stood on a small, round hill northeast of the intersection of Troost Avenue and Dodson Road. The woods were about two hundred yards distant. The house was a five-room structure with three rooms downstairs and two rooms upstairs. There were others in the house besides Mrs. Lee, including her daughter Lizzie and the Young family. Two of the posse members stopped along Dodson Road to approach from the south. The other two stopped on Troost Avenue to approach from the west. They labored through deep snow to reach the house. They were all armed with pistols except one city detective who had a rifle.

Reportedly Lonie and Aunt Lee were sitting at the kitchen table eating breakfast when they saw the detectives approach. Logan decided to make a run for it instead of either making a stand inside the house (endangering the occupants) or surrendering. Logan put on his overcoat and hat and bolted out the south kitchen door, possibly with Mrs. Lee calling after him. Seeing only one carriage, Lonie went around the east side of the house toward the south gate on Dodson Road. At that point, officers appeared and shouted for Lonie to stop in the name of the law. Instead, Lonie drew his revolver and apparently ran for the timber to the south. His heavy clothes and the deep snow must have slowed his escape efforts. Both groups of lawmen opened fire as Lonie ran through the gate, firing twelve rounds in all. On a dead run, Lonie was not able to return fire with his Colt .45. (A second revolver, a Smith & Wesson .38, was later found secreted on Lonie's body.) He staggered, regained his balance, and pitched forward onto a snow bank. He fell on the south side of the road at the edge of a cornfield. The fatal bullet had entered the back of his head at about the height of his ears, passing through his brain and coming out his right cheek.

Lonie's body was bundled in a heavy carriage blanket and taken to Stewart's undertaking parlor on Walnut Street in Dodson. Later the body was taken to Kansas City, accompanied by a local justice of the peace, Alvin Douglas, and a coroner named Leslie. Lonie was described as being about thirty years old and 155 pounds, five feet seven inches tall and of slender build with a dark complexion, dark brown hair, and hazel eyes.

In all the years Lonie had been gone, he apparently hadn't written or paid a visit to the aunt who had raised him. She later said Lonie had told her that he was only wanted for moonshining. When the detectives entered the Lee house, they found her burning materials in the wood-stove. Some writers have suggested these materials might have been currency from the train robbery, although Lonie had had other money sent to him by Jim Thornhill. The house occupants testified that she was burning old underwear. The detectives were able to find at least one envelope with Bob's return address on it.

The body was positively identified by Sheriff Tom Clary of Chouteau County, Montana. It was viewed in Kansas City before being buried in the family plot at the Forest Hill Cemetery in Kansas City. Supposedly Mrs. Lee, upon viewing the body, said, "They have killed my little boy." In another version of the story, she said, "I want to tell you that you did an awful cowardly trick to just come down and shoot my little boy."

Lonie's death was not the only shock for Mrs. Lee. Her son Bob was later arrested for complicity in the Wilcox Train robbery. The actual charge should have been accessory after the fact, but he was tried in federal court in Cheyenne, Wyoming, for participating in the robbery. Like Lonie, he carried with him a clipping of the Wilcox affair, perhaps as a badge of honor. Mrs. Lee had to mortgage the family farm in order to pay for his lawyer.

The prosecution proved that Lee had handled the stolen funds, but not that he was at the scene of the robbery. In fact he was able to provide a solid defense that he was in or near Black Hawk, Colorado, at the time of the robbery. Interestingly a former partner of Lee's not only gave him an alibi but also told of their previous mining experiences in Arizona and Mexico. Some of the jury must have been impressed, too, because initially the jury saw it eight to four for guilty, but by the end of the day it was all for guilty. Bob received a ten-year sentence on May

1, 1900, but was released in February 1907 for good behavior. He reportedly returned to the Dodson area and worked as a bartender.

Lonie's Aunt Lee moved away from the Dodson house to the community of Dallas on James Road. She could not face the cornfield outside the house where Lonie died, plus she probably wanted to keep a lower profile.

The bounty on Lonie (it had increased with the crimes, and now stood at three thousand dollars) went to the Kansas City policemen since Pinkerton men could not accept rewards.

On May 5, 1900, Pinkerton Detective Agency Western Superintendent John C. Frazer, along with U.S. Marshal Frank Hadsell and attorney R. W. Breckons, met with Bob Lee in Laramie's Wyoming State Prison. After an hour and a half, he began to talk freely to the officers.

He denied any involvement in the Wilcox train robbery, saying he only learned of the details from cousin Lonie. He said only three men had been involved: Harvey Logan, George Currie, and a Frank Scramble (although Lonie had been identified). He said the Wilcox money in their possession had come from Scramble, who had paid Lonie for supplying horses for the Deadwood, South Dakota, jailbreak. The description of this man doesn't completely match any member of the Wild Bunch, so perhaps Bob was protecting the third man's identity.

Lee said he knew nothing about the Roberts brothers or anyone else. He did say that Harvey Logan had used the name of Frank Jones.

They asked Bob if he knew the last known whereabouts of Harvey Logan. He replied that Lonie had said Harvey had been living in Kansas City last January, but had left to join Frank Scramble in New Mexico. Bob thought the two might have been involved in a bank robbery in that state. In describing the aftermath of that robbery, Lee said, "They killed the Marshal who was close to them, also wounded an officer in the posse who subsequently died." This could be a garbled version of an incident in southwestern Arizona in which George Scarborough died and a deputy sheriff, Walter Birchfield, was wounded.

After Lee was released from prison, he returned to Jackson

County, Washington Township. In the 1910 U.S. Census, he was listed as the unmarried, forty-two-year-old proprietor of a pool hall. He died about two years later. His obituary named a wife, Minnie, and said he had been employed as a construction superintendent in Jackson County. The causes of his death were heart and kidney trouble.

Meanwhile, back in Landusky, Siringo, still calling himself Charles L. Carter, was doing his level best to learn more about Harvey's whereabouts. Fortuitously, Siringo ran into Jim Thornhill when Siringo's horse shied as he was riding by a saloon with a number of rough-looking men standing outside. The horse bucked, causing Siringo's Colt .45 revolver to fall out of his holster. Thornhill had observed the scene, and now returned Siringo's gun. They became friendly and Siringo went to work for him as a ranch hand. He learned much about the Logan brothers, including how Thornhill, watching Landusky try to fire his pistol, had told Harvey to shoot Landusky, and for that reason would always be Logan's friend. Thornhill and his wife had a three-year-old named Harvey in honor of Harvey Logan. (The boy carried a small toy pistol buckled around his waist.) The detective also met Julia Landusky and her family, including twenty-year-old daughter, Elfie, and Elfie's three-year-old son by Lonie, Lonie Jr.

Siringo injured himself in a runaway wagon accident and spent some time at the Thornhill place. He learned very little more except that Harvey sent mail to Thornhill via Chinook instead of Harlem because the Harlem post office was being watched. Of course Thornhill was bitter about Lonie's death and Bob Lee's prison term. Siringo also learned that Harvey was in the Southwest, and was preparing to rob another Union Pacific Railroad train. The Pinkertons decided that Harvey probably wouldn't return to the Little Rockies, and so directed Siringo to join Joe LeFors in Denver to follow up on a report that George Currie was in Mexico with a former Powder River outlaw, "Black" Henry Smith. The report turned out to be false.

By February of 1900, three of the Logan brothers were dead (Lonie and Johnny Logan by gunfire, and Hank from natural causes); Bob Lee and Elzy Lay were in prison; and the hunt was on for Will Carver, Harvey Logan, and George Currie. Rumors regarding their wherabouts abounded. Carver and Logan were erroneously spotted practically everywhere in Arizona, New Mexico, and Texas, and were credited with a number of major crimes. There was even a 1900 report that Tom Horn had killed Logan in the Hole-in-the-Wall after a fierce fight. Logan's name also surfaced in March when a mailman in Apache County, Arizona, reported seeing two suspicious individuals, resembling Harvey and Will Carver, camped about three miles north of St. Johns by the Little Colorado River.

Posses were organized and a chase ensued, at the end of which two posse members, Andrew Gibbons and Frank Lesuer, had been killed. The outlaws initially escaped, and the murders were laid at the feet of Harvey Logan and the Sam Bass gang, which no longer existed. Tod Carver, a member of the Jack Smith gang (which operated between St. Johns in Apache County and Holbrook in the adjacent Navajo County), later admitted to taking part in the killings. Carver, whose real name was T. C. Hilliard, was also implicated in the death of Sheriff Jess Tyler. He was arraigned for that killing but never went on trial. Author Charles Kelley believes he probably escaped.

But at least one murder of a lawman might have actually been committed by Harvey Logan. George Scarborough was a respected law officer in the region, having worked as a town constable, sheriff, and deputy U.S. marshal. (He was most known for his killing of John Selman, the notorious killer of John Wesley Hardin.) Scarborough lived with his wife, Mollie, and seven children in Deming, New Mexico, where he now worked as a stock detective.

A friend of Scarborough's, Walter Birchfield, was a foreman of the huge Diamond A ranch in the Aprinas and Playas Valley of southwest New Mexico. In April of 1900, Birchfield requested Scarborough's help to help chase Mexican cattle thieves on the border. Scarborough took a train from Deming, New Mexico, to the San Simon station, just over the state line into Arizona. After he met up with Birchfield, the two men followed a traditional outlaw trail into the San Simon Valley, then farther south yet to Rustler Park in the Chiricahua Mountains. At first they thought they might be on the trail of some Mexican smugglers operating across the borders, but then they noted the type of horseshoes that were making the tracks. They also discovered some Winchester shells.

As the trail led deeper and higher into Chiricahuas, the two men became increasingly wary. They found where the suspected outlaws had stopped for lunch, leaving behind a lard pail that had been used as a coffee pot. Meanwhile, near a place called Triangle Springs, the outlaws realized they were being followed and set up an ambush. When the two officers arrived at the springs about 2:00 p.m., they saw a pair of saddle horses. When they went to investigate, the outlaws opened fire from about seventy-five yards away. Scarborough and Birchfield took cover behind some rocks. When they later mounted their horses and tried to get in a better position, they ironically became perfect targets. Scarborough took a .30-40 bullet in his right upper leg, shattering the bone. His horse reared up and threw him off. Birchfield, meanwhile, was hit in the left arm. The two sought cover again, exchanging gunfire with the outlaws until nightfall. Scarborough had lost his rifle with his horse. Birchfield backed up thirty paces and piled up a rock shelter for Scarborough. After dark, Birchfield wrapped him in a blanket, left him behind the shelter, and went for help. First he tried a local ranch, but it was deserted. A storm came up, and he rode on to the railroad station at San Simon where he wired for a doctor. Afterward, he started back to the site of the shootout with four more cowboys and a wagon. They reached Scarborough at daybreak. The outlaws had long since departed. Scarborough was conscious but weak, still lying behind the improvised shelter. The base of a nearby tree was splintered from rifle fire. He was given water and a stretcher was improvised to take him down the mountain to the wagon. At the San Simon railroad station, the group met the doctor, Swope Broadneck, and Scarborough's son, Ed. The doctor dressed the wound and gave Scarborough morphine for the pain.

They put Scarborough aboard the train for his home in Deming. Doctors finally had to amputate his leg, but he was already weak from exposure and blood loss. He died from the trauma of the surgery. After he died, his former employer gave his family a year's salary to help them out.

Arizona and New Mexico newspapers attributed Scarborough's murder to Will Carver and Logan. Author Ed Bartholomew claimed that Carver was definitely one of the men, but the identity of the others was only conjecture. Although the death occurred in Cochise County, Arizona, a Sheriff Blair of Grant County, New Mexico, responded with a posse. After three weeks he finally had to give up the chase. Sheriff Beeler of St. Johns also tried to track the outlaws. After Birchfield received first aid for his wounded arm, he joined Beeler's posse. There were soon three Arizona posses in the field, from Silver City, St. Johns, and Bisbee. On April 17, 1900, the *Silver City Independent* proclaimed that "[t]he identity of the outlaws is thought to be known." But there was a long list of suspects. One such list included John Hunter (alias, Dick Smith), Bob Johnson (alias, Max Stein), one Wilson (alias, Smith), Tod Carver, and one unknown. Some lists included Logan calling himself Capehart and Ben Kilpatrick (alias, Bob Johnson). As Logan most likely intended, this was confusing since there was a real Tom Capehart who was a cowboy, a bronc rider, and a minor criminal. Then there was the theory that the remnants of the Butch Cassidy gang had deliberately set out to kill Scarborough because he was crowding them, and that they hadn't killed Birchfield because they knew him from the Diamond A Ranch days.

While no one was ever brought to justice for Scarborough's murder and while Will Carver and Harvey Logan came to be associated with it, the Pinkertons drew no such conclusions. There were too many outlaws and outlaw gangs operating in the area to lay the blame so specifically at the feet of two men.

The killing of both good and bad men continued. George "Flatnose" Currie, now calling himself Jim King, was the next victim.

After nearly being captured for the Wilcox holdup, Currie had decided that train robbery was not for him. He left the Hole-in-the-Wall country, which had become too hot for comfort, for Utah and the Castle Dale area south of Price. He then moved southeast to the Green River country in the latter part of 1899.

But then ranch manager Fullerton of the Webster Cattle Company north of Thompson on Hill Creek complained to Sheriff Tyler of Moab that he was losing cattle. They suspected men on the governor's list of wanted men from Robber's Roost, including Tom Rose, Will Roberts, and Tom Dilly. Around the same time that a posse formed by Tyler was making a complete sweep of the ranch, a Webster cowhand found a man changing brands on one of their cattle. The cowboy ordered him off, but the rustler drew his revolver and ordered the cowboy to leave instead. The cowhand met Sheriff Preece of Uintah County who was answering a call to assist Sheriff Tyler in his search efforts. A rider was sent to find Tyler while Preece and his posse went to the place the cowhand had described. From the Webster ranch on Hill Creek, the two posses rode together to the McPherson ranch on the Green River. They eventually found a deserted camp and the tracks of the rustler's horses running off and of the rustler following on foot.

The next day about noon they came up on George Currie walking with a bedroll and a rifle on his shoulder, bridle in his hand. The Preece posse exchanged gunfire with him, but no one was hit. That night Currie constructed a crude raft that allowed him to cross the river and find one of his horses. The chase continued the next day until the posse caught up with him again. Currie saw them coming and went up a hill, working from rock to rock, finally hiding behind a large boulder near the top. Sheriff Tyler with a second posse had moved up on Currie from behind and begun firing from the outlaw's side of the river. By 4:00 that afternoon there was no return fire, and the lawmen cautiously climbed up the hill. They found Currie dead, Winchester in his lap. He had a bullet through the back of his hat as well as a bullet through his cartridge belt that had come out through the back, so both posses could make a claim that they had killed him. The date was April 17, 1900.

Upon examining the body and possessions, they found a recent model Winchester, a fine Miles City-made saddle, and an exceptional quilt in his bedroll, made by a feminine hand. They strapped the outlaw on a mule and started across country to Thompson while Sheriff Preece and his posse continued to search for the other members of the rustler's gang. At Thompson, Currie's body was packed in ice. He was identified as George Currie by Pinkerton Agent Frank Murray. Currie's sister in Casper was notified, and John, Currie's father, picked up the body for burial back in Chadron, Nebraska.

Over Preece's objections, Sheriff Tyler received the reward from the Union Pacific for bringing Currie to justice.

Back in southern New Mexico and Arizona, Will Carver, Harvey Logan, and someone named Wilson were still roaming the country. They were suspected of robbing the Bauman and Son Bank in Las Cruces, New Mexico. With Carver and Logan were also (supposedly) a Mack Stein and Frank Loughlin. But then newspaper reports had them splitting up, with Carver and Logan going north into Wyoming.

The search continued for the rest of the rustlers who had operated with Currie. Sheriff Jesse Tyler, three thousand dollars richer thanks to the Union Pacific Railroad, was now after Tom Dilly, who was wanted for murder. Tyler had heard that Dilly was operating north of Thompson in the rugged country of Roan Cliffs and the East Tavaports Plateau. Sheriff Preece also joined the hunt. After reaching Post Canyon, they divided into two groups. Sheriff Preece and Fullerton went west while Sheriff Tyler, Sam Jenkins, and Deputy Sheriff Herbert Day, along with a boy named Mert Wade, went south.

East of the Green River, on the morning of the April 27, 1900, Tyler spotted a small bunch of horses near a camp in the willows. There were three men wrapped in blankets, squatting before a fire. Tyler initially believed them to be the Ute Indians they had helped cross a creek the day before. He rode up with Jenkins, hoping they could return the favor with information. As Tyler and Jenkins started to dismount, Tyler said something to the effect of, "Hello boys." These were his last words. The three men opened fire with their rifles. Jenkins was shot down as well. The officers had no chance to draw their saddle guns. Day supposedly started to join the fight but was fired at and rode away. He met the rest of the posse four miles away. Mert Wade safely hid in the surrounding bushes.

Day wasn't too coherent in his belief that there had been more assailants than three, having noted first the size of their horse herd. He did report that Jenkins had called out the name Dilly before dying. Preece mistakenly believed the shaken Day and went back to Moab for reinforcements. The trip required two days. When Preece and his men arrived at the camp, they discovered part of the outlaws' camping equipment, left behind to make it look as if they were still around. The posse lashed the bodies of Tyler and Jenkins onto mules and brought them out to civilization. Autopsies later revealed that Tyler had been struck twice in the back on the right side and Jenkins shot five times in the back.

Sheriff Preece notified regional law enforcement officers by telegraph, including Indian Agent Myton of Vernal who worked with the Unitah and Ouray Tribes, Superintendent Welby of the Rio Grande Western Railroad, Governor Wills, the sheriffs of Rock Springs, Wyoming, and Meeker, Colorado, and several others. The railroad furnished transportation for all the posses traveling to Thompson. The fact that the two men had been shot in the back and were unarmed caused the outlaws to lose favor with the public. The greatest manhunt in Utah's history had begun.

The law enforcement officials learned that three men had been in the area five days after Currie's death. Incredibly, they rode into the Webster ranch, claiming they were looking for money that George Currie had stashed in the vicinity, an amount that was about equal to the reward that Tyler had collected. Shortly after the Webster ranch visit, they were seen to the southwest, crossing the Colorado River. They resurfaced again about one month later, passing through Moab toward Thompson Canyon. On several occasions, they asked about where Currie was killed. Their leader was described as having dark skin, and possibly being Indian or Mexican. They were well equipped with high-quality horseflesh, and had a yellow packhorse. They also showed interest in knowing who the sheriff was who had killed Currie. They were seen entering Thompson Canyon two days before the murders of Tyler and Jenkins.

At first the authorities believed they were looking for Butch Cassidy, Harvey Logan, and Charley Hanks. But Cassidy wasn't a killer, and Hanks was in a Montana prison. It was more likely that Logan was being accompanied by Will Carver and Ben Kilpatrick.

The manhunt, although extensive—with the governors of Utah, Colorado, Wyoming, and Arizona involved, and with men guarding every known trail to Brown's Hole, Hole-in-the-Wall, Robber's Roost, and other haunts—was handicapped by a late start. Sheriff Preece and four men, getting an earlier start than others, went north through Uintah County.

The killers stopped eight miles to the north at the Turner Ranch, taking four of the owner's horses, saying they were going northeast up Hay Canyon and across the White River, and that they would pay for the horses as soon as they got some money. The White River flowed northeast, just south of Brown's Hole. Preece followed an old Indian Trail north and found the outlaws had changed horses at the Turner Ranch. The posse next stopped at the K Ranch on the Utah and Colorado border. They learned that three men had been camped there and now were supposedly heading for Brown's Hole. The search next centered around Rangley, at the confluence of the White River and Douglas Creek, about forty miles south of Brown's Hole. Preece camped on Bitter Creek near Rangley, losing five horses to thieves overnight. The search spread out from there. They picked up a trail about thirty miles beyond the White River where a camp that might have belonged to the outlaws was found, but then they lost the trail. The trio of fugitives could have gone to the Hole-in-the-Wall, but it would have been a dangerous trip. Brown's Hole was a possibility, although so was Arizona.

Logan was credited with two killings, although rounds had been fired by more than one man.

Pike Landusky, killed by Harvey Logan during a saloon brawl in December of 1894, was known for his fierce temper.

Jim Thornhill, center, is shown here with Pike Landusky's family in Landusky, Montana, ca. 1890. Julia Landusky is seated in the foreground. To the immediate right of Thornhill is a woman believed to be Elfie.

Above: *Harvey "Kid Curry" Logan's ranch near Landusky, Montana, is shown here in a photo taken ca. 1920.*

Below: *After being shot near Kansas City, Missouri, in 1900, Lonie Logan lies in state.*

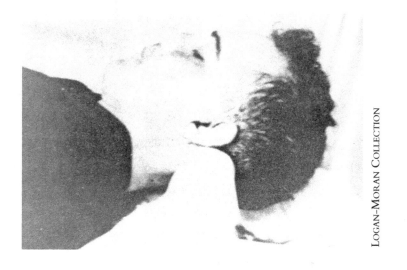

*Elfie Logan with her two children by Lonie, daughter
Mayme and Lonie Jr.*

Top: *The famous "Fort Worth Five" photo of Butch Cassidy and the Wild Bunch, taken in 1901. From left to right: Harry A. Longabaugh (The Sundance Kid), Will Carver (News Carver), Ben Kilpatrick (The Tall Texan), Harvey Logan (Kid Curry), and Robert Leroy Parker (Butch Cassidy).*

Bottom: *Harvey Logan and his girlfriend, Annie Rogers.*

The Dynamited Express Car after the Curry "Hold Up" between Malta and Wagner, Mont. July 3, 1901. "Kid" Curry's gang got away with $80,000.

Above: *The dynamited express car after the Curry hold-up between Malta and Wagner, Montana, July 3, 1901.*

Left: *Harvey Logan, after his arrest for the 1897 Belle Fourche bank robbery.*

*In this rare, previously unpublished photo, the three young
Logan brothers—Johnny on the left, Harvey center, and
Lonie—are shown in a moment of camaraderie, well before
they each set off on their unfortunate and bloody paths.*

*This photo of a man killed
near Parachute, Colorado,
in 1904, is argued by some
to be Harvey Logan,
despite the conspicuous
absence of certain identifying marks.*

The manhunt for Harvey Logan after the killings in Utah didn't detour the outlaw from continuing on his path of murder and mayhem. Authorities in several states had him at the top of their most wanted lists. It was perhaps unexpected, then, that he would return to Wyoming for his next robbery.

Some researchers have claimed that Butch Cassidy planned the Tipton, Wyoming, train robbery in retaliation after his Wyoming amnesty had fallen through. But Jim Thornhill had made it clear to Pinkerton agent Charles Siringo that Harvey had been planning such a robbery in revenge for Lonie's death and Bob Lee's imprisonment. Harvey's prime motivation was still more likely greed and glory, although perhaps the family deaths had made him more reckless.

Logan apparently stayed in the area of Brown's Hole after the killings of Tyler and Jenkins. Lowell Spence, assistant superintendent of the Pinkerton Agency's Chicago office, became the major pursuer of Logan after the famous "Fort Worth Five" photograph was taken. (This was a photo, taken in Fort Worth, of Harry Longabaugh, Will Carver, Ben Kilpatrick, Harvey Logan, and Robert "Butch Cassidy" Parker.) Spencer's log in which he kept track of Logan between June of 1899 and December of 1901 shows Harvey killing Sheriff Josiah Hazen after the Wilcox train robbery. Spence also describes six more killings through 1901. He credits Logan with the killing of Gibbons and Le Seur in a St.

Johns, Arizona, posse, but not the killing of George Scarborough. The authorities in Arizona had it exactly the opposite.

Spence's log has Logan in Rawlins, Wyoming, immediately before what would come to be known as the Tipton Train Robbery. This is reasonable since saloon owner Jack Ryan, previously from Dixon, had located his new saloon in Rawlins and was later thought by the Pinkertons to have helped with the logistics of the Tipton robbery operation. Jim Hanson of the Twenty Mile Ranch was located twenty miles southwest of Rawlins. Hanson and Jim Ferguson were friends. Outlaw historian Donna B. Ernst found that Ryan was also a part-time brakeman with the Union Pacific Railroad, the intended target.

This time, however, there wouldn't be any George Currie, Joe Walker, Lonie Logan, Elzy Lay, or "Bub" Meeks. And Butch, Will Carver, and Harvey Longabaugh would also be absent, planning and executing a bank robbery in Winnemucca, Nevada. But even while the dynamic of this holdup gang would be different, logistical help would come from several Little Snake River Valley residents.

On the evening of August 29, the second section of the Union Pacific train 3 was boarded west of the Tipton siding. An outlaw with two revolvers and wearing a red bandanna as a mask apparently climbed on the train there while they were taking on water. Near Table Rock, he took command of the engine cab, ordering the train to stop at a small campfire by the tracks. Engineer Henry Wallisten and Fireman Weaver obeyed. Table Rock was two and a half miles west of Tipton, and Tipton was about fifty miles west of Rawlins.

Conductor Ed Kerrigan got off the day coach and went forward to find out why the train had stopped. He encountered one of the four bandits, who told him to disconnect the mail and express cars from the rest of the train. Kerrigan began to climb back on the day coach. The same holdup man told him to uncouple the cars immediately. Kerrigan set the brakes of all the cars since the head brakeman had run off behind some nearby bushes and told all the passengers not to put their heads out of the windows. One hearing-impaired passenger did stick his head out but quickly withdrew it when he saw the flash of gunfire. Another passenger left his car to see the robbery scene and received a gun barrel over his head for his trouble.

With all brakes properly set and the mail and express cars separated from the coaches, the crew was herded into the cab and sent down the tracks another mile or two. One bandit watched the crew and postal employees while the other three worked on the express car, which again was occupied, as it had been at Wilcox, by Charles E. Woodcock. Conductor Kerrigan told the man to come out or dynamite would be used (again) to get him out. After several attempts Kerrigan was able to convince Woodcock to open the doors. The bandits set three charges on the through safe, demolishing the express car and damaging one end of the mail car. They scooped up the contents of the safes into a gunnysack, mounted their horses, and fired a few farewell shots into the air. They headed off toward the southwest. One bandit had asked Kerrigan the time. As he was removing his pocket watch, he remembered that the bandit probably wanted it, too. "No," the man replied, "we want nothing from you railroad boys." The robbery was over in twenty minutes, but the train arrived two hours late in Green River, pulling the mangled cars. The crime was reported at the Bitter Creek railroad station, which had the nearest telegraph.

In addition to Harvey Logan (the "profane one"), the train crew mistakenly believed that the robbers included Butch Cassidy, Harry Longabaugh, and another, unidentified man. Engineer Wallisteen and the mail clerk, Pruitt, had heard a rambling discussion from an unknown bandit guarding the train crew, who said that the robbers had done well at Wilcox, even though it hadn't been the original target. They had wanted the gold shipment from the week before but hadn't stopped the train because of two cars that had hoboes aboard who the robbers had thought were officers. He didn't know what they would find here, but they were short of money. He talked of not wanting to hurt anyone, but it could happen. He said they should have killed the engineer on the Wilcox run because he hadn't been cooperative enough. And Sheriff

Hazen had to be killed, he explained, because he wouldn't stop following them. The bandit said that they were not scared because they knew of back roads that no one else knew about, and they would shoot anyone who got too close, anyway. He also said that they had all agreed that any member of the gang who killed unnecessarily would in turn be killed by one of their own members. He was probably referring to Logan, who had a reputation for violence and profanity.

According to Donna B. Ernst, three of the train robbers were Harvey Logan, Ben Kilpatrick, and William Cruzan, an ex-convict and resident of Rawlins. Cruzan had replaced Longabaugh, who was on his way to the Nevada bank. The identity of the fourth man, while he had apparently also been at Wilcox, remains unknown, although many writers have speculated on it. There might have also been a fifth participant, Laura Bullion, who often accompanied Ben Kilpatrick on his expeditions and held his horses.

The amount of money the gang obtained has also been a subject of debate. The official amount taken was either $50.40 or $154.00. (They apparently didn't get the six hundred dollars that Woodcock had hidden behind some baggage.) Others said unofficially it was more like $55,000. The train was scheduled to carry $100,000 of government money, but that shipment had been delayed. However, there is an interesting story in *Wyoming Place Names*. Author Mae Urbanck says they got less than fifty dollars in cash and three bags of coins they thought were gold. When they stopped to divide the loot, they found the sacks contained only pennies. Logan supposedly let out a war whoop and said, "They can't make us take that kind of money." In disgust he poured the pennies down a prairie dog hole.

The official loss according to Pacific Express Superintendent Rogers was $50.40 in cash and two packages of jewelry. The robbers obtained thirty-nine separate packages from the safe. Among other things, they contained canceled baggage checks and express company communications. The money came in amounts of $42.00, $5.00 and $3.40. The damage done to the car was estimated at over $3,000.

The Union Pacific Express Company offered a reward of a thousand dollars per man, and the Union Pacific Railroad matched the reward, making the total eight thousand dollars.

Joe LeFors and U.S. Marshal Frank Hadsell happened to be staying overnight in a hotel in Rawlins when the robbery occurred. Frank Wheeler of the Union Pacific Mounted Rangers was also in town. Several posses were formed under the leadership of Wheeler. A group from Rawlins was delayed because of mechanical problems with the special train near Creston, and they arrived late to the scene. But they had wired Sheriff Swanson at Green River to also organize a posse, and he was soon following the trail. With LeFors and Hadsell's group were Sheriff Daniels and Deputy Sheriff Horton of Carbon County.

In the interim reports were coming in that some suspicious characters had hung around the company restaurant at Tipton before the robbery. A rancher, who grazed cattle near the robbery area, claimed to have seen Butch Cassidy and four others about two weeks before the robbery. Based on this evidence, it's possible that Cassidy was involved in the planning of the robbery, although not its execution.

The outlaws' trail was taken up at daybreak by Sheriff Swanson across the Red Desert, where, according to *Wyoming: A Guide to its History, Highways and People,* "Patches of alkali alternate . . . with clumps of sage and greasewood, occasional jutting red rocks disturb the monotony of gray salt shale and greenish-gray shrubs. Winter winds sweep the snow into deep arroyos and gulches, leaving the sparse plants uncovered for sheep feed." Then there were the higher geological formations to cross, such as Delaney's Rim, the Haystacks, and Horseshoe Bend. This is the country where the outlaws were sure they could ditch the posse, or even lead its members to their deaths.

Hadsell, LeFors, Wheeler, Sheriff Daniels, and eight more men quickly followed Swanson, soon catching up with him. The trail led southeast toward the Little Snake River Valley. The Haystack Flats slowed Swanson's large posse, the hard ground making tracking difficult. When Swanson lost the trail, LeFors swung to the south, picking it up again. The men were soon strung out behind him for two miles. A number of the posse members dropped out due to poor horses, halving its size to twenty men. LeFors determined he was following three men and a pack animal. The outlaws had obviously hoped that the posse would water its horses at Soda Springs, thinking that the bad water would harm or kill their horses. As recounted by Brown Waller, the outlaws used every evasive trick they knew to elude the lawmen. They followed the rocks and ledges and dry creek beds and, once in Colorado, drove range horses over their trail to help cover their tracks. At that point they were about twenty-five miles from water, and the outlaws hoped the posse would quit. But they didn't know LeFors. The outlaws reached the eastern edge of Brown's Park and turned south to a creek of running water, one of at least three major creeks in the area that flowed north into the Little Snake River.

LeFors and Deputy D. S. Harlen, having the best horses, went ahead of the worn-out posse. By sundown all members of the posse had reached the Little Snake River Valley. The two lawmen saw the outlaws going up a long slope on the other side of the river. Since they hadn't had any sleep in twenty hours and the horses hadn't rested for twelve hours, they decided to camp and pick up the trail at daylight instead of risking an ambush. LeFors believed the bandits must have divided the loot at their camp because of the quantity of torn paper from express packages. Also there were the burned remains of holdup masks, and evidence of a sandwich breakfast.

The twelve men who were left in the posse followed a trail on the Little Snake River to an area south of Baggs called Horsehead Buttes. Near Timberlake Creek between the Little Snake and Yampa Rivers, they discovered an old gray packhorse in poor condition, barely able to stand. The posse found a trail south that they felt would eventually lead west into the eastern edge of Brown's Hole. Within another fifteen miles, the trail led through a patch of willows and across swampy, low-lying ground. Posse members readied their weapons since this was a perfect place for an ambush. They then saw horses' legs in the willows. The men surrounded the area, while LeFors went in with two law officers, Harlan and Osborne. They found three horses that had been replaced with fresh ones. As author Richard Patterson put it, "It was a clever Wild Bunch maneuver." LeFors claimed they had traveled about 120 miles.

The posse members decided it was time to quit and head for "the big Perkins ranch" for something to eat. They were probably right, since their played-out horses couldn't have caught the bandits now. The robbery had occurred on August 29, and the chase was over on September 4. Rains came to the broken county, erasing the trail and seeming to confirm their decision to quit. Sheriff McDaniel, Deputy Sheriff Horton, and three posse members continued the search, but to no avail. Soon after, a lawman supposedly found a trail leading south toward Hahn's Peak, Colorado. This report might have been connected with an earlier incident at the copper mining town of Encampment, Wyoming. A woman reported seeing a man peering into her woodshed. She described him as wearing overalls, a dark coat, and a soft black hat. She saw him ride off with three other men.

But this was yet another rumor, as at least two of the bandits were quite comfortable on Jim Ferguson's ranch at the foot of Black Mountain above Dixon, just across the Colorado line into Wyoming. The outlaws were camped where Ferguson could bring them supplies and gave them information on the movements of the law.

The Pinkerton Agency had sprung into action when the Denver office received a tip from an ex-convict who said that he had talked with Harvey Logan and a tall companion (Ben Kilpatrick) at their camp on a mesa twenty miles south of Grand Junction. This would have been after September 23, according to Lowell Spence's log of Logan's activities. The ex-convict had told a Pinkerton man that Logan was heading south where the climate would fit their clothes. Siringo took the train to Grand Junction and stayed with C. W. "Doc" Shores while he put an outfit together for the trip. Shores had been a Gunnison County sheriff, a stock detective, Pinkerton detective, and was a railroad special agent.

Siringo first stopped at the Elliot ranch east of Gunnison, learning that the suspects had passed through a week earlier. From there he went to Paradox Valley and the Young ranch where he learned that the two had gone south with Lafe Young, who was also wanted by the law. The elder Young claimed that the three had gone over the Colorado state line to the La Sal Mountains. This turned out to be the wrong trail, costing Siringo a week of lost time. He next headed for the Blue Mountains where the Carlise ranch was located, near Monticello, Utah. The owners, Edmund and Harold Carlise, often invited outlaws to stay with them in order to ward off rustlers. The foreman, Bill "Latigo" Gordon, told Siringo that the boys had said they'd failed to get any money from the Tipton train robbery, and so he had supplied them with a grubstake. In addition he learned they had intended to continue south. Siringo also visited a camp of tough characters at a place called Indian Creek. From someone called "Peg Leg," he learned that the outlaws had been camped in the area. When Logan and Kirkpatrick started south, Young had returned to his family's ranch in Paradox Valley.

After learning much about the out-of-the-way trails used by outlaws in the area, Siringo continued to Bluff City near the San Juan River where he and Sayles previously had tried trailing the Wilcox robbers. He received orders to head to Circleville in Utah's Sevier Valley to learn more about Butch Cassidy's past. From there he headed for Arizona and New Mexico, ultimately returning to Grand Junction before setting out to find Jim Ferguson (who had been run out of Dixon by the vigilantes for aiding the Wild Bunch). Siringo later wrote that he found him on "a small patch of land in an out-of-the-way place on Grand River near Palisade, twenty miles above Grand Junction with his young wife and two pretty little girls."

Ferguson was an ex-convict from Keystone, South Dakota. A dangerous man with a violent temper. But Siringo became his buddy once he convinced Ferguson that he was a wanted outlaw. This was probably the closest that Siringo had so far come to the Wild Bunch. Ferguson had furnished horses and grub prior to and after the recent train robbery at Tipton. (Jim Hanson of the Twenty Mile ranch had also supplied horses.) Ferguson confirmed the three secreted outlaws had been Logan, Cruzan, and Ben Kilpatrick. Cruzan had elected not to go south and had returned to Grand Junction area where he had met Bert Charter, the man who had carried letters or messages between the gang's associates and members.

In the meantime the Pinkertons had other problems to deal with. On September 19, 1900, the First National Bank of Winnemucca, Nevada, had been robbed of $32,340. Involved were Butch Cassidy, Will Carver, and Harvey Longabaugh, besides those who held the horses and set up the horse relays. The robbery was over in five minutes, but the chase lasted several days. The trail was finally lost in the valley of the Owyhee River, thirty miles from Tuscarara, north of Elko on the Oregon border.

Now it was time for a going away celebration in Texas, after which the Wild Bunch would disband, never to be reunited.

The log of Pinkerton detective Lowell Spence places Harvey Logan in both Fort Worth and San Antonio in October. Harvey (going by the name Bob Nevilles) and Will Carver (as Will Casey) were visiting the San Antonio Exposition, a yearly event held at the International Fairgrounds. There they met Lillie Davis (using the name Callie May Hunt) and Annie Rogers (using one of her many aliases) of Fannie Porter's local bordello. They got along so well that they decided to travel to Fort Worth, Houston, and then back to San Antonio. Carver must have been the man with the money since Harvey had gained nothing from the Tipton, Wyoming, train robbery.

They returned to Fort Worth for Will Carver's sudden marriage to Davis. The most prominent members of the Wild Bunch all met at Maddox Flats apartments in Fort Worth to celebrate. Historians initially said this was a pretend marriage, but then author Donna B. Ernst came up with a record of the marriage actually having taken place in Tarrant County on December 1, 1900.

But the fun the Wild Bunch had in Fort Worth eventually came at a high cost. The duded-up party—including Harry Longabaugh, Will Carver, Ben Kilpatrick, Harvey Logan, and Butch Cassidy—had stopped off at John Swartz's gallery, a few blocks from the Maddox Flats, to have their picture taken. This was the famous Fort Worth Five photograph, and it was an image welcomed by the Pinkertons, Wells, Fargo, the Union Pacific, the U.S. Marshal's Service, as well as city and county law officers.

Author Richard F. Selcer in *Hell's Half Acre* explains why the famous picture was taken. According to Selcer the boys had purchased derbies for the wedding. On the way back they walked by Swartz's gallery-studio and, on impulse, had their group photo taken. The boys received the prints, Swartz kept the negative, and later placed the famous photograph in his window. Then a lawman, possibly Fred Dodge of Wells, Fargo, whose office was only a block away, noticed the picture. Soon the Pinkertons and lawmen had the photo, and sent one to the Winnemucca Bank in Nevada for identification. Selcer quotes Logan, in an interview with a Bert Vincent of the *Knoxville News-Sentinel* conducted in Logan's jail cell, as saying, "One day one of us saw a Pinkerton detective on the street, and in thirty minutes the [Fort Worth] apartment was empty." The Pinkertons made the photograph a high priority, putting out a wanted poster that was circulated all over the country. But apparently, even with the picture, the Pinkertons had trouble putting a real name to some members of the gang.

After Fort Worth, it was honeymoon time for Carver and Davis, with Harvey and Annie going along. The first stop was Denver, where the group stayed at the famous Victor Hotel. The last stop was the McFall House in Shoshone, Idaho. In Harvey's Tennessee court disposition for Annie Rogers at Nashville, he also mentioned going to Helena and Butte, Montana.

But the boys had other things on their mind besides touring. They disappeared for five days and returned with several sacks of gold coins from the Winnemucca, Nevada, bank robbery. (Foolishly, Butch, Will Carver, and Harry Longabaugh had decided to dispense with masks for the Nevada bank job, a decision that later made it easier for witnesses to identify them.) Flush with cash, the two couples returned to Denver to stay at Brown's Palace and rooming house. Harvey bought some new clothing—and the others probably did as well. The trip ended at the Bank's Hotel in Fort Worth. Lillie received a set of diamond earrings and a fur sack from Will, which cost $275. He sent her home with $167, and then sent another $70 in currency just before his death in Sonora.

Harvey gave Annie one hundred dollars and sent her back to Fannie Porter's while he and Will headed for the country south of San Angelo. The couple would stay in contact through her father's family at Kennedale, a suburb of Fort Worth.

Cassidy, Longabaugh, and girlfriend Etta Place had left for New York. Carver, Logan, and Kilpatrick went back to Porter's for Christmas in San Antonio and then to the San Angelo area. Lillie went home to Palestine—now a respectable woman—where her father lived, and Annie apparently remained at Porter's.

Butch had not been able to convince Logan to go to South America with them and try to become a legitimate rancher. Logan planned on making one more big robbery, go on a tour of the South with Annie, and then start another gang in the West. Kilpatrick and Carver were probably part of that plan.

In San Angelo Carver supposedly tried to kill a Rufus Thomas, who had helped capture Elzy Lay near Carlsbad, New Mexico. Carver stalked Thomas, intending to kill him, but Thomas stayed in a poker game for two days with a sheriff and two Texas Rangers, and Carver eventually abandoned his attempt. There is the story that on Carver's next try, the target was laid up with some malady in a hotel room.

After visiting Knickerbocker, Carver, Logan, and Kilpatrick moved on to Christoval. They may have also stopped near Bandera where Carver's mother and stepfather lived. Their hoped-for place of retreat was the Kilpatrick home in the [Cedar] Hills settlement, about seven miles from Eden. The county seat was at Paint Rock, twenty miles to the north. The area to the south and east of San Angelo had been home to several outlaws, including the Ketchum brothers, Carver, some of the Bullion and Kilpatrick families, and Dave Atkins (according to Barbara Barton in *Den of Outlaws*).

Laura Bullion's older sister, Viana, had been married to Carver, but she had died in childbirth in 1892. Laura's brother, Ed, was believed to have been killed with the Ketchum brothers' gang during a hold-up. Carver and Laura became serious, and she accompanied him to San

Antonio and Fort Worth. This was before he took up with Lillie Davis. However, the 1900 census shows her both residing at the Lamberts in Sonora (Sutton County), Texas, and with the Byler family at Dove Creek in Tom Green County, so their relationship must have been of a short duration.

Harvey and Carver were actually camping in an area adjacent to the Kilpatrick family on the old Mollery Cattle Ranch pasture. The boys took it easy until conflict found them again. The Kilpatricks were having trouble with a neighbor and former lawman, Ed Dozier (or Dorier), who lived about a mile away. On March 27, 1901, Dozier's hired man, Oliver Thornton, was killed at the Kilpatrick place. The story generally goes that the Kilpatrick hogs were wandering onto Dozier's property, and he sent Thornton to warn them about it. Then the story turns murky, with several unanswered questions: Was Thornton unarmed? Was he killed by Logan or Carver or by one of the Kilpatricks? Did Dozier complain to the sheriff that there were outlaws staying at the Kilpatricks? Did Carver threaten to kill Dozier if he didn't shut up? And lastly, if Dozier thought the men were dangerous, why did he send only one man? (According to nearby rancher John Loomis in his memoirs, Carver threatened to kill Dozier, and "this news made Ed somewhat nervous.")

The Kilpatricks claimed that Thornton had been armed and made demands about the boys and their wandering hogs. Ed supposedly told Thornton that the hogs belonged to his brother, Boone, and they wanted no trouble. Logan must have decided that Thornton was a threat because he waved a rifle at them, and he shot Thornton in the chest. Then Logan shot him again when he tried to run away. Thornton fell over a log near the spring, firing a third time. The Dozier-Thornton people claimed that Thornton was unarmed and not a threat. However, it is hard to believe that Logan would shoot an unarmed man and completely blow the gang's cover.

In a later telling, Thornton's rifle became a shotgun, and Carver . . . no, a Kilpatrick killed him. Another theory advanced for the shooting was that the boys suspected that Thornton was an undercover lawman.

When her husband didn't return, Mrs. Thornton got worried, and, taking a dog along, checked the Kilpatrick place. She found the house deserted and locked. Her dog ran off down to a shed at the back of the house and continued running, barking to the spring. She followed the dog to the spring, finding her husband's body spread out over a log with three bullets in him. However, there was no evidence of blood loss, hence he must have been killed elsewhere.

Ed Kilpatrick reported the incident to a deputy at Eden after giving the others time to escape. They had also had more time to escape because the telegraph line north to Paint Rock had been cut, coincidently located in the same pasture where they had been camped. Another telegraph line was later cut at El Dorado, about forty miles to the southwest in Schleicher County.

The delayed posse headed for El Dorado. The description put out for "Walker," described him as a small man, from 135 to 145 pounds, with a dark complexion, a heavy brown mustache, and a bald head. He was estimated to be between thirty-five and forty-five years old. In reality, "Walker" was quite husky and probably weighed more than the witnesses described. Ben and George Kilpatrick were wearing cowboy gear, but Walker had on suit pants with a matching vest and a narrow-brimmed felt hat.

The men may have stayed at the Jake Byler ranch at Dove Creek, near Knickerbocker. It was said that Byler went to town for their supplies, being paid very well by the fleeing outlaws. The Bylers were Laura Bullion's grandparents. Five days later, the fugitives were seen riding down the valley of the Buckhorn Draw tributary of the Devil's River, toward Sonora, another twenty miles to the south. They camped for the night just out of town, near the Sixes Ranch, where, according to Donna B. Ernst, Carver and Kilpatrick had once been employed. Carver and George Kilpatrick rode into town for supplies.

The gang had been in Sonora four months earlier in their rubber-tired buggy, posing as Iowa horse buyers. Although Sonora was quite a sheep and cattle center, at the time they had seemed more interested in the First National Bank. They may have still been interested in the bank, but for now they needed supplies, even though going into this town could be dangerous if anyone recognized them from the earlier visit. They rode into the west side Mexican section on the edge of town and bought baking powder, flour, and other staples. But the merchants there didn't have any grain for the horses. This meant a trip downtown. First they unsuccessfully tried Beckett's livery barn, then Owen's bakery by the bank. Inside the bakery they were recognized by a brother of a deputy sheriff, who left to inform Sheriff E. S. Briant that two of the "rubber-tired buggy gang" were back in town. The sheriff and three deputies entered the bakery with guns drawn, ordering the gang to put up their hands. Carver went for his gun. Kilpatrick may (or may not) have made a hostile motion as well. Bullets struck Carver in the lung, arm, leg, hand, and temple. He tried a border shift (throwing his pistol to his other hand) but he was too far gone to fire. Several shots also put Kilpatrick down. The town doctors were not able to save Carver, who only lived for about another three hours.

Sheriff Howze of Concho County identified the men as Will Carver and George Kilpatrick, who were both wanted in the murder investigation of Oliver Thornton.

In Carver's gear were found one Colt .45 revolver, one hammerless .38 Smith & Wesson revolver, and a derringer. Other articles included one gold Elgin watch, a silver compass and case, a diamond ring, and a gold band. In one pocket were two U.S. gold currency certificates. Both the outlaws' horses were sold to pay for Carver's funeral. George Kilpatrick was released after surviving his many wounds, since he was not connected to any crimes of the gang. There was also a five thousand dollar reward for the capture of Carver that the lawmen would split.

The arrest warrant for the murder of Thornton, issued by the local Justice of the Peace K. W. Goher, was for a man calling himself Bob McDonald or Charles Walker, two aliases used by Logan. Ben and Ed

Kilpatrick were also named as accessories. The defense attorneys were able to get a change of venue, moving the trial from Paint Rock to Ballinger in nearby Runnells County for March of 1902.

Back in Fort Worth and San Antonio, the Pinkertons had been busy following up on the Fort Worth Five's celebration. The trail led to Fanny Porter's bordello at 505 South Saba Street. The twenty-nine-year-old Porter (whose family name was actually Walker) cooperated with the agency, even describing one night when a drunken Logan tore her satin sheets with his spurs.

Lillie Davis, the widow of Will Carver, would also be helpful (after the Pinkertons caught up with her in Cameron, Texas). She had gone home after her wedding but had then returned to Porter's in April of 1901 to wait for Will. Logan had returned with the news of Carver's death but didn't have the heart to tell Lillie. It was left to Fanny Porter to inform her that her husband was gone. The Pinkerton detective, Lowell Spence, who finally questioned her, still thought her name was Callie Casey, the name that Carver had used as an alias and that was on their marriage certificate. She was only able to name the five in the photo by their aliases, but this was more information than the Pinkertons had had before, and it eventually helped lead to the outlaws' real names.

During the spring of 1901 Ben Kilpatrick apparently spent time with Laura at the Lambert Ranch, located at College Peaks near Douglas, in southern Arizona, and the Mexican line. It was quite isolated, being fifty miles from any railroad. As for Harvey Logan, there appears to be no public information as to where he spent part of April, May, and June of 1901.

By the time the Great Northern Railroad robbery occurred near Malta, Montana, there were few friends or hideouts or associates of the gang that the Pinkertons didn't know about. And most importantly, they had the gang's photograph, some real names, and even personal histories. Perhaps wishfully, Logan told Cassidy there were still places left where he could hide when he started his new gang. Lowell Spence, assistant manager of the Pinkerton Chicago office, was now Logan's chief adversary. The two would play cat and mouse for three more years until Logan's Colorado death (if you accept his death as fact, as most researchers do). However, Spence would still be trailing far behind as Logan pulled off the legendary daytime train robbery that is still talked about today.

The Exeter Creek Train Robbery

In the late spring of 1901, the Curry Gang had been through some tough times. Most of the original crowd was either dead or in prison. A new group, however, soon came to form around Logan, including members of the Ketchum Gang, as well as Orlando Camillo "Deaf" Hanks, just out of prison.

Hanks had been serving time for the robbing of a Northern Pacific train west of Big Timber. He and two conspirators had forced it to stop after Greycliff. Not only was the robbery mostly unsuccessful, but three of the men, including Hanks, were traced to Augusta, Montana, by former Sweet Grass deputy Sam Jackson. A posse at Blackfoot City found them at a cabin on Two Medicine Creek. After wounding two members of the posse, they escaped, only to be cornered near Summit by a reinforced posse. One was killed, one was captured, and the third, Hanks, was captured soon after.

In Helena Hanks had been convicted of "obstructing movement of the U.S. mail," receiving a ten-year sentence to be served at the state penitentiary in Deer Lodge. He did only six years, leaving prison on April 21, 1901, soon to strike up a partnership with Logan.

Times were changing. The West was becoming closed to outlaw gangs—as Butch Cassidy had already figured out. The killings by these gangs, especially of lawmen, had turned people—who had sometimes viewed these robbers as "Robin Hood" types—against them.

But there was maybe one last caper on the horizon. Logan's idea of taking a group of outlaws and robbing a Great Northern Railway train wasn't a bad one, if only because Great Northern wasn't on the outlook for Logan, and so there would be no special trains of rangers and trackers to deal with. In theory, it should have been much like the earlier days of outlawing—in other words, easy.

So Logan formed a new group. Whether they knew what money would be carried on that particular train is not known, but there were certainly enough railroaders along the Hi-Line for Logan's friends to talk to. (Logan himself was keeping a low profile, since his face and name were becoming so well known.)

Hanks showed up in Malta about the first of July, hanging out at the Shade Denson Annex Saloon across from the railroad tracks, watching the westbound Great Northern Overland Coast Flyer 3 as it stopped for water. On July 3 the train rolled to a stop as usual, running a little late at 2:30 p.m. It carried passengers in a festive mood, looking forward to celebrating Independence Day in either Havre or Great Falls.

Hanks left the saloon, walked the half block to the station, and, as the train began to move, boarded it between the blind baggage car and the coal tender. Conductor Alexis Smith spotted him and asked for the fare. Instead, he got a revolver in his face and an order not to stop the train. Hanks crawled over the coal tender into the engine cab. He directed engineer Tom Jones and fireman Mike O'Neil to stop the train at the eastern edge of the Exeter Creek bridge.

When the train stopped, two more outlaws appeared from under the bridge—Ben Kilpatrick and Harvey Logan. Logan switched places with Hanks and led the engineer and fireman back to the first baggage express car. He had them bang on the door until the express and baggage men opened up. Kilpatrick and Hanks positioned themselves on each side of the train, firing down the sides to keep the passengers inside, while Logan attended to the robbery. A fourth gang member stayed with the horses. While going about his business, Logan cheerfully commented on the fine condition of the surrounding county and the great hay crop in the nearby fields. Instead of disconnecting the cars, he had the baggage man Morton tell the passengers to move back one car, away from the dynamite blasts.

There were a few complications as Logan worked to open the safe. First a sheepherder, John Cunningham, appeared, thinking he might be able to help with the broken-down train. He ignored the gang's first warning shot, only retreating when a second round hit his saddle. Cunningham rode for Wagner, west of Malta, to sound the alarm. In a sad coda to this story, brakeman Woodside and traveling railroad agent Douglas were shot when they tried to put up warning flags on the gradual curve, so the following freight trains wouldn't slam into them. Both men received attention, but one died.

The hot sultry day made it hard to want to close the windows. A bullet accidentally struck eighteen-year-old Gertrude Smith as she looked out a window, two cars behind the baggage and express cars, while the northwest side of the train was being peppered with rifle fire by the two bandits. Smith was on her way from Tonah, Wisconsin, to Everett, Washington. She survived, after apparently being treated at the Columbus Hospital at Great Falls, 113 miles southwest of Havre.

Sheriff Griffith strutted up and down the aisles, showing his badge and revolvers, but the passengers knew he was no match for the robber's rifles. Ira Merritt, another passenger, said the steward disappeared and was later found hiding in the ice storage room at Havre, almost frozen.

Logan was busy attacking the safe, and the passengers were busy hiding their valuables. Logan commented to the train crewmen that the through safe was the hardest safe he had ever tried to open. (The local safe was empty.) It took at least three charges to blow it open. The explosives shook the day coaches and broke the windows in the smoking car. Passengers huddled in the rear of their cars and didn't believe the conductor's explanation that fireworks were being lit. The grips and trunks of several passengers—including the unfortunate Smith family—were in the baggage car and broken open by the blasts to be saturated with black lubricating oil also stored in the car. (Afterwards, the trunks and contents were transported to the railroad's headquarters in St. Paul, Minnesota, and, at no expense to the passengers, were rebuilt and cleaned.)

First the conductor, Alexis Smith, then Fireman O'Neil, helped hold sacks for Logan while he filled them with banknotes and a box of eight gold watches that were being shipped to jeweler H. F. Skusa in Havre. Logan promised to send O'Neil a watch for his cooperation, but never did. Logan also took a bolt of silk, saying it would be for his old lady.

Express messenger Smith asked Logan for a souvenir of the hold up, and Harvey gave him one of his pistols, minus the bullets. The crewmen went to the rear of the train as ordered, while the three outlaws disappeared off the train. Four riders were seen crossing the Milk River toward the Little Rocky Mountains to the south. Sheriff Griffith apparently fired two rounds once the outlaws were safely out of range. The whole thing was over in forty minutes.

In an interesting sidebar, the outlaw guarding the crew on the north side, as well as firing down the line of cars, had been asked by express messenger C. H. Smith why the gang robbed this train since it was running six hours late. The outlaw replied that they wanted it for the Fourth. Logan supposedly told the railroad men, "We ain't going to hurt anybody, we just want Jim Hill's [who built the Great Northern] money."

A story went around that the express car had carried a quantity of silver dollars that were bent by the explosions, and that the passengers had got them for souvenirs. It was also said that when the local part of the train arrived in Great Falls, the souvenir dollars began to appear all over the city. Nice stories if true, but they didn't get into the official records of the robbery.

The money taken in the robbery was in the form of brand new ten and twenty dollar bills in sheets. Forty thousand dollars of this was bound for the National Bank of Montana, Helena, and five hundred dollars was meant for the American National Bank of Portland, Oregon. There was also an unconfirmed report that the robbers also made off with 360 blank Great Northern Express money orders.

The trainmen described the three as speaking in a very marked Texas cowboy dialect. One of the gang was about five feet nine inches, 175 pounds, with dark eyes, a projecting brow, and had about two weeks growth of a sandy-colored beard. He wore new tan shoes, a black coat, and corduroy trousers. His handgun was a silver-plated Colt revolver. The second man was about six feet tall, 175 pounds, with a sandy complexion, dark eyes, and a slight cast in the left eye. He wore workingman's shoes and blue overalls over a black suit of clothes. They used sewed-up boot legs for rifle cartridge pouches, suspended around their necks. The third man, undoubtedly Logan, looked to be part Indian, had large black eyes, a smoothly shaven face and a prominent nose. His weight was estimated at about 180 which, if correct, meant he'd been eating well while in Texas.

Their horses were described as one black or bay, one white, and one buckskin. A fourth rider, on a gray or white horse, was seen by Mike O'Neil. After the robbery the train pulled ahead into Wagner, three miles away and nine miles west of Malta, where the damaged car was unhooked from the train. Sheriff Griffith wired for posses from Glasgow, Malta, and Fort Benton after getting authorization from the railroad to pay for a fifty-man posse. (He also notified surrounding counties to be on the lookout for the outlaws.) The Glasgow posse came on a special train to Malta, and Sheriff Charles Crawford of Fort Benton brought men from that county seat as well as Chinook. Unbelievably, the railroad's express company rejected the use of the Malta posse because they said that Malta was full of outlaws, and one of the robbers was said to be from Malta (perhaps because Hanks had waited in a Malta saloon). Meanwhile Fergus and Dawson County posses to the south and east were watching for the gang.

What isn't usually described by historians is how the bandits had waited at the Exeter Creek ranch of the man who ran the coal chute in

Wagner. His name was also Mike O'Neil, and he was the first cousin of Fireman O'Neil. They were about the same age and came from County Clare, Ireland, on the same boat. Over the years, he had co-owned a hotel in Malta, had worked as a Great Northern section foreman, and a deputy sheriff and jailer in Malta. Fireman O'Neil soon became an engineer, and his family moved from Glasgow to Havre.

When cousin O'Neil went to his ranch that morning, he found the outlaws hiding in his barn. His horse shied at the sight of the men and one man, Logan, thought it was funny. O'Neil said he didn't think anything of seeing the men in his barn. He believed them to be hoboes, riding the rails. Fireman O'Neil and Section Foreman O'Neil were not implicated in the robbery as accessories, but it made now-Engineer O'Neil nervous to testify in Knoxville, knowing Logan's friends could retaliate back at him. Fortunately, neither family suffered any consequences.

Although Griffith claimed he took his posse all over the Little Rockies country, the official report was that three outlaws crossed the Missouri River at Forsyth within forty-eight hours of the robbery. On July 5 they reportedly stopped at the Morton ranch on a Montana trail paralleling Little Porcupine Creek in Rosebud County. They told the rancher that they had to be at Forsyth (to the south) on the following day to apprehend some horse thieves with a stolen herd. They traded four horses and gave him one hundred dollars in stolen bills. In another of many supposed sightings, they boarded a train at Park City, between Billings and Columbus.

The local newspapers came up with two unofficial theories: the first, that the gang headed for the Hole-in-the-Wall after crossing the Missouri River, and the second, that they hid in the Missouri River Breaks until the law gave up searching for them.

After the train robbery, William Pinkerton of the Chicago office moved to Denver to oversee his field agents. The agency represented both the Great Northern Railroad and the Northern Express Company. Pinkerton said the gang would be hard to capture, in that they knew every cow patch between Canada and Mexico.

The rewards for Logan's capture were mounting as a result of his activities in Hole-in-the-Wall, Wilcox, and Tipton, Wyoming; Wilcox, Wyoming; Belle Fourche, South Dakota; Paint Rock, Texas; and now Wagner, Montana. The Great Northern Express Company offered a five thousand dollar reward for the arrest of the four robbers, including Logan and two others (who were wrongly identified as Butch Cassidy and Harry Longabaugh), and another five hundred dollars per outlaw for each conviction.

Sheriff Griffith spoke to the newspapers on a regular basis. It really didn't look like he was serious about collecting the rewards, however, just the cheap publicity. Considering that the outlaws only had four hours of a head start, they really had a relatively easy time of it. Griffith also had to get his horses from Glasgow since the people of Malta—who had been slighted by the railroad's rejection of them as posse members—were hardly going to cooperate. Finally, a number of sightings by cowboys with overactive imaginations added to the confusion.

Meanwhile at the Coburn Circle C ranch, Walt Coburn, the youngest son of the owner, was overseeing a herd of ranch horses on a remote pasture near Coburn Buttes. This entailed driving them out the west gate and letting them graze on the Fort Belknap Indian Reservation near the East Coburn Butte. The twelve-year-old Coburn was just closing up a gate when he saw four riders approaching. He'd been expecting to see Jim Thornhill or perhaps Thornhill's sons, but this was Harvey Logan and three other riders. Logan approached the boy with a rifle across his saddle, a revolver in his belt, and a sewn up boot top slung over his saddle horn. He told Coburn that Jim Thornhill said he knew how to keep his mouth shut. Walt replied, "Yes sir."

After querying Walt as to which horses were Thornhill's, the gang rode up to a nearby rimrock where they exchanged their horses for Thornhill's. Logan told Walt that if anyone asked if he'd seen them, he was to say that he hadn't seen or heard anything. Logan also assured him he would have the horses back "inside of a week." Then he cautioned him again to keep his mouth shut and "dummy up like a loco sheepherder."

As Logan's bunch was continuing south on the reservation, far from any pursuit, Sheriff Griffith's posse claimed to have found signs of them on Beaver Creek. Further erroneous evidence of the gang's trail was discovered southeast at the "Houchette River." (This was actually Fourchette's Creek, between Third and Dry Fork Creeks.) There were also mistaken reports of the sign being found near the Allen Ranch at Beaver Creek and Dry Creek, just east of the main trail. These reports would lead a person to believe that, not only didn't the posse know where the outlaws were, they weren't real sure where they themselves were, either. The sheriff even later reported, again erroneously, that he had the outlaws bottled up. As his mistakes were uncovered, he became a laughing stock to residents and legitimate lawmen alike.

The sheriff and the posse had had their big day. Now it was evening, and they were tuckered out. The main ranch in the area was the Coburn place. They headed for it not knowing that the Coburns were friends of Logan. They were also unaware that the chuck wagon full of supplies they'd been waiting for hadn't shown up because it was being driven—very slowly—by friends of Logan.

As evening came, according to Walt Coburn's remembrances, he told his brother Bob that all had gone well that day. In order to create an alibi, Bob had spent the day at the Coburn's Ruby Gulch mines. He had also (and uncharacteristically) allowed Walt to sit in his house, even though they weren't on friendly terms. They both pretended to be reading. Bob was also wearing his Colt pistol, seemingly waiting for someone to show up.

Griffith and his Glasgow Valley County posse eventually knocked at his door. Griffith demanded supper and fresh horses for the posse. He said the Great Northern train had been robbed, that he was hot on the trail of the robbers, and that they had suffered a setback because the chuck wagon and relief horses from Malta hadn't showed up. Besides that, two pro-Logan men from Malta, Jim Maloney and Bryan Harley, had to leave the posse because they had supposedly forgotten their guns.

Bob Coburn told Griffith that the posse was welcome to turn its horses out in the pasture below the barn and sleep with them. Bob told Walt to tell ranch cook Al Taylor to feed the posse if he wanted to; and if he did, to charge one dollar per man, cash in advance. Lastly as Walt went out the back door to have ranch hand Pete Olson show the posse to the pasture, he heard Bob tell the sheriff that drinking alcohol would not be allowed while they stayed and that he didn't want posse members going into the barn, smoking. Then he slammed the door in Griffith's face.

Taylor had a meal ready for them about 10:00 p.m. Walt didn't think much of the posse, writing in his memoirs, "a sorrier-looking motley crowd would have been hard to find in any man's cow country." Bob must have taken some pity on the posse members because he allowed them to use the empty bunkhouse. But the next morning Bob sent them on to the Winter's Gill ranch where lawmen would be welcome and fresh horses would probably be available.

The posse got a late start, and they only made it to the foot of Bear Gulch Hill, staying on the stage station road across from Zortman. They had another setback, the beans they'd been eating turned out to be bad, making the men quite sick. However there could have been another cause: Some of the boys snuck off to Zortman for some cheap rotgut whiskey. Whatever the truth, a story spread that the Coburns had tried to poison the posse. Adding to the posse's problems, there were notices put up around the Little Rockies by Logan's people warning people not to help them. In the five days the posse was in the Zortman area, no trail was found, but again, they didn't travel very far off the main road, either. Zortman folk would remember the posse for shooting up the town, one posse member shooting himself in the foot and another shooting his horse. They also cut wire fences and trampled grain and hay fields. Jim Thornhill said if any of the posse members were caught on his ranch, they would probably be shot, since they could easily be mistaken for prowling coyotes.

There were two professional posses on the scene, one from Great Falls and another from Fort Benton. They worked quietly and presumably stayed far away from Griffith. Two Pinkerton men reportedly came by stage, possibly also going out to the Winters-Gill ranch (the owners of the ranch were sympathetic to lawmen, and might have some information).

Most local peoples probably thought the wanted men had hidden at Thornhill Butte or East Coburn Butte. Actually, according to Walt Coburn, they were staying at the Coburn Circle C line camp on Rock Creek near the Missouri River. After the lawmen left the area, Logan would have some freedom to go north to one of the two buttes.

There is another story told about Harvey Logan's activities after the robbery. Since the currency was unsigned by local bank officials, Logan went to Great Falls looking for someone to forge the signatures. He rented a room in the Minot Block and went to the Mint Saloon. An acquaintance from his past ranching days, former sheriff Sid Willis, wasn't there, so Logan went to the adjoining Herald Café, had too many drinks, and caused a disturbance. Willis appeared and took Logan to his room. Logan asked Willis to help him find a forger. Willis said no, then told Logan to leave and never come back. Willis had had enough trouble explaining Lonie's Wilcox robbery bill that he had passed in Great Falls, without being involved in forging banknotes, becoming an accessory to the robbery after the fact.

At about the same time, circumstances were heating up, according to historian James Horan. In Dallas, Texas, a bank cashier reported taking in a forged note from the train robbery. Pinkerton agent Lowell Spence's log gives no specifics, but he does note something much more serious—the Montana killing of a Jim Winters on July 25.

Supposedly Jim Winters had told Charles Siringo that he expected to be killed by Harvey Logan. He was not confident that Logan had left the country after the train robbery. It was July 25, 1901, twenty-two days after the train robbery when Winters awoke at his usual time (about 6:15 a.m.) to feed the chickens, eat his breakfast, perhaps air out his bedding and brush his teeth on the porch. He probably next headed for the outhouse to the southwest of the back porch. Unknown to him, three men were watching from the edge of the brush southwest of the house. They initially held their fire, perhaps because they wanted to kill Gill, too. (They weren't aware that Gill had left for Fort Benton the night before.) Finally the ambushers lost their patience. Two rounds were fired, one after another. The .30-30 bullets hit Winters in the belly. He lay in a pool of blood, dying a slow painful death.

Inside the house were students from Gill's Brooklyn, New York, college (they were spending a vacation summer in the Wild West). After the rifle fire quieted, the kids brought Winters inside. Two of them rode to Landusky for help, returning with mine owner J. P. "Guy" Manning. Another rider was dispatched to Harlem for a doctor. Winters died within three hours. There was too much blood loss for the doctors to be effective. Investigating officers arrived from Fort Benton about two days later. The main suspects, besides Jim Thornhill and sons, were the Coburn brothers. Thornhill had an alibi, as he was visiting a neighbor at the time, but nothing was said about his sons.

A posse stayed from Chouteau County at the ranch. They soon lost the trail of the attackers near Bull Creek, and no further leads developed. An examination of the assassin's hiding place produced shell casings and the stubs of hand-rolled cigarettes. Speculation had it that after Logan shot Winters, he left two men to put down a covering fire to give him a head start and ensure that Winters didn't receive any immediate help.

The college students were sent home, their romantic cowboy notions ruined, yet they did have something to talk about for a lifetime. Winters was buried at the ranch, about one and one-half miles from Johnny's resting place and only a few miles south of Landusky's grave.

Even with a $1,400 reward for the train robbers being offered by Chouteau County officials, as well as a $6,500 reward from the

Pinkertons, the state, and the railroad express, there were no takers. Whatever amount was added for Winters brought the same lack of response.

Some people doubted that Logan had killed Winters, but the Pinkertons believed it and so did the Chouteau County officials. The Denver Pinkerton office felt that Logan had killed him because, "Mr. Winter[s] had for some time previously taken an interest in his capture and location and had given some information to the officers in regards to him, and out of revenge for this Logan killed him." The Chouteau County grand jury charged Logan with both the train robbery and Winters's death.

On the other hand, the skeptics said that if Logan had wanted to kill Winters, he could have done it not long after the train robbery and then left the country. Besides, the murder weapon was a .30-30, not the .30-40 rifle Logan carried at the train robbery. However rifles can be changed, and Logan would have had to wait until all the posses searching for the train robbers were out of the area.

Gill was the one who had to worry now. He had few local friends, but did have influential acquaintances at the county and state level. He apparently played the law and order card, informing on all lawless acts committed in the area, and he continued his job as U.S. Land Commissioner, helping homesteaders file on lands that had once been considered open pasture for the use of the large ranchers only. The Gill ranch continued to be the headquarters for lawmen who had business in and around Landusky and Zortman. Gill was shot at on occasion, but this didn't deter him.

According to Spence's log, Dodson, Missouri, was the next stop on Logan's itinerary. He apparently made a mid-July trip to visit the Lee family. This would have been after the Great Northern train robbery but before the killing of Jim Winters. The log also showed a second trip to Kansas City, Missouri, starting on August 30, 1901, to visit a Carrie Hunter, who Logan had met seven years earlier. Apparently she had gone to Cripple Creek with Harvey and Bob Lee earlier in the year. If the information is correct, then Logan did leave the Little Rockies after the robbery and returned to kill Winters on July 25, after which Logan returned to Fort Worth. The log next shows Logan going back to Fannie Porter's bordello in San Antonio on September 14. Since Annie Rogers had a home at Kennedale, a suburb of Fort Worth, perhaps the couple spent the time there with Ben Kilpatrick and Laura Bullion before going their separate ways.

Thus September 14 was departure day for at least Harvey and Annie. They journeyed to the cool mountain country of Mena, Arkansas, near the Oklahoma border, as Mr. and Mrs. Bob Nevilles. It is quite possible they intended to get married on this trip. According to author James Horan, Logan wanted to marry Annie when Carver and Lillie Davis were married at Fort Worth, but Annie said it would have to wait until she knew what kind of man he was. It is possible they planned to wait for the other couple at Mena since they rented a small duplex. Kilpatrick and Bullion, now calling themselves the Arnolds, were believed to be spending time at the Byler-Lambert ranch in remote Arizona before heading for Arkansas.

One of Logan's jobs, besides relaxing and spending money, was to sign the banknotes from the train robbery and make them look as if they'd been in circulation. He and Annie knew enough to spend only a small amount of the stuff and then move on. They left town on September 18, perhaps because Logan felt they couldn't afford to pass anymore of the stolen money. For whatever reason, Logan was right to leave because a Pinkerton man soon found their abandoned rental on his house-to-house rental check, and a neighbor identified them. They next traveled to the Serwich Hotel in Shreveport, Louisiana. Shreveport, on the Red River, was south across the Arkansas border and near Texas. Spence shows them there from September 18 to September 25. They moved on to Memphis, Tennessee, as Mr. and Mrs. R. T. Moore, spending three hundred dollars at Corinna Lewis's house of prostitution and similar establishments, saloons, and a clothing store. Such places were somewhat safe establishments where they could relax in the fancy, upper-class atmosphere. Their last stop was Nashville, Tennessee, although they may have made a brief stop at Jackson, Tennessee.

Meanwhile Laura and Ben showed up at Hot Springs, Arkansas, to start their vacation, traveling as Mr. and Mrs. J. W. Rose. From there, they went to Memphis. In Hot Springs their photo was taken by a reporter as they rode in a horse-drawn carriage through the Happy Hollows area. Perhaps they had Logan's itinerary, but they gave up when they missed him again, taking a train to St. Louis, arriving in November of 1901.

In Nashville, Harvey and Annie registered as Mr. and Mrs. Logan at the Linck Hotel, taking room 2. This was about October 8. Annie spent a lot of time in their room while Harvey preferred saloons, staying out late at night.

Annie had accumulated about five hundred dollars of the stolen money. She decided, wrongly, to take that large amount to of all places, a bank, to change it for larger bills. It is doubtful Harvey knew of this as he would have stopped her. But since they had spent hundreds in stores, brothels, and hotels, she obviously felt no fear.

She picked the Broadway branch of the Fourth National Bank of Nashville, entering about 2:45 p.m. on a Monday, just before the 3:00 p.m. closing. She was described as well groomed and well dressed with several rings on her fingers. She was considered an attractive young woman, with dark auburn hair, high cheekbones, and dark eyes. Her smile showed front teeth that were made of gold. Teller J. S. McHenry described her as "somewhat good looking, of light build with a heavy head of dark hair." McHenry was suspicious of her, probably because of the amount of crisp, new bills, which she wanted to turn into fifty and one hundred dollar bills. McHenry excused himself and showed the bills to cashier J. F. Howell and bank president Samuel J. Keith. The serial numbers matched those on the Pinkerton circular and they called the police. McHenry probably engaged her in some small talk, saying it would take a few minutes for the bills to be exchanged. Soon a police lieutenant and two city detectives arrived, placing her under arrest.

At police headquarters she identified herself as Maud Williams— a name she apparently used at Porter's; both Porter and Lillie Davis referred to her as "Maudie"—claiming that she had been given the money by a blonde man she knew only as Charlie, whom she had met in Omaha. Rogers insisted that she hadn't done anything wrong, and she knew nothing about the money being stolen or forged. Annie claimed that she and Charlie had traveled together until recently, and she believed Charlie was on his way to New Orleans. Meanwhile, "Charlie" had a feeling that something had gone wrong, and he decided to leave town by train for Alabama.

Obviously Logan soon learned of her arrest through the newspapers. At her preliminary hearing she had been charged by Justice of the Peace Hiram Vaughn with passing the forged bills. Bail was set at ten thousand dollars, and she was remanded to jail since she couldn't make the bail. When Justice Vaughn asked her what her plea was to be, she went on at length that yes, she took the bills to the bank, but she had come by them honestly. Furthermore she couldn't see why she was arrested because she had spent some of the bills before. She began to cry hysterically saying the charges should be dropped because she wasn't guilty of any crime. She was able to regain her composure after a few minutes. It was evident she needed a lawyer at this point to advise her to keep quiet.

Meanwhile, Harvey was heading west for Rawlins, Wyoming, eventually to meet up with saloon owner Jack Ryan and Jim Hanson of the Twenty-mile ranch. Logan went out to the ranch, and dug up the rest of the stolen railroad express money (buried after the robbery as he was heading south) so he could hire an attorney for Annie. In the two days he was around Rawlins, he saw Siringo and suspected he was a detective. Luckily for Siringo his new outlaw friends vouched for him. Harvey said he looked too bright and wide awake for a common rounder. Again, as former outlaw Emmett Dalton had written, the ability to make fast, accurate judgments about men would help an outlaw detour an arrest or a bullet in the back.

Logan returned to San Antonio, knocking on Fanny Porter's door one night. She turned down the hallway lights and he entered, going into her bedroom. Lillie Davis later told the Pinkertons that Porter was crying, "Poor Maudie," and at the same time blaming her for taking the bills to the bank. Porter left with Logan, presumably to retrieve the three thousand dollars he had left in her care. Fanny returned unaccompanied at about 3:00 a.m. Logan stayed in town overnight, going the next day to Kennedale and apparently reported back to Fanny that he had not found any help there. He stopped one more time to speak to Fanny before heading back to Tennessee. According to author Donna B. Ernst, Harvey also gave Fanny his diamond ring to pawn.

Back in Nashville, more of the stolen money showed up at another Nashville bank. Some also appeared in St. Louis, New Orleans, Chicago, and Baltimore. The local Nashville authorities were beginning to believe Annie's story since no one had stepped forward as her attorney, financed by "the gang" or otherwise. Hence Annie looked like someone just being used to pass the money.

A little more was learned about Annie when she had her police mugshot taken by a local photographer named Giers. He reported that he found Annie to be quite charming, witty, and good humored. Annie told him that she had previously worked as a secretary and photographer in Texas. She liked photography, except for the messy photo development process.

Annie continued to stick to her story, only admitting that she'd been with "Charlie" in Shreveport and Memphis. A bizarre fake story appeared in the local paper, claiming that she, as Annie Williams, was wanted for strong-arm robberies in Cincinnati, Ohio.

Her life was made somewhat easier in that she was allowed to stay on the second floor of the jail rather than being immediately transferred to the county lock up. Her meals came from restaurants and she was supplied reading materials and care by a church's women's group. On October 25, 1901, Annie had her first interview with a *Nashville American* reporter. She continued to claim that she was innocent, stating that she came by the money honestly and didn't know anything was wrong with it until she was told so at the bank. Also, she continued on about the mysterious stranger she met at Shreveport called Charlie, expanding that story somewhat. She did say more about herself, telling the reporter she was born in Texas, and she had never been anywhere else before except Fort Smith, Arkansas. She had married a farmer at eighteen, and she left him when she was about twenty-one years old. Annie admitted her name wasn't either Annie Rogers or Maud Williams, but she was afraid to reveal who she really was because of her family finding out. Later, as lawmen continued their interrogations, she yielded more information. Again, she badly needed an attorney to advise her.

The following day, October 26, Annie was transferred to the Knox County jail. She now had two attorneys, the first, General W. H. Washington, hired by "the gang"; and the second, Richard West, hired by a local cigar salesman, Morgan Roop (who may have only felt sorry for Annie).

Tennesseeans were in for more excitement from an associate of Logan's. His new partner in crime, Hanks, was soon to escape from the law in Nashville. (Hanks apparently kept in loose contact with Logan. Spence's log shows Harvey meeting with Hanks about ten miles out of town the day after Hanks's escape from the Nashville police.)

Hanks's problems began at 10:30 a.m. on October 27 when he went shopping for clothes. He presented a new twenty dollar bill at the Newman and Company store in east Nashville. He later was described as being five feet ten inches tall, florid complexion, raw boned, and shabbily dressed. His purchase amounted to about two dollars for a pair of pants and smaller articles. Clerk Gillock didn't have much cash on hand, so he sent a Mrs. Newman to Horwells Drugstore and then Zickler's grocery store to find change. Charles Zickler was suspicious of the bill and took it to the nearby police station. Sure enough, the bill was on the stolen list for the Montana train robbery. The police had Zickler enter the store and speak to the suspect as a signal for the police to arrest him. "How are you today?" asked Zickler. But instead of grabbing Hanks unawares, detective Jack Dwyer, who had entered the store, began a conversation with him, asking him his name and where he was from. Hanks replied Memphis. At that point Dwyer and another detective named Dickens tried to arrest him, but Hanks pulled two .45 revolvers, ordering the men out of his way. Instead, they grabbed for him and his weapons, using their lead saps to try and subdue him. Hanks finally threw both officers off him and ran off down College Street. Nearing the corner, Hanks commandeered an ice wagon. Dwyer fired at him but missed, and Hanks whipped the ice wagon horses into a gallop, careening at full speed over the Cumberland River Bridge, weaving in and out of traffic.

The speeding wagon went up on a sidewalk at Bridge Avenue and First Street, hitting a fire hydrant. It had four bullet holes in it, and there was blood on the seat from a head wound Hanks had sustained. Hanks next switched to a stolen horse and buggy, heading up Woodland to Fourth Street and to Fatherland Avenue. He took Ninth Street toward the river, driving through a telephone pole storage yard. He took the buggy over the poles and through a fence, over gullies and ravines. At one point the carriage overturned, but Hanks simply righted it. The poor horse finally gave out, forcing the fugitive to run through Shelby County Park. He also threw away a wallet containing $1,280 in stolen money. The fugitive was last seen going into a thicket opposite the river pumping station about two miles upriver from town. One story had Hanks crossing the Cumberland River on a skiff. The authorities scoffed at this, yet two hundred men couldn't find any trace of him on the north side of the river. Someone named J. T. Johnson later reported giving him such a ride across the river.

A later investigation revealed that Hanks had been in the North College Street area for several weeks and had even been arrested for vagrancy (although he had served only a few days). He had apparently been using several names, including "Red." The police decided that after all he was Butch Cassidy. But then, no, he was Harry Longabaugh (even though their descriptions hardly matched).

Meanwhile, Ben Kilpatrick and Laura Bullion were arrested in St. Louis on November 5, 1901. He bought a diamond-studded watch at the Globe Loan Company. They were nabbed on their way to the train station. (Sylvia Lynch, Donna B. Ernst, and Brown Waller have written in depth about their capture.)

After Annie's arrest, the Pinkertons traced Logan to Birmingham, Alabama. It was a large industrial city that had the major railroad connections Logan needed for potential escapes. He used the railroad to travel to Knoxville via Chattanooga, approximately 145 miles east of Nashville. He probably felt that Knoxville was as close to Annie as he dared get. Knoxville also had a large red-light district where he perhaps felt he would be fairly safe, and he could perhaps find a fence who could help with peddling the stolen money.

At one point his explosive temper almost resulted in the shooting of a hotel clerk at the Franklin House in Birmingham. He had the presence of mind, however, to talk his way out of that situation without shooting anyone. He even apologized for his aggressiveness, saying he was under a lot of tension because his wife in Nashville was suing him for divorce.

According to author Sylvia Lynch, the Bowery area in Knoxville consisted of cheap hotels, seedy saloons, restaurants, pawn shops, small drugstores selling narcotics, and vice of every imaginable kind. Logan picked Ike Jones's Central Saloon at the junction of Central and Commerce Streets as his headquarters. He ate at a restaurant next door. Logan also kept an apartment upstairs in Jones's building, shared with two women, as well as a room in the Central Hotel where he kept his belongings secure. He briefly had a good situation in Knoxville.

The old, dimly lit, musty smelling Central Saloon had a bar on the left as you entered. At the rear right side was a single billiard table operated by a Frank Humphreys. At the rear was a stairway that led down to a bank of the First Creek. Owner Ike Jones described Logan as "a drummer [salesman] type, just passing through; a quiet man, standing treat many times and playing many games of pool." Calling himself William Wilson, he drank nothing but apricot brandy, smoked the most expensive brand of cigars, and wore Denver-bought clothes. He was usually friendly, although not talkative. When asked what he did for a living, he would say that he was a railroad man, which was true in a way. According to a later police report, Logan entrusted bartender J. D. Finley with $3,500 in stolen currency.

To his new acquaintances he boasted of having money and also said that he had killed at least three men. This was not smart behavior for a wanted man. Later when in jail, he only claimed to have killed two men (Spence credited him with at least six). Logan also excelled at the nearby shooting gallery on Gay Street in which he shot a circle around the target. He was known to carry at least two handguns, a .45 Colt and a concealed .38 Smith & Wesson. Logan was seen in the company of a saloon owner, Luther Brady, and pals Jim Boley and John Whipple, probably trying to find a connection to exchange the money. They possibly made a trip to Ashville, North Carolina, just across the state line.

The boys at the saloon were getting along well until the night of Friday, December 13, when Logan's mood turned black. Before Logan went to the pool hall that night, he quarreled with his two lady companions, Mayme Edington and Lillian Sartain, possibly striking them or at least scaring them in his fiery, drunken condition.

His pool partners were enjoying their liquor that night, also. The stakes weren't particularly high for the players, twenty dollars a game. Luther Brady and an unidentified black man were playing Logan and John Whipple. During one of Brady's turns, he slipped and broke the tip of the pool cue. Logan protested, though their initial argument was short, with Logan calming down until Brady tried to use the cue on his next turn. Logan grabbed it from Brady, and began to trim the splintered end of the stick. Humphreys then entered the quarrel, objecting to Logan trimming one of his pool cues. Logan told Humphreys to butt out, grabbing him as if to strike him. Humphreys quickly pointed out that it wouldn't be a fair fight because he had only one leg. Logan said no harm done and shook his hand. Then Brady opened his mouth, arguing, egged on by the saloon crowd. Logan went over to the bar and downed a shot of whiskey. He returned and he and Brady exchanged further words in lowered voices.

Suddenly Logan grabbed Brady and pushed him into a corner of the saloon where a sugar barrel was located. He pushed Brady into the empty barrel, strangling him in the process. Jim Boley rushed over to aid Brady, planning to use his pool cue on Logan's head. The crowd cried foul and prevented Boley's further involvement. After all, this was good Friday night entertainment!

While this was occurring, veteran police officers Robert T. Saylor and William M. Dinwiddie were walking by on their "Bowery beat." Both officers had been injured a few months before and were still recovering. The officers heard the noise and went to investigate. Usually these fights either fizzled out by themselves or the officers broke them up and hauled the drunks in for a night in jail. When the noise level increased dramatically, they decided to intervene. First they had to move the crowd out of their way, which they succeeded in doing with the display of their billy clubs. By this point Brady was barely breathing.

The next thing Logan knew he was facing two big police officers. Officer Saylor ordered Logan to let go of Brady saying, "You'll have to stop that." Logan then pulled a gun, telling Saylor, "By God, I am here to protect myself." He shot Saylor. Witnesses at first thought Logan had shot through the pocket because he fired so quickly. He held his gun close to his body to prevent the officers from grabbing it. In spite of the wound, Saylor rushed Logan, hitting him over the head with his night-stick. The second .38 round hit Saylor on the right side of his body. The third round punctured his left arm below the shoulder. Saylor went down but regained his feet, only to be shot again on the left side of his body—this time his body sprawled on the floor, his billy club split from hitting Logan.

Dinwiddie hit Logan on the head with a blow that brought Logan to his knees. He regained his feet, brushed the club to the side, at the same time shooting the officer near at close range. The bullet lodged near Dinwiddie's neck arteries. Dinwiddie, too, went down, but not before wrenching the pistol out of Logan's hands.

Logan stood weaving, blood pouring from his head wounds. He saw that the front door was blocked by the crowd, leaving him only the back door through which to make his escape. Logan bypassed the stairs and leaped from the doorway the ten to fifteen feet to the stream bed below. The saloon crowd rushed to the back door, watching Logan stagger into the night, leaving his fine May store overcoat and blue hat behind.

The authorities came quickly after someone made a phone call for help. With the police were doctors N. C. Carter, W. S. Nash, and C. E. Jones. They administered to the fallen officers, stopping the flows of blood and giving stimulants. Saylor was placed on the billiard table and Dinwiddie on the carpet, the hammerless .38 Smith & Wesson long-barreled revolver he had grabbed from Logan next to him. Dinwiddie had powder burns over his body from that weapon. Dinwiddie was taken to his home, and he was expected to recover. The outlook for Saylor, however, was more bleak.

The police sent every available man out to look for the fugitive. The Knox County Sheriff's Department provided bloodhounds. The lawmen probably believed "Wilson" had little hope escaping with his wounds, plus it was freezing cold and wet outside. But they were unaware of Logan's "Tiger of the Wild Bunch" reputation. His strength, courage, and endurance were unmatched

The dragnet continued throughout the night, hoping to turn up some trace of Logan. Those with bloodhounds followed his trail on First Creek. He then possibly crossed the Tennessee River, going east two miles to an abandoned East Knoxville barn. Here the trackers found blood on a rock where Logan had apparently rested his head. The trail vanished at this point, and he was supposedly seen back in town. A local merchant, N. Miller, claimed to have seen someone who looked like the bloodied Logan exiting from an alley near Mabry Street at about 11:00 p.m. Also a janitor on his way to work said he saw a bloody, bare-headed Logan on Reservoir Hill; another thought she saw Logan at Chilhowee Park. And so the Logan sightings went. Among those reports was one that reported that Logan took a hack coach (taxi) from Central near the fairgrounds to the Southern Railway tracks. This report might not have been far from the facts since the authorities now believed that he had doubled back to town, found a druggist to dress his wounds or sell him medical supplies, and then engaged a driver to take him out of town. The suspected driver had nothing to say, however.

The police in Knoxville continued to track Logan's movements prior to his "outburst." They found his room at the Central Hotel, which contained his clothes and two suitcases, as well as the possessions he had left in the girls' room and at the saloon (including a black silk-lined overcoat, a pair of kid gloves, a silk handkerchief, and a pair of silver-rimmed smoked glasses). The suits, shirts, and underwear he wore were expensive, probably all from the May store in Denver.

Using the testimony of witnesses, police put together a description of the fugitive that they said fitted that of Harry Longabaugh. "Longabaugh" had replaced Cassidy as the suspected ice-wagon bandit in Nashville. However the description of William Wilson was of a man with a swarthy complexion, heavy set and muscular, about five feet eight inches tall, 170 pounds, about thirty-two years of age, with a prominent nose, two missing teeth from the lower jaw, and a well-groomed appearance; this was hardly Harry Longabaugh.

Two days after Logan disappeared, the doctors, assisted by the medical students, continued trying to save Saylor. They decided if infection didn't set in, he had a chance to live. The medical team were amazed that the chloroform used during the surgeries hadn't killed him. One of Logan's bullets had entered Saylor's body on the right side, turning downward toward his stomach, while two others had lodged in the left arm below the shoulder and in the left side. He still had a bullet in the chest, near the spinal column. After the surgery Saylor developed a high fever, and he was on morphine for the pain.

Besides the search for Logan and the efforts to save the policeman, another drama was unfolding. Logan's pals, Brady, Boley, and Whipple, were spending funny money all over town, buying clothes, going to restaurants and saloons, and generally having a good time. When one store notified the police that the trio was spending the stolen money, the police followed their path from the Central Bar, to Finley's Bar, and then to Whipple's house. When arrested, the three were trying on their new suits of clothes. Four thousand dollars was found in a large red wallet one of them had picked up after the fight. They claimed to have won the money in a poker game with a stranger. After the three went before a judge, Brady and Boley were able to make bail, but not Whipple.

The policemen were both still alive, Boley and his partners had been arrested, the stolen money had been collected, and the banks assured everyone that it would be replaced. Now if they could only find William Wilson or whoever he was.

The break came three days later when a man wearing an old hat and overalls, his head bandaged, was spotted in Jefferson City, about thirty miles to the northeast of Knoxville. An unnamed black man mentioned the sighting to a merchant, William Carey, who then walked by the man and took note of the blood on his clothes. He telephoned the Knoxville Police Department at 4:00 p.m. Four officers responded, taking a train that the police chief had stopped so that the lawmen could board. Chief of Police J. J. Atkins strongly encouraged Carey to apprehend the fugitive before he disappeared. Carey organized a group of men armed with shotguns. Logan and a John Drees were now camped just outside of town. Carey and his men caught Logan's companion when he neared town to buy supplies. They held him at the train station while the others went after the other man. They spotted him, his shirt and head blood soaked, in a patch of brush where he'd made a campfire. He refused to raise his hands as they apprehended him, only putting them horizontally in front of him, saying he refused to be taken with his hands up. He apparently hoped to strike his captors with fists full of cartridges—though how much affect that would have was questionable. Logan then complained that the lawmen hadn't given him a chance to defend himself. Carey responded that he hadn't given the policemen in Knoxville a chance, either, a point which Logan agreed with. Carey's group, with Logan in tow, returned to the station. The other man, Drees, was eventually let go since he was working as an iron molder, following the railroad to his home in Bristol.

The city of Knoxville was electrified by the news that the man who had shot two of their police officers had been captured. And he might be the famous outlaw, Harvey "Kid Curry" Logan. The *Knoxville Sentinel* described his capture as "one of the biggest catches ever made in the country."

Despite the cold, wet weather, a large crowd was there to meet Logan when his train arrived in Knoxville about 6:35 p.m. The crowd had to be cleared so the paddy wagon could be backed up into the station driveway. A number of young gawkers climbed the nearby roof of the Union News Company and clung to the latticework of a depot storage building. Because of the pressing crowd (now being forced back) and the wagon's being overloaded by its police escort, the wagon was forced into a gutter, requiring several men to put it back on the street. One exuberant crowd member fired a round into the air.

Throughout it all, despite his blood-soaked shirt and blood-encrusted hair, Logan appeared calm and cool. The crowd that met him at police headquarters was almost as large as the crowd at the station. Once inside, after a more thorough search, his clothes yielded a package of $2,000 in stolen currency wrapped in a newspaper, an old wallet with another $240.00 of the Montana money, $50.00 in legitimate currency, two baggage room checks, and a cash fare stub for $6.85 issued November 3 by the Union Pacific Railroad.

Logan gave his name as Charles Johnson, using his mother's family name, and he said he was from Chelsea, Iowa, adding that he had left there when he was ten years old. At the time of the arraignment, he decided he didn't have a name, and he didn't know where his cuts and bruises had come from. When asked if he wanted a doctor, he said no, he just needed some water to wash his head. But then he didn't object to a doctor examining and bandaging his head. Along with the doctoring, Logan received a meal of steak, potatoes, eggs, hot rolls, and coffee. He finished up with a cigar and a glass of whiskey. The new celebrity said he hadn't eaten since Friday night.

Logan became more talkative as he felt better, saying his actions were only in self-defense, and that the police had no right to interfere. Logan explained his "philosophy" to a *Knoxville Sentinel* reporter: "I never harmed an innocent or helpless man or woman. I believe those large corporations are squeezing the life out of people, and it does no harm to take a few thousand or even a million from them. When a man gets out and takes his life in his hands and on his nerve robs an express car, he earns what he gets." After the shooting, he said, he followed the railroad out of town, but discovered the next morning that he was going east instead of west. He rested under some trees by the tracks all day Saturday, and traveled only at night. He remembered a hard rain that froze his clothes. But he related nothing further as to where he got the clothes, and how and where he got his head bandaged. When captured, Logan was wearing two gold rings and a pocket watch. He gave one ring to an officer, Sid Giles, and the watch to Sergeant Will Malone. He figured he wouldn't need them where he was going, and they had been civil to him on the train back. The pocket watch contained a photo of Logan and Annie Rogers, which would be used in evidence against her.

After the arraignment Logan was transferred to the Knox County jail, with his trial set to begin on December 18, at 2:00 p.m. Bail was set at twenty thousand dollars.

Meantime, Drees, captured with Logan, was trying to get out of trouble. He explained his occupation and described how he'd spent all his money in Knoxville with a James Burton. He had been riding the rails with Burton, but had lost him near Jefferson City (his jump for the train had apparently been blocked by Logan). Drees had been on his way back to the depot when he'd been arrested. He claimed that this had been his only contact with Logan. Nevertheless, the officials decided to keep him until the Pinkertons could get a look at him.

Sheriff Fox introduced Logan to reporters and onlookers as "Charley" and allowed them access to the corridor area in front of their cells. A local reporter extended his hand, saying, "Good evening, Mr. Longabaugh." Logan responded that his name was Johnson. He asked that the reporter who shook his hand only take three fingers because the rest were sore (from having Dinwiddie wrench the revolver out of his hand). When it came time to set up a hammock in his cell, he pretended to be inept, since he was supposed to have never been in jail before. However the authorities weren't buying it. William Pinkerton wired to Chief of Police, J. J. Atkins that if the man they had in custody was Harvey Logan, he was "undoubtedly the most desperate murderer, train robber and outlaw in the United States." Pinkerton said that Lowell Spence was on his way from Chicago to identify the prisoner.

Meanwhile, the Knoxville police weren't idle. They searched the remainder of Logan's baggage, finding his Colt .45, writing materials, and more Montana banknotes wrapped in a Cincinnati newspaper dated December 4. The total amount of the money now collected from St. Louis, Nashville, and Knoxville came to about $18,000—far short of the $45,000 taken.

Neither the reporters nor county officials were finding Logan cooperative in allowing his photo to be taken. As he was being examined by Dr. E. C. Lones, an artist, Lloyd Branson, painted his portrait. Lones had coincidentally also worked on the policemen Logan had wounded, but Logan apparently never showed any concern about their fate. In his mind, they had got what they deserved. (The two men would continue to improve, but neither would return to normal, and neither would live as long as he might have otherwise. In fact their deaths would eventually be attributed to Harvey Logan.)

As the doctor stitched the worst of his head wounds, he found Logan to be in a good mood but rather quiet. The longest cut was three inches long and revealed the bone below. A wound on his right temple didn't require stitches. The doctor said the prisoner had lost a good deal of blood, and his weakened condition was made worse by exposure to the extreme weather. Lones couldn't help but admire Logan for his grit and overall nerve. He also commented in his notes that Logan was an outdoorsman who was lean and muscular. The doctor also observed that Logan's legs were slightly bowed and his feet slightly pigeon toed; he noted his finger wounds, the results of Dinwiddie's work. The doctor stated that he used "good language, well-framed sentences, not as much slang as might be expected and very little profanity." The doctor also noted a scar between his right wrist and elbow (a scar that would later come to play undue importance—given that in a 1904 robbery attempt of a Rio Grande Western train, a bandit who committed suicide was identified as Harvey Logan, but the body was absent a wrist scar). The doctor was amazed at the large crowds that came to see Logan, especially women. He jokingly said it would cost ten cents a peep to look at the prisoner.

Spence came to Knoxville from Chicago, accompanied by Police Chief Atkins and Sheriff J. J. Fox. When they arrived at the jail, the prisoners were exercising in an inner corridor. Sheriff Fox called for "Charley Johnson" to come to the outer corridor bars so that Spence could have a look at him. Spence whispered to Fox that Johnson was in fact Harvey "Kid Curry" Logan. Spence next asked to see Logan's right arm, confirming his identity by his bullet scar. Looking at Drees, he said he was not Butch Cassidy. Before leaving, Spence asked if Logan wanted anything. Logan replied that he'd like a cigar. Spence said he had none but he would get some for Logan when he went uptown. Meanwhile, John Drees was released and allowed to go home to Louisville, Kentucky.

The newspapers focused on Spence's remarks concerning Logan, especially his praising of the law officers' capture of the fugitive, and how lucky they were not to have any more policemen hurt or killed. Spence described Logan as a "deadly bandit who had a total disregard for human life." He also recounted the background story of Logan's connection to Annie Rogers, Fanny Porter, and others.

Logan inquired who this Spence was who had looked him over. He was told about Spence, and how he was Logan's main pursuer from the Pinkertons. Another Pinkerton Detective Agency superintendent, Andrew Irle, also tried to talk to Logan, but Logan wouldn't cooperate, going to his hammock and partially hiding behind a newspaper. Other guests were luckier, though. Logan met with Governor Benton McMillan, U.S. Marshal Hadsell from Cheyenne, and a Union Pacific chief detective, W. T. Canada, among others.

In the midst of this commotion, the sheriff was cautioned that Logan was capable of escape from anywhere. "Hold on to him tight," one law enforcement official warned. But Logan was likely in no condition to attempt an escape. His head wound was inflamed and causing him great pain. Otherwise, he was being treated better than he perhaps deserved. As the old saying goes, an outlaw is admired once he is captured. He received a variety of food and even had visits from ministers and the Christian Temperance Union. He claimed he came from a Methodist church background. And while he was denied the purchase of an expensive pair of Douglas shoes (size 7E) because they had a steel shank, he was given a new hammock after his ripped, as well as whiskey and cigars.

Logan also received the daily papers, had clean laundry, and was kept groomed to meet the public. He still enjoyed talking with the reporters and reading his own press notices. He would talk about most subjects, except his outlaw life. His visitors now numbered in the many thousands. The sheriff kept parading them through. Close to one thousand visitors showed up on December 22 alone. Only Teddy Roosevelt's visit to town attracted more people.

After seeing visitors, Logan would go back to his cell to play solitaire. He also enjoyed playing ragball, football, and leapfrog with the other prisoners.

This casual atmosphere was all to change just before Christmas when Logan received a letter carrying a local postmark. He was quoted as saying he had received an important message from a friend whom he wanted to see to learn more about a subject the stranger had addressed. The sheriff decided to take this as a security threat, restricting Logan's visitors to "officials and only prominent citizens." But this wasn't before a tall man with reddish hair and whiskers visited Logan. After the visitor left, the guards discovered that the combination locks in the outer corridor had been played with to learn the number series.

Logan received a pillow from one female visitor, along with a love letter in a scented pink envelope. This may have been from a woman named Catherine Cross, who was shot to death in a saloon for singing a song about Kid Curry one too many times. She had told people that she and Harvey were going away together.

We don't know if he ever heard the song himself, although he liked the newspapers calling him "The Napoleon of Crime." Supposedly a fellow prisoner dared to call him a "common cowboy," which resulted in Logan going into one of his rages and trying to strangle the man. Another of Logan's almost-strangled-to-death victims, Luther Brady, was also in jail for passing the stolen money. Logan and Brady had a three-sentence conversation before Brady was moved upstairs. Logan supposedly asked Brady if he had hurt him. Brady said no, and Logan said he was glad. The Pinkertons' Mr. Spence brought forth the theory that Brady had stolen money from Logan, making the argument over a pool cue incidental. Brady was able to make bail, easing his concern that he might come down with something fatal at the hands of Logan. Brady also took the time to visit with the police officers, thanking them for saving his life.

Logan was given a chance to help instruct a constable from a rural town in the Great Smoky Mountains about law enforcement. The constable told Logan that people said he was a "plumb good detective." Logan said he was glad that he hadn't met him on the outside. The constable agreed. He tried to guess Logan's weight, estimating it at about 160 pounds, which was Logan's regular weight, but it was now 180 pounds, thanks, Logan said, to all the good food women were bringing him while he was in jail. Logan asked the constable if he had made many arrests, and he replied a few. When he said he had studied law enforcement, Logan replied that studying was the safest part of his business. They both laughed at that and shook hands. Logan told him not to be in a hurry to graduate, saying, "Some farmer might beat you to death with a cornstalk." Logan laughed and laughed, even when the visitor was gone.

Logan's legal predicament wasn't quite the fun as some of his visitors. By December 19, Logan had hired Reuben L. Cates, a lawyer; his cousin, Charles T. Cates Jr.; John C. Houk, a former state Senator and an experienced trial lawyer; and an E. F. Mynatt. Reuben L. Cates was the Knox County registration and election commissioner while the other three were city attorneys. He had the best attorneys and was being supplied by law officers with cigars, pipe tobacco, and whiskey. But not everything was going well for him. The case was put on a back burner because of the two policemen's health. This delay worked against Logan in keeping the criminal charges local.

In the meantime Sheriff Fox, Logan's attorneys, and Circuit Judge Sneed (a political ally of Cates) wanted the case tried by the state in Knoxville. The Great Northern Express Company, the Pinkertons, and federal authorities wanted it tried in a federal court, where the penalties would potentially be more severe, given that the charges would include train robbery and passing banknotes. The preliminary hearing was held in the jail on December 28, conducted by Squire William Sellars. Several officers were in attendance, as was the press. The authorities had the contents of Logan's luggage spread out in front of the cell. The prisoner politely answered the judge's questions, except when it came to his personal life and the train robbery. (He did say, falsely, that his parents, four brothers, and three sisters were still alive, but not where they lived.)

It was February 1902, and the officers were still not healthy enough to appear. Spence returned to Chicago, but not before telling Fox that Pinkerton would pay for an extra guard to keep watch over Logan. Fox said no, but eventually accepted a similar offer from the Great Northern Express Company.

While local, state, and federal authorities fought it out for jurisdiction over the trial, the *Nashville American* speculated on where Logan was getting the money to fund his defense. They mentioned "a wealthy sister" who was helping him, but not Jim Thornhill, who was also contributing. The sister was probably Arda in Kansas City, Missouri, who might have been selling horses (like Thornhill) to fund the defense.

Through it all the press continued to write about Logan—reporting on his health and what his favorite foods were, how he passed the days playing cards and reading papers and novels. On January 21 a grand jury charged Logan with intent to commit murder (referencing Saylor and Dinwiddie) and assault and battery (with regard to Brady). Also in January the *Knoxville Sentinel* got around to interviewing police officer Robert Saylor. He expressed his appreciation for the kind way the community had treated him and his partner Dinwiddie. (The city paid the two officers their monthly pay of fifty-five dollars in spite of their inability to work.) Saylor mentioned his earlier dealing with Logan the Wednesday before the shootings. He had gone to the apartment of the two women with whom Logan was staying to speak with him about the loud noises coming from the room. He also saw Logan at Finley's Bar and the nearby restaurant, even having a cigar with him. He concluded that "he had never seen a man as cool as Logan." The public also learned that Saylor was still weak and could barely use his injured arm. The momentum of the bullet had destroyed a large portion of bone. He didn't expect to ever have full use of the injured arm again. His partner, William Dinwiddie, still had a bullet in his chest, which apparently couldn't be operated on.

According to authors Brown Waller and Sylvia Lynch, Logan's popularity began to fade in February, and his disposition began to sour.

He became intolerant of visitors, even at times covering the bars of his cell with a blanket. He told reporters that he didn't want to be stared at like a wild beast. He complained of a sprained ankle from playing football and a lack of food from the community, which Fox had apparently stopped for security reasons. He exercised daily in his cell to keep in shape, often climbing up the sides with the agility of a jungle animal. Learning about the sentencing of Ben Kilpatrick and Laura Bullion on federal charges could certainly have contributed to his low morale. (Kilpatrick was in prison in Columbus, Ohio; and Laura in Jefferson City, Missouri.)

Reporters and law enforcement officials were learning more about Harvey Logan than they'd learned about any other member of the Wild Bunch. He apparently had an enthusiasm for music, for example. When Joshua and Moutrie Jones were housed in Logan's cellblock, Logan mentioned that he had read about their brother "Ole Bull" Jones, who was considered one of the best solo violinists in America. Logan even gave a discourse on great composers and their works. According to author Sylvia Lynch, when Moutrie brought out his violin and played classical music and then a reel, "Harvey positively squeaked with delight and laughed as he hadn't done since his incarceration. The encounter brought out yet another side of the mysterious man."

On April 5, O. C. Hanks was shot and killed by law officers in a San Antonio saloon. He was carrying $440 worth of currency from the robbery. His mother came from Abilene to identify the body. Spence arrived on the scene and also announced that he was the man who had been chased by police in Nashville, as well as the man who had boarded the Great Northern Train at Malta. Now all the participants in the Exeter Creek train robbery were either dead or in jail. Even some of Hanks's relatives were arrested for spending the stolen money.

Sheriff Fox received a letter from D. S. Elliot, the general manager of the Great Northern Railroad Express Company. He cautioned Fox that Logan was more likely to try and escape now that Hanks was dead.

Annie Rogers's trial for possessing and passing stolen currency started on June 14, before Judge W. M. Hart. Testifying were local bank employees, a United States Treasury man, express messenger C. H. Smith (who was on the Great Northern train at Exeter Siding when it was robbed), the local police, and even Corrine Lewis, the Memphis madam. The prosecutor was able to show that Annie's signature matched the signature on some of the forged banknotes. Lowell Spence produced Annie's and Harvey's picture that had been found in the pocket watch that Logan had given away to one of the Knoxville police officers. Enough evidence now linked Annie to Harvey that her story of not having known him from before fell apart.

As the police produced information regarding Annie's relationship with Logan, her defense switched from the alleged crimes to her poor treatment at the hands of the officers, including her "sweatbox" interrogation and denial of counsel. The cigar merchant, Morgan Roop, who had hired a lawyer for her, added that the authorities had tried to intimidate him into dropping his help.

Meanwhile Harvey was following Annie's case in the newspapers and worrying about her. Annie's defense wanted Logan to be brought to Nashville to testify, but Sheriff Fox wisely said no. Davidson County Assistant District Attorney G. B. Kilpatrick and Annie's attorney instead came to Knoxville to take Harvey's deposition. Also present were two Knox County deputies and a stenographer. Logan freely told of his relationship with Annie and their travels together. Most importantly, however, he said that Annie had not known where the money had come from (he would still not answer as to what the source of the money was).

Harvey's deposition, when combined with her defense attorney's efforts to show that she'd been denied her civil rights, won Annie a verdict of not guilty.

Meanwhile, apart from his deposition, Logan was turning into less than a model prisoner. At one point, according to the local papers, he went into a tirade because of supposedly bad food and poor treatment by Sheriff Fox and his men. It started with Logan dousing a day guard,

Sam Callaway, with a bucket of water, breaking a window, tearing out a light, and swinging back and forth on his cell door, "making an unbearable noise and yelling like a Comanche Indian." He threatened to get even with all of the jail's staff. He then went to bed and slept soundly. The next morning, after apparently promising to calm down, he was given breakfast. But he was soon striking the bars with a broomstick and making wild noises again. In addition he sang a cowboy song that ended with, "In the saddle of my favorite bronco I will die."

Other prisoners were soon removed from his cellblock, he was denied the use of the corridor, and visitors were prohibited. Harvey retained his broom, but as the sheriff said, he had no more lights within reach to destroy. Sheriff Fox believed that the tirade had been over the day guard, whom Logan disliked. Logan also was hosed down at one point.

Perhaps Logan was wondering what was happening with Butch, Harry, and Etta in South America. There had been no mention of them in the newspapers since they had left the country. He could not have known that the three had filed on homestead ground in the province of Chubet, District 16 of Octobre, near Cholito, Argentina. Like some other outlaws, they were still living with the impossible dream of settling down somewhere with their ill-gotten money. Logan no doubt spent many long nights, staring at the stone ceiling, envying his friends their freedom.

Harvey's trial was slated for June. The authorities were hopeful that Knoxville Circuit Court Judge Joseph Sneed would drop the local assault and attempted murder charges, in effect turning Logan over to the federal authorities. At the trial six men lingered in the back of the courtroom, waiting to take Harvey into federal custody. Instead the city's misdemeanor charges were ruled on, and Logan received a six-month jail sentence and a fifty dollar fine.

On September 4, 1902, Judge Sneed announced that the federal court would have joint jurisdiction. The federal trial would begin in November. Logan would be charged with forging and counterfeiting stolen bank notes, forging signatures of bank officials, and passing and possessing stolen currency. The train robbery charges were dropped, since Harvey would have had to have been transported to Chouteau County, Montana, to be tried. The judge's decision to allow joint jurisdiction may have had to do with Logan's attorney, Reuben L. Cates, being elected Knox County district attorney. Because of this new conflict of interest, attorney Jerome Templeton was appointed a special prosecutor. Templeton in turn requested that Logan be turned over to the federal court. Judge Sneed granted Templeton's request.

Between Logan's federal court dates, an Edwin Jackson Harrison, "Uncle Jack," received a small package wrapped in sand-colored paper. It contained a measure of Duke's pipe mixture, Queen's Smoking Tobacco, some twist tobacco chew, and six corncob pipes. Harrison had owned a restaurant at a location that Logan had frequented before the shootings. A note inside, signed by a Martin Roberts, directed Harrison to take the package to Charles Johnson at the county jail. The September 19 postmark on the package appeared to be Nashville, and the writing in a female hand. The note said if Harrison made the delivery, he would receive a box of cigars. Harrison obediently took the package to the county lockup the next morning. The package contents appeared okay, until the pipes were examined a second time. It was discovered that the pitch beneath the paper trademark had been removed and replaced with a hacksaw blade, which when extended, measured about twenty-three inches long. Sheriff Fox detained Harrison, but there was no evidence of his wrongdoing. A woman in black wearing a veil had been appearing everyday at the trial, but this was almost certainly Harvey's admirer Catherine Cross. Annie probably left town after the package had been examined. In a letter to Harvey, she said there was nothing further she could do for him, and going to his trial would only create a media circus.

There are different versions as to what finally happened to Annie Rogers. Donna B. Ernst, in her book *Women of the Wild Bunch,* reported that Annie worked as a prostitute at Dee Picchi's Saloon in Hot Springs, Arkansas. Ernst cites a 1908 Pinkerton report that also places her near Lander, Wyoming, as a Mrs. Warner. Yet another report has her spending time in a women's home (detention center) before escaping south again.

A different Pinkerton report, cited by author James Horan, describes her pawning a diamond ring given to her by Logan and telling the pawn-broker that she was tired of being a prostitute and intended to go to St. Louis where her mother and brother owned a department store. This Pinkerton report said that she was never heard of again. Hopefully she did escape "the life" and was reunited with her family under her real name, Beulah Phinburg.

Logan's federal trial—Case 3472, *U.S. v. Charles Johnson*—ran through November. (Interestingly, while Spence had correctly identified Logan, Harvey had stayed with his Charles Johnson alias and was tried as such.) Over thirty witnesses were called, including Great Northern Railroad officers and employees; law enforcement, bank, and railroad express officials; and Treasury Department people from Washington, D.C. The railroad employees were express messengers C. H. Smith, who had testified at Annie Rogers trial, and Michael O'Neil, the fireman at the time of the holdup, now an engineer. O'Neil was quite nervous dur-ing his testimony, apparently worried about Logan and others taking retribution against his immediate family, but neither Smith nor O'Neil had any trouble after the verdict was reached.

The defense said that Logan was in France from June until August 1901. They claimed a James Stewart, possibly of Chicago, could verify this. However no such man could be found. The defense also claimed that the prosecutors had not proved that Logan had signed the currency. They cited a case of a national bank in Oberlin, Ohio, issuing unsigned banknotes. Logan's attorneys did everything in their power to slow the proceedings, objecting to documents offered into evidence and to cer-tain procedures, including jury selection. In addition they asked for con-tinuances and postponements.

Chouteau County had tried extraditing Logan back to Fort Benton for trial. Apparently the Union Pacific and U.S. Marshall Frank Hadsell in Cheyenne had contemplated the same thing on behalf of two train robberies committed in Wyoming. The Union Pacific claimed to have spent a million dollars looking for Logan.

The prosecution introduced a parade of witnesses. Logan was identified by the trainmen, the two injured Knoxville policemen, the bartender at Ike Jones's saloon, and others. The presentation began with a Treasury Department official who identified the seized currency as part of the stolen shipment on the train. Notaries were called to confirm that Logan's handwriting was found on some of the money. All told, there were twenty-seven government witnesses while the defense only called seven. Logan would not testify himself. A girlfriend, Lillie Martin, whom the prosecution planned to call, had disappeared.

The defense seemed confident about the jury voting Logan not guilty, and they were very surprised when he was convicted on ten of the nineteen counts. In fact Logan was more than surprised, he became very angry. The judge sentenced him to twenty years at the federal prison located in Columbus, Ohio. (There had been an unsubstantiated report that he turned down a plea bargain for a sentence of fifteen years.) Of course the defense immediately appealed, claiming bribed and perjured witnesses. Logan's legal representation had already cost him (and his relatives and friends) three thousand dollars; now he had to come up with at least another five hundred dollars. Logan had thirty days to raise the additional funds, being he was ruled ineligible under the Pauper's Oath (which was not valid in appeals). He also asked to be sent to a southern prison if his appeal failed, since he had developed a case of bronchitis and was taking medication and a warmer climate would be better for him.

The Pinkertons, express companies, and U.S. marshal's office had warned Sheriff Fox about Logan potentially trying to escape. However, the court ordered him held in the local Knoxville jail during the appeal. He was still confined to the second-floor cellblock by himself. A steel-lined mail car waited to take him to prison.

The Circuit Court of Appeals ruled in favor of the state on June 2, 1903, with only minor changes. Logan now had about thirty days before being transferred to prison. (Sylvia Lynch and Brown Waller have written exhaustively about the trial. See Lynch's *Harvey Logan in*

Knoxville, and *Last of the Great Train Robbers,* by Waller. A trial transcript is also available from the National Archives, Southeast Region.)

Butch Cassidy had always claimed that Harvey Logan was the bravest man he had ever met and was the type to wager everything on one card. Logan was about to prove it.

Saturday June 27 dawned like any other day in Knoxville. Logan had taken to waving to a small girl in front of a white house near the jail. She would wave back from her chair on the edge of the lawn. Vendors had set up for a Saturday farmer's market, dressed in shirtsleeves on a pleasant seventy-nine-degree day. Sheriff Fox was attending the funeral of a J. C. Roberts.

Despite the pleasant day, there was still a tense undercurrent. As long as Logan was in jail, there was a chance he could escape. Fox continued to reassure the Pinkertons that all was secure, and he would not lose him. Meanwhile, for his recent good behavior, Logan was being allowed visitors, including local society and church women who brought him books and food. Fox was also allowing Logan the use of the outer corridor (Logan's attorney's had threatened to make an issue out of the restriction). The outer corridor went entirely around the inner corridor, which separated six cells on the east and four cells on the west, including Logan's. It was quite normal for guard Frank Irwin to make a round of the outer corridor, and then stop to talk with Logan on the south end between the cellblock and steam radiator below the window. That day Logan may have called Irwin's attention to the unusually high and muddy Tennessee River, or maybe Irwin just stopped to muse, staring out the window.

In any case, the next thing Irwin knew, Logan had tossed a lasso made from broom wire around his neck and slammed his head back against the hard metal bars. Logan made it clear that this was a desperate situation for them both, and if Irwin caused any trouble, he was dead. Irwin did as he was told, turning around so Logan could tie his hands through the bars, using strips torn from an old hammock. Now Logan released himself from his cage and hurried to the bathroom, just north of the dungeon, to retrieve a nine-foot-long pole made of broken window molding.

The pole also was held together with strips from the torn hammock. On one end he had a hook fashioned from the handle of the bucket he had destroyed during a recent tantrum. Logan went to the northwest corner of the cellblock, stretched out flat on the floor, and used his pole to hook the shoebox in which the guards stored their weapons before entering the cellblock area. He drug the box back to him, removed the pistols, and pushed the box back to its original position so as not to tip off anyone making rounds. Logan checked Irwin's watch. It was about 4:30 p.m., and close to time for guard Tom Bell to bring his cough medicine. Logan repeated his promise to Irwin to kill any jail personnel who wouldn't cooperate with him.

Next began the second phase of his plan. He impatiently rapped on the bars until Bell came up the stairs to the second floor, entering through the double doors. Logan held out his cough syrup container, asking that it be filled. But before Bell could react, he had a revolver in his face. Next, with one of his wrists bound with hammock pieces, he commenced to unlock the cellblock entry door. It took longer than usual for Bell to make the combination work because he was rattled. It wasn't helpful to have a gun barrel pressed against his head. Bell asked Logan not to point the gun at him because it might go off. Logan replied that he didn't have to fear it's going off accidentally, adding that he wouldn't harm a hair on Bell's head. Once they moved out of the cellblock, Bell preceded Logan down the stairs, past the sheriff's and guard's offices, and out the kitchen to the backyard.

Once outside they met a third man, R. P. Swanee, a former prisoner who helped out around the jail. Swanee had been on his way to the kitchen, but now, at gunpoint, helped Bell saddle the sheriff's mare. Swanee found the saddle in the stable but no bridle. Logan kept a hat low over his eyes as the men worked. Bell next unlocked the outer gate onto Prince Street. Logan changed his mind about taking Bell with him and using him as a shield since he faced no opposition.

While these events were occurring, housekeeper Sallie Robinson had noticed that Bell was outside and not looking well. She reported this to Sheriff Fox, who had returned from the funeral and was in the dining room. Fox stepped out on his upstairs porch, seeing Bell in an agitated state. Bell waved at him to go back inside. But Fox had noticed Logan riding his mare, and would later claim that he then ran up to the third floor to retrieve his pistol. By the time he returned, Logan was heading up Hill Street toward Gay Street and the bridge across the Tennessee River. Meanwhile Bell and the jail cook, Jim West, had freed Irwin. The time was about 5:05 p.m. People on the street noted Logan riding off with the little girl he had exchanged waves with. He indicated to her that she should keep silent. Logan was last seen by townspeople turning right onto the Martin Mill Road.

At about 5:15 p.m., U.S. Marshal R. W. Austin and U.S. Attorney W. D. Wright met Sheriff Fox walking casually down the street. They asked about Logan, only to learn that he had escaped just a few minutes before. They went to Austin's office to learn the particulars. Fox told them he had recently learned that Logan had a map of the country to the south across the river. More importantly, he told them that he had given Logan the run of the inner corridor against Wright's orders because of Logan's lawyers insistence. He said a posse was being formed. Austin put out the alarm to all deputy U.S. marshals, county sheriffs, and even had the telephone company call their subscribers with a description of Logan. The posse didn't leave town until about 6:00 p.m.

Sheriff Fox returned to the county jail about 6:00 p.m. Austin and Wright notified Judge D. C. Clark of what had happened, and the judge directed them to make a careful examination of how Logan had escaped. Fox's casual attitude about the escape evoked suspicion of conspiracy. Hadn't Logan's friends supposedly offered ten thousand dollars to anyone who would help him escape? Pinkerton special agent Charlie Siringo would be even blunter, claiming that Jim Thornhill had been on hand with a good supply of "the long green" which makes the "mare" go. Siringo went on to say that Thornhill had sold another five hundred broken horses in 1903, had cash available, and may have been at the jail shortly before Logan's escape.

An inspection of Logan's cell revealed that he had taken his razor, soap, combs, razor strap, and a small looking glass, perhaps to read maps. The cell contained old clothing, papers, magazines, and trash. Apparently the accumulated trash had allowed Logan to conceal items he'd saved to help him in his escape. He also left a book behind, *The Life of Napoleon Bonaparte*. Inside the cover he had written a list of the books of the Bible. Perhaps the visiting men and women of the Christian faith had influenced him—or maybe he was just killing time.

Austin and Wright were to meet Fox again that night at about 8:30, but Fox didn't show. Instead the meeting was held in Charles T. Cates's office with Logan's other lawyers present. Austin and Wright did not agree with Fox's contention that Logan had been well guarded and were suspicious about the circumstances of the escape. On Sunday the mare that Logan had stolen was found near a railroad trestle that crossed the Tennessee River. It was missing a shoe, had a strained forefoot, and the saddle was gone. The following morning U.S. Marshal R. W. Austin and U.S. Attorney W. D. Wright, along with the Pinkertons, began their own investigation, holding Sheriff Fox responsible for the escape.

During his escape Logan kept up a quick but steady pace, knowing that the Knox County posse (led by deputies Hardin and Epps) was at least an hour behind. Two young women saw Logan ride by, but couldn't get his attention. He was too busy urging on his horse. A farmer tried to talk with him, but again Logan rode past. According to one account, he turned east on the Valley Road that connected the Martin Mill Pike with the Sevierville Pike. He stopped at the Giffin store and post office about 6:30 p.m. to smoke a cigar and chatted with the men on the porch, leaving abruptly when they seemed to grow suspicious of him. He stopped again near the Sevierville Pike to ask a farmer where the Maryville Pike was located. He backtracked and turned onto a side road into the McCall Woods. From there the trail crossed Brown's Mountain, toward Neubert Springs, about seven miles from Knoxville. Here it vanished into the mountains. Posses thought they picked up his trail at different times and places but were not definite.

When the sheriff's mare was found by the road, it was obvious that Logan had circled back. It was surmised that he had spent the night in a cedar grove and cane breaks by a wood-processing mill near the river, then doubled back to a railroad trestle near a corn lot. A man in a nearby house had heard noises and found the horse. It appeared that the horse's front legs had gone off the trail into a gully and that it had thrown the rider. Logan had probably thrown the saddle in the river so that, finding a saddleless horse, the posses would believe Logan had changed horses and the sheriff's horse had returned on its own. However, the human tracks around the horse told a different story. Two Pinkerton men did search into the mountains, crossing into North Carolina. They followed several false trails before giving up, just as Logan had hoped they would.

Besides the now-national search (which put Spence back in the center of things), the spotlight was focused on the Knox County jail and Sheriff Fox, who had drawn suspicion for three reasons. He had gone back to get his gun, but hadn't followed Logan; he hadn't put out an immediate alert; and he had given tours of the escape scene instead of concentrating on the escape.

The government conceded the escape was possible without assistance, but it could have been prevented. Austin filed a civil suit for negligence against Fox for ten thousand dollars in the United States Circuit Court. It was later settled out of court for three thousand dollars. Fox and Irwin lost their jobs at the next election.

It seems doubtful now that there was true collusion on Fox's part. Thornhill was having enough problems just raising the legal fees without coming up with bribe money. His allowing Logan freedom in the corridor and reacting slowly to his escape were mistakes, but probably not arising from ill intentions. Maybe some part of him only hoped Logan would get away so he could be done with him.

On July 2, 1903, the Pinkerton Agency released a wanted poster of Logan, offering $1,100 as a reward (not enough for a person to risk a life for). Logan was now the number one wanted criminal in the United States.

Chicago-based Pinkerton Lowell Spence had spent a year in the field looking for Logan. And Spence now understood that if they met, Logan would try to keep his promise to kill him.

There are several versions regarding what Logan did next and how and when he died.

First there is a version by Frank and Bruce Lamb wherein he spent two weeks in a safe house—provided by Thornhill in Knoxville—before hopping trains to Montana. They also have him stopping to see his sister, Allie, in Minneapolis (even though she lived in the Dodson-Kansas City, Missouri, area, until moving to Texas, where she died). But Logan certainly could have hidden out at Allie's Missouri horse ranch in the southwest corner of McDonald County near Noel.

He arrived in Montana, staying in Landusky until he moved on to Wyoming, picked up both a partner and a bullet in his leg from stealing horses near Kaycee. After some locals gave him first aid, he and his partner moved on to spend the winter at the Lambs' ranch in Sand Gulch, Colorado. There the Lamb family members wrote never-to-be-sent letters to the Knoxville papers, as dictated by Logan. In them he criticized the office holders in Knox County and the Great Northern Railroad, including judges, his lawyers, the prosecution, the sheriff, his deputies, jailer, and others. Three letters were written in a single-entry bookkeeping ledger.

The editor of the *Great Falls Tribune* received a special column from its Malta correspondent, stating, "Kid Curry was visiting here last week." No one disputed this. He had both the caves on East Coburn Butte and Thornhill Butte in which to hide out. The Little Rockies country was certainly full of lawmen and Pinkertons, but like Valley County's Sheriff Griffith, they stuck to the main trails.

In a more documented version of Logan's tale, the ledger letters were written by Logan (and others) in jail just after the verdict was announced. He had given the ledger to Jim Thornhill, who had then passed it on to their friend, writer Walt Coburn, the son of the Circle C ranch owner, Robert Coburn, who had played an earlier part in Logan's story. This perhaps happened after the Thornhill and Coburn families moved to Arizona in or about 1916. Coburn kept the ledger, passing it on to his nephew Coburn Maddox. (Maddox's daughter, Mary Grandell, passed it on to the Montana Historical Society in recent years.)

The *Daily Journal and Tribune* of Knoxville received a tongue-in-cheek letter, supposedly from Logan, printed August 23, 1903. The return address was Perkins, California, in Sacramento County. He even gave a street address of 401 Pacific Avenue, where the writer claimed to be leisurely spending the summer. Recalling his escape from the Knox County jail, he gave credit to the sheriff's mare for his escape, claiming not to have taken a train or to have thrown the saddle in the river. Instead, he wrote, he'd walked south into the Great Smoky Mountains. He claimed that he easily could have ambushed the posse but declined "out of respect for the government."

Writing as Charles Johnson, he jokingly defended Sheriff Fox, saying he didn't know about the escape for a whole twenty minutes. He thanked the guards for their pistols and also requested the return of the lasso he had used to escape and one thousand dollars for returning the horse. All of this, he said, could be forwarded to his liveryman and herder, Mr. Gotthere.

Johnson praised the newspapers for accurately stating the facts of his escape. He regretted he couldn't return the favor to a Knoxville police officer named McIntyre, who abused him when he was captured at Jefferson City. He expressed the hope that officers Saylor and Dinwiddie would fully recover. He said he would return sometime, ending with, "Tell the boys not to follow my footsteps and keep out of trouble. Respectfully Charley Johnson." The Monday paper ran an article, discussing whether locals thought the letter was real or bogus.

Jailer Thomas Bell expressed mixed feelings, believing some of it sounded like Charley Johnson (Logan), some not. He further commented that it sounded like someone who was at least familiar with the case. The article mentioned there were reports coming out of Montana that Logan had been visiting his old haunts in the Little Rockies country. The article writer said there were legal samples of his handwriting, but they had not been compared with the letter yet. The reporter speculated on whether Logan would return to the Hole-in-the-Wall country, probably having gotten the idea from Spence of the Pinkertons.

Presumably the Pinkertons and local law enforcement people checked the California street address in Perkins, if it existed. It wouldn't be the last time that Pinkerton dealt with reports of a Logan sighting. Rumors of appearances by Logan persisted for years, some of them even extending down to South America.

One story that several researchers have recounted had its start in a June 1927 article in *Frontier Stories* magazine. The author was Edgar Young, and the article was entitled, "The End of Harvey Logan."

The author claimed to have met Logan "far up the Yguazzie River in Brazil" where the author had managed a logging camp. Young claimed that Logan showed up in his camp in terrible shape, having hiked from Buenos Aires, Argentina, "across pampas and desert and through jungles." Young had a bunk built for him in his shack. When Logan recovered his strength, he went to work for Young as an assistant foreman. Logan saved Young's life when a Brazilian whom he had discharged was going to stab him in the back.

Logan told his story to Young. After escaping from the Knox County jail, he had obtained money from his sister in Minneapolis and headed for Seattle, where he hired out on a Dutch windjammer and jumped ship in Valparaiso, Chile. From there he eventually crossed the Andes into Argentina and began robbing railroad stations. In his travels, he told Young, he never ran into Butch Cassidy or Harry Longabaugh.

Wanted by the law, he recrossed the Andes to Valparaiso by train, boarding a steamer there for Punta Arenas at the southern tip of Argentina. He then traveled northeast to Río Gallegos where he mined for gold. He wound up in jail for drunk and disorderly, but escaped using the Knoxville wire-around-the-neck trick. He headed north through the vast arid plains of Patagonia, robbing outlying trading posts, sheepherders, and ranchers. Once he hit the transcontinental railroad, he began robbing train stations again. The army was now out in force, and he headed for Buenos Aires, again going on an "immense spree." While bar hopping, he met up with some international counterfeiters and he joined them in spreading bogus paper money. With money in his pocket again, he went on another drunk and ended up in jail, escaped, and found Young.

Young's story went on, including time spent on the Uruguay frontier and Chile, with more gold mining and a number of drunken sprees. Young naturally received letters about his Logan article and in one changed the river's name to the more correct Iguazzu. (There is a Iguaçu River in southern Brazil plus a Iguassu Falls and Iguazú National Park.) But his portrayal was of a man who clearly wasn't Logan (having called him stupid, slow-witted, slow on the draw, and a poor rider—just the opposite of the real Logan).

There were many other Logan sightings, a number of them taking place in the months after his escape from Knox County jail. The Pinkertons dealt with reports placing Logan in Malta, Landusky, Yantic, Chinook, and Havre. One of the more credible Logan sightings was by Ruel Harner, a driver for the stagecoach running between Zortman and Malta. Harner had property near the old Curry spread, and he told of seeing "Kid Curry" with a local Landusky rancher after his escape from Knoxville. Other bizarre rumors had Logan killing a local deputy sheriff, as well as working as a section hand on the Great Northern.

A man who claimed he spent a couple hours with Logan was James T. Moran of Yantic (later Lohman), Montana, located between Havre and Chinook. He and his partner, Robert Main, had operated a trading post there. Moran heard a knock at his door one night, opening it to a "hobo" who had just gotten off the westbound train. The man wanted to borrow a horse, saddle, and bridle. It took Moran, an old acquaintance of Logan, a few minutes to recognize Harvey through his getup. For the next two hours, Logan talked about visits to Fort Benton and Havre, and even of seeing former sheriff Buckley and old soldiers Bailey and Purnell at their Havre saloon. He said no one recognized him. Logan returned the horse that Moran had lent him one day later with a small package of money. Moran said Logan stayed a few nights at a ranch a few miles to the east near Chinook. Reportedly several men had seen Logan and wanted the reward, but the Pinkertons would not guarantee their safety afterward.

"Sleepy" Tom Conant had been a roundup foreman with the Simon Pepin P-Cross in the Bear Paw Cattle Pool, south of Chinook and Lohman. He later told a story of a hobo he had hired to help with the horses, and how good the man had been with animals. The man drew his pay every day, spending it in the saloons. Conant thought he had looked familiar but couldn't tell through the scraggly hair, beard, and dirty clothes. One night, after too much to drink, the new hand told Conant about his early days in northern Montana. The man left the next day, and Conant finally put two and two together. It had been Harvey Logan.

September 1903 saw the last Montana sighting of Logan. In mid-February of 1904, however, there was a supposed sighting in Denver (this one made the national news). A hotel runner had met a man at the train station to take his bags. The man decided to take the bags himself but handed the boy a dollar anyway. The runner arrived at the hotel first, telling the staff what had happened. When the man arrived, the employees curiously looked him over. The desk clerk recognized him from his boyhood days in Missouri but said nothing. Then the newcomer asked for a pitcher of water, which was brought to him in his room about fifteen minutes later. The bellhop entered the man's room without knocking. The valises, now open, contained stacks of new-looking currency.

There was a revolver lying beside one of the bags. When the man became aware of the bellhop's presence, he cursed at him and ordered him out of the room.

While the suspect fled before the police arrived, he supposedly matched the Pinkerton description of Logan to the smallest detail. The newspapers speculated whether the money the bellhop saw could have been the remainder of the unsigned banknotes from the Exeter Creek, Montana, train robbery. (Of the $45,000 taken, after all, only about $19,000 had been accounted for.)

A month later, in March 1904, there was another sighting to the northwest of Denver in Rock Springs, Wyoming. The Union Pacific Railroad, taking no chances, outfitted a special train with rangers and horses and put it on the ready between Laramie and Green River. Nothing ever came of this scenario, however.

In late spring of 1904, a train was robbed near Parachute, Colorado, between Glenwood Springs and Grand Junction. One of the robbers, after being severely wounded, committed suicide. Pinkerton agent Lowell Spence identified the robber from a death photo as Harvey Logan. Some authorities agreed with Spence while others weren't so sure. More importantly, however, there were people from the Hole-in-the-Wall country who certainly didn't agree. Their uncertainty throws an enticing shadow of doubt over the final chapters of Harvey Logan's story.

The descendants of those local residents who were involved in the drama still take very seriously the discrepancy between the official version of Logan's death and the folk story version.

In May 1904 Logan showed up back in his old haunts in Kaycee, Wyoming, gateway to the Hole-in-the-Wall country. He and an unknown companion arrived on spent horses, apparently coming up from the Casper area to the south. He and his partner stole several horses, saddles, a revolver, and other gear from the ranch of Kenneth McDonald in the Big Horns. McDonald notified the Johnson County sheriff department about the thefts, and a deputy sheriff named Beard and another man from Kaycee responded. The thieves' trail led south along the Red Wall of the outlaw valley and around the southern edge of the Big Horn Mountains toward the Wind River country. The day after the theft, two of the horses were recovered, leaving the duo with only one.

On May 21, when Deputy Beard approached the ranch of former gang member, Walt Punteney, on Bridger Creek, he saw two men fleeing up a nearby hill. A shootout ensued, during which Beard believed one of the men was seriously wounded, perhaps in the groin. (Apparently, the wounded outlaw was Logan himself.) Beard called for more assistance from Sheriff Walter Webb before continuing on the chase. Reportedly, Punteney had told Beard that one of the fugitives was Harvey Logan. The other was known as Stevens.

Sheriff Webb arrived with three men. Sheriff Fenton of Bighorn County also brought a posse. They either trailed the thieves to their next location, or as reported in the *Natrona County Tribune,* Sheriff Webb (after several weeks of searching) received a letter as to the suspect's location.

It was nighttime when the outlaws sought refuge at the 2B ranch in the Lost Cabin country. This ranch was owned by Dave Picard and Vince Hayes. They had previously known Logan as Ed Howard, and he had frequented their ranch. The men were on a roundup, so their wives dressed the outlaw's wound and hid him in a cellar with his partner on guard. The next day the ranchers moved him to the other side of Lysite Mountain on Lake Creek, where they had an old winter camp. Again the wounded fugitive was put in a cellar with his partner on guard. A Thermopolis doctor was called, perhaps a Dr. Richards. (A story went around that a Dr. Hale covered with the authorities on behalf of Dr. Richards.)

Next Logan was moved to a place on the Bighorn River where the ranchers kept their milk cows. They took supplies to him twice a day, helping him to eventually recover.

Sheriff Webb quizzed Punteney about the identity of the two men.

Supposedly Punteney said one of them was Harvey Logan. Webb went to the second location where Logan had been hidden, finding bandages in the cellar, but at this point the sheriff showed no further interest in trailing him.

David Picard and Vince Hayes were arrested by Joe LeFors, Sheriff Webb, and Deputy Sheriff O'Brien, supposedly for giving Tom O'Day a false alibi (helping O'Day beat a rustling charge). They were later found not guilty, and both men claimed that the arrests were in retaliation for helping their old friend Logan.

The historical importance of this story, as far as Picard, Hayes, and the other families are concerned, is that Logan was still in the Hole-in-the-Wall country, recovering from his wounds, when the Parachute, Colorado, train robbery took place.

Thus far, we have stories of Logan hiding out in Landusky in the summer of 1903, showing up South America at various times between fall of 1903 to 1911, Denver in February of 1904, and Rock Springs in March of 1904. One branch of the trail then leads to Colorado, in June of 1904.

Most serious Wild Bunch historians look at the robbery of a Denver and Rio Grande Western train near Parachute, Colorado, in the Grand River valley, and accept the notion that Harvey Logan was severely wounded in the course of the caper and then committed suicide. But this line of thinking ignores several potentially important loose ends.

Author James Horan has a man called "Tap" Duncan arriving in the Grand (now Colorado) River country, riding a poor horse and a worn saddle. A loner, he was hired by a small ranch east of Parachute. The other ranch hands looked down on him as an old drifter and saddle bum. But then one day, as the ranch crew was target practicing at a whiskey bottle, Duncan couldn't stand watching them miss shot after shot. He shattered the bottle with a lightning draw. The townspeople and railroad station attendants later recalled that the stranger had quite an interest in train schedules. And just before the robbery, he'd been joined in town by some "rough-looking cowhands."

This robbery also supposedly involves the Lamb family of Sand Gulch, Colorado, whose ranch was located in Fremont County. The story of the Lamb family's supposed relationship with Harvey Logan is anonymously told by Frank Lamb in the 1966 book *The Wild Bunch,* and by his son, F. Bruce Lamb, in a 1991 book, *The Life and Times of Harvey Logan and the Wild Bunch.* The latter work is listed as "Western fiction" but includes endnotes and a bibliography. It is a strange blend of fact and fiction.

According to the Lamb family, they first got to know Logan and cousin Bob Lee in the mid-1890s when the two men arrived in the Sand Creek area looking for a remote place to set up a horse relay station. Logan and Lee were disguised as miners. Logan stayed for a while, becoming friends of the family.

The Lambs then claim that Logan returned a year or two later with Butch Cassidy and Harry Longabaugh, using the aliases Jim Lowe and Harry Alonzo. This would have been no earlier than 1897.

Logan and a man calling himself Charlie Stevens (his name was actually Charlie Howland, according to the Lambs) showed up at the Lambs' in the fall of 1903. Logan told the family about his Knoxville capture and jail break, bitterly relating how he and his family had been treated by the law and the Pinkertons. At first he tried dictating his complaints to this man, Stevens, but his work was unsatisfactory; so the Lambs took over.

According to the Lambs, Logan had received a leg wound (not a groin wound) in his confrontation with the law, and then spent the winter at the Lamb ranch (instead of with the ranchers elsewhere documented by local researchers). The Lambs also provide dates that are different from other researchers.

According to Bruce Lamb, the trio went to Wild Bunch confederate Jim Ferguson's new Colorado ranch near Palisade for horses. Ferguson was off on a roundup, however, so the men were forced to steal horses. (There are differing versions of this story in the father's and son's books.) Charlie Stevens (or Howland) stayed at a hideout in

Rincon, New Mexico, while Logan went to Texas, returning with Kilpatrick. They had decided that the Texas trains had too much security, and so made a plan to rob a Colorado Midland train instead (it also discharged more express packages at Grand Junction).

For their part the Pinkertons described three train robbers traveling north from the Ozona, Texas, area, identifying two of them as Harvey Logan and George Kilpatrick. R. Brunazzi, a detective with the Denver and Rio Grande Western Railroad, identified the third man as Dan Sheffield, a Kilpatrick brother-in-law.

According to the Lambs the three men finally decided to rob the train at Parachute where the train took on water. Two of them temporarily took jobs for the railroad section crew between DeBeque and Parachute. They left their jobs on the last day of May, prior to the June 1904, robbery. There are different versions of this story in the father's and son's books.

The Lambs' accounts have several problems with them, the most significant being the identity of Charles Stevens (or Howland). First, while there was a Holland ranch in Johnson County, there were no Howlands. And while William Holland did have two sons, Albert C. and Charles F., Charles Holland had died after his horse fell on frozen ground. He was only ten or eleven years old!

At this point, about the only thing regarding the Parachute Train Robbery that various researchers can agree on is that three men robbed the train, and one of them committed suicide. The rest of the story remains controversial to this day, even down to the amount of money taken in the robbery.

The Parachute-Grand Valley Train Robbery

It all began on Tuesday night of June 7, 1904, when the seven-coach Denver and Rio Grand Western Mail train number 5 neared Parachute, Colorado, a fruit shipping station on the Colorado River (then called the Grand River). It was about 10:45 p.m. A passenger got off and the engine probably took on water for the tough pull to Glenwood Springs, high in the Rockies.

The caper began in the usual Wild Bunch fashion. One robber climbed aboard the blind baggage car and moved toward the engine tender. The fireman heard a noise, but perhaps he thought it was just a hobo who had slipped aboard. (In another version, the fireman got off the train to dislodge the unwanted passenger.) Fireman John Anderson learned differently when the bandit appeared and pulled a pistol. The same bandit then ordered the engineer, Ed Allison, to blow the whistle as a signal and pull up to a bonfire two and one-half miles east of Parachute at a place called Streit Flats, near the Una Railroad Siding. The engineer did as he was told, stopping near the small bonfire where two more men appeared. Fireman Anderson later remarked that the shining barrels of their revolvers looked as large as stovepipes.

Conductor Charles Ware and head brakeman Ed Shellenberger came forward to find out why the train had stopped. They were met by gunfire that shot out their lantern and wounded Shellenberger in the thigh. The robbers ordered the crew to separate the passenger cars from the express and baggage car, then move the train forward to Streit Flats.

Most of the crew was ordered to stay with the coaches and not to move. So far, so good, except the bandits hadn't noticed that the conductor was running back to the station.

As mail agent Fred Hawley realized what was happening, he hid some of the registered mail between his outer overalls and trousers, and tossed the remainder in a sack behind some bags at the end of the car. Meanwhile express messenger D. M. Shea piled heavy trunks and other baggage against the express car door. Shea refused to open the door, so the outlaws had to blow it open. They then went after the through safe with dynamite, as it could only be opened at Denver or Salt Lake City (for security reasons, the combination was apparently not given out). The bandits asked if the safe was Wells, Fargo. To their chagrin, they learned that it was Globe Express. They had stopped the wrong train!

The train they had been after was the Colorado Midland, carrying a reported $150,000 in gold bullion bound for the Philadelphia Mint. The Midland train had been running late, and was passed by the D&RGW train. The two trains used the same two miles of tracks in this area. (The outlaws' chances of robbing the Midland would probably have been poor anyway, since it would have carried several guards.)

After taking two charges, the safes yielded only a single complete bag of coins worth about a hundred dollars or less, plus fifty-cent pieces scattered everywhere—and some "sealed packages." The expressman had his gold watch taken.

A disappointed bandit told the engineer he could now back up to the rest of the train. The gang was not aware that Conductor Ware had already sounded the alarm.

The outlaws abandoned the train. The crew assumed they swam the river, but later it was found that they had stolen a boat from the O'Toole family. On the south side of the river, the outlaws mounted their horses and rode toward the thickly forested, ten thousand foot Battlement Mesa. They had trouble finding the main trail south, and their horses were tiring from traveling through the thick brush/trees and rugged, broken country.

Meanwhile the train had backed up to Parachute and Conductor Ware had sent out an alarm to the railroad's offices at Denver, Pueblo, Salida, and Grand Junction. The Globe Express company offered a reward of only three hundred dollars since the holdup men didn't get anything of substantial value. Posses were sent out from Glenwood Springs, Grand Junction, and Meeker. The Grand Junction posse was made up of "Doc" Shores, a D&RGW special agent, Mesa County Sheriff W. G. Struthers, deputies, and other men. The posse found the outlaws' rowboat sunk on the south side of the river.

The bandits first stopped at the ranch of Rollin (or Roland) Gardner. Along with his neighbor and brother-in-law, Joe Doby, Gardner soon joined the posse. The trail led to Battlement and Holmes Mesas, and then westward to the head of Cache Creek, to Spruce and Beaver Gulches, to Mumm and Divide Creeks, then up Gibson Gulch. The trio of robbers was easy to follow because two of their horses had recently been shod and left a distinctive track. The posse lost the trail in thick timber on Cache Creek. They thought the outlaws would head south to the Gunnison River, and they searched for their southward trail. The posse learned differently when the bandits stopped at the Joe Banta ranch for breakfast on Thursday, June 9, heading in an easterly direction.

The outlaws had cut Banta's telephone line, but he was able to splice it together and report that they'd been there and had stolen three of his horses. The telephone network went through a Mrs. Trumble, the Garfield County operator, who kept all informed where the pursued outlaws had last been and the direction of their travel. The Todd ranch reported in, and more horses were taken from a Fred Toland and the "Gus" Gustafson ranch near Rifle.

Locals didn't get very excited about the robbery until the bandits started taking their horses. By now every local rancher and farmer had been notified, and they were all waiting by their telephones. The outlaws finally stopped at the Larson ranch in Divide Valley, south of Silt. The Larson men were all out with the posse, leaving Mrs. Larson and her young sons behind. Mrs. Larson saw the trio at the corral getting fresh horses. She ran out of the house, only to retreat back to the house when threatened by the gang. This didn't deter her for long, though, as she soon sent her sons out with rifles. Luckily the posse arrived at this point. The outlaws rode to a nearby gulch by the Nuckoll and Sweitzer ranches. The posse tried to surround them in the gulch on upper Divide Creek, but there weren't enough men, and the outlaws escaped into a deep gorge on Garfield Creek Canyon. There they abandoned the horses and started climbing the steep, boulder-covered hillside.

As Rolly Gardner described it, before the bandits retreated up the hillside, the three jumped out in front of the posse and one of them said, "Okay you SOBs, that is far enough. Just turn your horses around and head down the mountain. If you try to follow us again, I will shoot the first man that comes in my sights around that corner down there."

One bandit was apparently standing out in front, pointing a chrome .45 Colt with pearl-handle grips. He also had another weapon in a shoulder holster. The posse stayed mounted, and two of their horses were shot and killed, perhaps in retaliation to their demand that the bandits surrender. Undersheriff Mahn was also wounded.

The dead horses belonged to Gardner and Joe Doby, who were within fifty feet of the outlaws. When the shooting started, Gardner dropped behind his fallen horse while Doby ran back toward the retreating posse, firing at the outlaws as he went. The same bandit who had done the talking now aimed at the retreating Doby. But Gardner fired first, hitting the man in the right arm, tearing off the top of his bicep, grazing the chest, and breaking his left arm. Gardner heard the other two men encourage "Sam" to keep climbing, but he replied in a weakened voice that he was too badly wounded and to go on without him. The posse sat tight, waiting out "Sam."

The wounded "Sam," rumor had it, stood up from the rocks and shot himself in the head. A vivid story, but Gardner said it never happened. The bandit stayed behind the rocks, waiting to see what the posse would do. Finally the posse heard a single shot, and then only silence. When they moved forward, they discovered the dead man.

The battle of Garfield Creek Canyon was over.

Gardner described the man as being underweight, and having a wrinkled, clean-shaven face and large, sunken black eyes. He resembled a sickly older man of about forty-two. His skin was tinted yellow, perhaps from jaundice. The man's finger was still wound tightly around a trigger. Also, he reportedly had scars on his legs caused by syphilis (according to an interview given by "Rolly" Gardner in 1994). The sustained standoff, plus the extra time the posse took to examine the dead outlaw, gave his two companions a chance to escape. A false report came in that the other two were surrounded by one hundred men in Gypsy Gulch near New Castle, that there had been a pitched battle, and thirteen horses and one member of the posse were killed. Bloodhounds were brought in from Leadville, Colorado, to join the pursuit. They found a trail, then lost it seven hours later, some four miles southeast of New Castle.

After the lawmen examined the clothes and possessions of "Sam," they found two revolvers and a Winchester rifle. His pockets contained a pair of field glasses, a large supply of ammunition, a compass, railroad timetables, and a crudely drawn map of the area.

The body was taken by horse, then by wagon to the train depot at New Castle, where it was to be put on the train to Glenwood Springs. The first misidentification of "Sam" came from D&RGW agent Folger, who identified the body as that of a J. H. Ross. The Globe Express agent, O. H. Barton, made the same identification. On Tuesday morning, Ross had signed his name to a discharge check for $1.75 for work he'd done as a section hand. Two other men, Charlie Stubbs and John Emmerling, had each received a final paycheck of $2.05. They had apparently taken a freight train toward Glenwood Springs. But when the real Ross heard he was a suspect, he contacted the sheriff's office at Glenwood Springs, apparently satisfying Sheriff Adams that he had been in town at the time of the robbery.

The search for the remaining two bandits was called off after it was learned that they had procured horses and ridden through

Glenwood toward Wyoming. They reportedly stopped for supplies in Shoshone, Wyoming, on their way toward the Big Horn Mountains. A local Grand River Valley rancher, Jim Cox, followed the two fugitives until they reached the mountains.

If the two were Sheffield and Kilpatrick, only Sheffield returned to Texas. Kilpatrick disappeared, perhaps moving on to Montana. Sheffield's family was contacted by author Arthur Soule, who was told that Sheffield never had any money problems after that robbery. Soule also believes that Kilpatrick sustained a wound after the robbery that resulted in his death.

The Lamb family had their own version as to what happened to the other two bandits. According to Bruce Lamb, Charlie Stevens and George Kilpatrick returned to the Sand Gulch ranch and rested up before hopping a freight train. Frank Lamb said that Kilpatrick went to Texas, but "no one knows where Charlie went." The other son of Frank Lamb, John, believes that Kilpatrick was wounded at some point, and died of his wounds at the Lamb ranch. Father Frank Lamb said Kilpatrick died in Texas in a steer roping accident in 1917. Author Jeff Burton states in his 1970 book, *Dynamite and Six-Shooter*, that Kilpatrick left home in the spring of 1904 to take part in the Parachute train robbery and never returned.

Authorities were still having difficulty in putting a name to the man who committed suicide. They had a body in the backroom of J. C. Schwartz's mortuary in Glenwood Springs. But who was he? Names that were attached to him included George W. Kendricks, alias James Keith, A. S. Keith, George W. Kayser, and others. Kendricks was eliminated when he turned up in jail in Omaha, Nebraska. Then a former Leadville resident, Brennick, was named as a possibility, but he didn't work out, either.

When the Garfield County coroner was examining the dead man's clothing, the bullet from Gardner's gun fell out. Whoever he was, without medical attention he would have likely bled to death from the wound in his arm. A week later, on June 14, "J. H. Ross" was buried in the old Glenwood Cemetery on Jasper Hill in a pauper's grave. He had been photographed in four different positions. A death mask had been created as well as full hand prints. The photographs were sent throughout the country to various law enforcement agencies, Pinkerton offices, and the railroad express companies.

Denver Pinkerton manager, James McPharland, sent the photographs to the Chicago office. Lowell Spence saw the photographs and proclaimed it to be Harvey "Kid Curry" Logan. He began an investigation to support his opinion. Meanwhile D&RGW special agent R. Brunazzi explored another course of action with cooperation from the Union Pacific's chief of detectives, William Canada. A piece of paper was found in the dead man's clothing with the name and Texas address of Ola Kilpatrick, a younger sister of Ben and George. Ola received a copy of the photographs from Brunazzi and was asked if she could identify the corpse. She replied it looked like "Tap" Duncan.

George Taplan Duncan had come from the Richland Springs area of San Saba County, Texas. He had two brothers, Richard and "Bige." Brother Richard had been convicted of a murder committed in Eagles Pass, Texas, while Bige was operating a ranch in San Saba County. He was married to Tom "Black Jack" Ketchum's sister. Tap Duncan was married to one of Ketchum's nieces.

Brunazzi continued his investigation, learning that neither George Kilpatrick or Dan Sheffield had been seen since the robbery; he also believed that the descriptions of the three train robbers matched those of Duncan, Kilpatrick, and Sheffield. The sheriff of San Saba County, Texas, said that Duncan had a nose wound (apparently similar to the one on the corpse) that had been inflicted several years ago by a deputy of his department. The sheriff also said that the buckshot wounds on the dead suspect's stomach had occurred during an arrest attempt, when Duncan had been shot off his horse by the county authorities. When other relatives and friends of Duncan's identified the unknown outlaw, Brunazzi really felt elated. (It was also believed that Duncan had visited the Kilpatrick family prior to the train robbery.)

Another acquaintance of the suspect, John Ring, identified Duncan from the photographs, describing him as "a disagreeable sort of fellow" with few friends and "possessed of unfortunate domineering qualities which brought to him a feeling of antipathy from people who might otherwise have been called friends." Ring also said the nickname "Tap" had come from his practice of claiming poker winnings—"tapping the pot"—whether or not he had the winning cards.

Meanwhile Pinkerton's Lowell Spence had been conducting his own investigation. Spence interviewed those ranchers for whom Logan had worked as a cowboy, using the name "Tap" Duncan. The descriptions of Logan and Duncan seemed to match. The detective also sent the photos to the Knox County sheriff's office, the police department, attorneys, and the like. They all identified the dead man as Harvey Logan.

Presenting his evidence, Spence was able to convince Garfield County, Colorado, officials to exhume the body. The exhumation was set for Saturday, June 16. Present besides Spence were Brunazzi, Canada, Undersheriff Mohn, Deputy Crissman, and possibly others. The key to identifying the body as Logan rested on being able to find the scar on the right wrist and arm. But after the body was exhumed, no wrist scar or any other distinctive mark on his arm could be seen. There was some disagreement in the newspaper reports as to the amount of body decomposition. The *Glenwood Springs Post* of July 23, 1904, said, "The body was somewhat decayed, but not so that it would prevent identification had the marks been present as is said to have existed." The article also stated that Spence said it was Logan, and the two railroad detectives said no, because the scar couldn't be seen.

Even though there were doubts among the Pinkertons, the detective agency reported to the U.S. State Department that the body was Harvey Logan "because of the impressive evidence." Thus the government could dismiss reports that he was in South America.

Contradicting the Glenwood paper, the *Denver Post* reported, "When the [cheap pine] coffin was raised to the surface and the lid removed, it was found that the decomposition had advanced to such an extent that identification was practically impossible." The *Glenwood Springs Avalanche Echo* also gave the opinion that the examination was unsatisfactory. Two days later the *Knoxville Journal and Tribune* wondered why the teeth weren't compared since Logan was missing two bottom teeth.

Spence made no definite identification, according to the *Glenwood Springs Post*, because of the body's decomposition, but he rested his case to the Pinkertons in his final report.

A doctor who had examined the body, R. R. Macalester of the Glenwood Springs resort, published a report in the *Denver Times* on July 19. He stated the dead bandit had undeveloped teeth and several teeth missing from the lower jaw. He also said, "There is no evidence of a scar on the right wrist, such as known to be carried by Harvey Logan." Unfortunately no one asked—or observed—whether the top of the head had scars from the billy club blows in the Knoxville saloon.

Others weighed in on the controversy. Charles Judd, a gun salesman, was on the Wilcox, Wyoming, train, and had a Colt revolver taken by bandits. He claimed the same weapon had been taken off the dead bandit by Deputy Sheriff Fred Carlson. Author James Horan stated that this revolver, in 1977, was in the hands of an Orem, Utah, gun collected named E. Dixon Larson. Horan wrote that Dixon "supplied impressive evidence that the body exhumed from the Glenwood, Colorado, grave at the turn of the century was that of Kid Curry."

Spence had continuing argument with Security Chief W. T. Canada of the Union Pacific Railroad. Spence said that Logan may have hidden at the Kilpatrick ranch, using the "Tap" Duncan name. He also said in a much later statement that W. G. Canada's claim that the body wasn't Logan's was based on a single observation of Logan in Knoxville. However the Knoxville papers had Canada visiting Logan's cell twice, as well as being in the courtroom.

In another muddying of facts, locals claimed that the train had actually been carrying a $10,000 to $15,000 mining payroll meant for Utah. Was this why Sheffield didn't have any more money troubles after the robbery? Also, Parachute area rancher Ed Walker said that the two remaining outlaws had returned a couple of weeks later looking for money they had stashed.

Another mystery attached to this robbery is why, if the body did in fact belong to Logan, the real "Tap" Duncan didn't step forward. Researcher Daniel Buck researched a history of the real Duncan, finding that George Taplin Duncan had died in Kingman, Arizona, at the age of seventy-five, survived by his wife, Ollie. He had lived in the area for forty-six years. He counted western author Louis L'Amour as a friend. Buck states that since Duncan had been gone from Texas for several years, and because of his brothers' reputations, his relatives and friends had jumped to the wrong conclusion. But Buck also asks the question, why hadn't he stepped forward like J. H. Ross had?

Denver's Pinkerton office had something to add to the Duncan story. A July 24, 1904, report has Duncan fleeing to Utah to escape arrest for cattle rustling and other offenses. The same report named Duncan, Kilpatrick, and Daniel Sheffield as the three robbers but was indecisive as to whether this outlaw was Duncan or Logan, or Logan *as* Duncan. The report, written by a Denver operative, claimed that the dead bandit was called "Tom" instead of "Sam." Texas researcher Jesse Cole Kenworth claims that Duncan was in the Brown's Park area at the time of the robbery, but he gives no documentation.

Logan's lead defense attorney, J. C. Houk, wrote a July 2, 1903, letter to Jim Thornhill in Landusky, informing him of Logan's escape. (As documented by Tennessee researcher Wayne Kindred, Thornhill had begun a correspondence with Houk and Logan's other attorneys in 1902, while supplying money for Logan's defense. He also corresponded with Logan, who was going by the name Charlie Johnson.) On July 25, 1904, Houk sent a copy of the dead bandit's picture, alleged to have been Harvey Logan. Thornhill acknowledged he resembled Logan, but he didn't believe that Logan would end his own life. "[H]e wouldn't have shot himself as long as there was any body else to shoot and that posse was coming up from the rear and if he was able to shoot himself he could have shot one or more of them and had company over the divide . . . and he knows that it will be a great pleasure to me to know that he [had] taken all of them with him." Houk replied, "I have no doubt in the world that he is dead." The lawyer also asked if he knew what happened to the saddle of the sheriff's mare, stolen when Logan made his jailbreak. Thornhill replied that the saddle had been thrown from the bridge into the Tennessee River. As Kindred theorized, this showed that Logan and Thornhill had been in contact after the escape, but when? Before or after Parachute?

While the outlaw name game continued, a bank robbery occurred that resurrected Logan's outlaw career for a brief time. On November 1, 1904, two men robbed the First National Bank of Cody, Wyoming. The afternoon holdup resulted in the death of cashier L. O. Middaugh after he tried to leave the bank to summon help. The two robbers engaged in a gun battle with some townspeople before galloping out of town. A posse of twenty men led by Park County Deputy Sheriff Jeff Chapman pursued them to the southwest. There was a continuous exchange of gunfire until the posse lost the bandits near Meeteetse, thirty miles to the south, where they turned into a canyon. Lawmen believed that the bandits had a relay team of horses waiting for them. The posse reorganized, and they continued the hunt later that night. They returned to Cody after following the trail of the outlaws as far as Thermopolis, another forty miles to the south.

Interest in the Cody bank robbery spread when Wyoming's Park County authorities said the outlaws had operated in Wild Bunch fashion using accomplices and relief horses. They reported that the shorter of the two men had been Kid Curry, and had led the robbery attempt. The sheriff speculated that the robbers were now hiding in the Hole-in-the-Wall country of Johnson and Natrona Counties. Ranchers in those counties refuted this, saying they had reoccupied the former outlaw valley. The *Sheridan Post* editor agreed with the ranchers, editorializing that "the Hole-in-the-Wall as an outlaw refuge no longer exists save in the novelists' fancy." Still some people used the supposed sighting of Harvey Logan as evidence that he didn't die in Colorado.

The Kid Curry rumor came unraveled on November 16, 1904, when the shorter of the two bandits was captured at the mouth of Owl Creek Canyon, north of Thermopolis. The suspect offered no resistance, and came apart emotionally—hardly the "Kid Curry type." The second suspect was captured by Bighorn County lawmen in late December near Basin, north of Thermopolis and Worland. He gave his name as Irwin, and witnesses placed him at the scene of the bank robbery. As each rumor of Kid Curry's endurance was debunked, it became more universally accepted that the dead Parachute robber was indeed Harvey Logan.

Back in the Little Rockies country on Rock Creek, land commissioner and rancher (and Logan antagonist) Abe Gill had been following Logan's story with interest. Gill hadn't felt threatened by Logan since Harvey's capture and confinement in Knoxville, but his escape must have brought Gill some concern, especially when he heard that Logan was back in the Little Rockies country. But even if Logan had wanted to kill Gill, law officers were using Gill's ranch as a headquarters while hunting outlaws in the area. There was probably too much commotion around the place. Not to mention that an assassination would have brought a massive influx of officers into the area, and that Logan didn't need. The killing of Gill's stepbrother, Jim Winter, had caused enough of an uproar.

Gill's seesawing emotions must have stabilized when he heard that Logan had died after a train robbery in Grand Valley. Two years later, however, the *New York Herald* and other publications announced that Logan was alive, and living in South America with Butch Cassidy, The Sundance Kid and Mrs. Harry Longabaugh. A Pinkerton Detective Agency representative said the story was absolute nonsense, and the agency clung to its tenuous belief—at least through 1906—that Logan was dead. At that point, a sighting of Logan in South America was reported.

Gill traveled to Argentina with fellow ranchers John Survant, James Peck, and William Coburn. These were men interested in potentially relocating their ranching operations to Argentina, where vast amounts of land were available under a law similar to the United States Homestead Act of 1862. The sandy soil of the high plains of Patagonia was much like that of southern Utah and other western cattle-raising states. Thousands of acres could be leased long term for only a few cents per acre, especially if a party knew how to deal with Argentina's politicians. This is where the gentleman Gill came in. He was handy as a Spanish-speaking diplomat to pave the way.

Gill stayed in Buenos Aires while his companions toured the vast interior. At the end of the rail line, Will Coburn continued on alone by pack train, supposedly making a 1,300-mile trip into the interior of Argentina. He supposedly stopped in the Cholila Valley in western Chubut Territory to visit with old friend Harvey Logan. This was reported by both Walt Coburn and Joseph Kinsey Howard in their respective books, *Pioneer Cattlemen in Montana* and *Montana: High, Wide and Handsome*. This is the only known "official" sighting of Logan in South America, although there were no other witnesses to verify it. Coburn returned to Montana in May 1906.

Reports of Harvey Logan's living in South America surfaced in the Montana newspapers in October 1906. They reported that Curry had been seen in South America by a "Montana man" within the last six months. Obviously they were referring to Coburn's visit. It was apparently because of this reported sighting that the Pinkertons showed a renewed interest in the Logan case. Addressing a 1907 Police Chief Association convention in Jamestown, Virginia, William Pinkerton said that Logan had turned up in Argentina. His brother and partner, Robert Pinkerton, expressed the same belief in an internal office memo dated January 1907.

Yet despite a number of circulars and handbills distributed in South America, there was never another confirmed sighting. Still, author Walt Coburn claimed that Abe Gill became "a troubled, worried man . . . " Gill finally decided to return to the states after selling his ranch and mining properties to Walt Coburn. He believed it was only a matter of time before he was killed. In October of 1906, Gill placed his luggage on the Landusky stage bound for the Harlem, Montana, train station, planning to follow on horseback the next day. He never arrived.

If Gill had been a local boy without political and social connections, perhaps the news of his disappearance would have quieted down more quickly. But he was a friend of U.S. Congressman Charles Pray of Fort Benton, a prominent member of the Chouteau County Republican Party, and had held a position as a U.S. Land Commissioner.

In August of 1906, former Havre lawman and brand inspector George Hall had told Gill that he believed Logan to be back in the states and currently residing in the Hole-in-the-Wall country of Wyoming. Hall further said that Logan would eventually show up in the Little Rockies. It's possible (if not likely) that Hall was part of a Coburn family conspiracy to scare Gill into leaving and selling his properties. Gill's leaving would also remove a U.S. Land Commissioner who was a potential obstacle to Coburn's idea of running off homesteaders, picking up their land at what were probably bargain prices.

The authorities tracked Gill as far as the Coburn ranch where he received $2,000 of his $10,000 selling price for his land; he was also due the balance of the $30,000 for two mines sold to the Coburns in 1904 and 1905. (Gill's family in New York would eventually have to sue the Coburns for the balances owed.) There was a great deal of speculation about how Gill died, and in spite of several manhunts, including those conducted by Pinkertons, Gill's brothers, and Chouteau County authorities, not a trace of Gill or his horse was ever found. Logan was mentioned as a suspect, but there were other suspects too.

In 1968, Walt Coburn wrote of Gill, "Sixty years have now passed, and to the best of my knowledge, the mystery of Abe Gill's disappearance has never been solved." He also wrote, "It was a foregone conclusion that Abe Gill met with foul play." He added that anyone who had been a friend of Kid Curry was under suspicion. This, of course, included the Coburns, their foreman Jake Myers, Jim Thornhill, and anyone who worked for him. In summary, Coburn said, "Gill played a minor role in the saga of violence and bloodshed in the feud between Jim Winters and the Curry boys."

Of course there continued to be sightings of Logan throughout the West, as there were of Butch Cassidy. Local Landusky historian John Ritch wrote of these, as did author Brown Waller. The most interesting sighting involved a robbery at Morenci, Arizona, on September 6, 1910. That morning, a solitary rider entered the town through Gila Canyon. He hitched his horse to a rail down the street by the post office and walked to the bank and hotel building. He was described as a seasoned rider having swarthy skin and a lean face. He weighed about 150 pounds and was about five feet eight inches tall. His hair and beard were dark; his eyes were a light color. His clothing and saddle leather were faded and worn. He entered the Gila Valley Bank and Trust Company about 11:15 a.m., ordering manager Efromson and bookkeeper Neptune to put up their hands. He pulled down the shade and locked the door. Efromson falsely told the bandit that he couldn't open the safe, perhaps saying it was on a time lock. Without threatening violence, the robber scooped up the bank's loose money, amounting to about three thousand dollars, plus two bags of silver. He backed Efromson and Neptune into the vault where the safe was located, but did not lock it on their promise to keep quiet. As he was leaving, they quickly forgot their promise and went after him with shotguns. In an exchange of gunfire, the bandit fired over their heads to drive the two men back inside. He tied the cash to his saddle horn but left the silver. He galloped out of town, two lawmen and a posse not far behind. At one point he jumped his horse off a twelve-foot cliff, landing in a sandy arroyo. The posse decided they couldn't make such a jump themselves and went around to the regular trail. They followed him to a place seven miles south of Morenci on the San Francisco River where his trail vanished.

The William J. Burns Detective Agency, Los Angeles office, hired retired Pinkerton detective agent Charles Siringo to investigate. Siringo believed the description, the exhibition of horsemanship, ability to lose a posse, coolness of manner, and other traits added up to Harvey Logan (since he didn't believe Logan had been killed at Parachute).

He had another reason for believing this bandit might be Logan: a letter he received from Jim Ferguson. As Siringo described it in his books, through his use of outlaw disguises and phony names, he had met many of the support members of the Wild Bunch. Jim Ferguson wrote to Siringo, who was using his alias of Harry Blevens, care of the Silver City, New Mexico, post office. The letter was forwarded to Siringo at his Santa Fe ranch. Ferguson recounted the Parachute train robbery and how the authorities had said the dead robber was Kid Curry. Ferguson said that the man who was killing "had stayed with me to the time the train was held up and I know he was not Kid Curry." Siringo turned this letter over to the Burns Los Angeles office with his report. (Sadly, some researchers, arguing for Logan's suicide after the Parachute heist, have felt they must dispute Siringo's competence as a detective, regardless of the twenty-two years Siringo had spent as an undercover operative in the lawless parts of the West, risking his life many times.)

There are some Curry-Logan stories that are of interest because they involve individuals who did cross paths with the outlaw. Ross Santee, author of *Lost Pony Tracks*, relates a conversation he had with Jim Thornhill, who supposedly said to Santee, the "Kid's alive, of course we don't dare write, but I've got word from him." And author Walt Coburn claimed that Thornhill told him that Logan had gone to South America. Others in the Little Rockies and eastern Montana claimed that Logan lived in Arizona for several years.

Mike O'Neil, the fireman on the Great Northern Railway train that was robbed between Wagner and Malta, testified against Logan in Knoxville. Much later, during prohibition, O'Neil was in the Mint Saloon in Great Falls, playing cards and having a soft drink. He noticed a man standing at the bar whom he thought looked a lot like Harvey

Logan. The more he studied him, the more convinced he became that this was indeed Kid Curry. And then he recognized that the man's companion was an old friend of Logan's. O'Neil promptly left the establishment, not wanting to meet the man he had testified against.

Rancher and Little Rockies historian and journalist, John B. Ritch, claimed that, in 1910, Harvey Logan had visited him in Landusky. Ritch even claimed that Logan had dined in his house.

Meanwhile, the Pinkerton Agency and federal officials received reports regarding Logan throughout the 1920s. (It wasn't until 1948 that Lowell Spence signed an affidavit for Pinkerton, testifying to his identification of the dead train robber as Harvey Logan.) In a letter dated April 8, 1919, B. F. Phelan, special agent for the South Pacific Railroad in Stockton, California, wrote that a friend of his had said that a man at a local hotel, using the name Davis, was actually Harvey Logan. Phelan began making inquiries, asking if there was still an outstanding reward for Logan. Phelan next said that Davis was living in a nearby city, where he was now using the name Rice. A Pinkerton circular with Logan's picture was sent to Phelan, but that was apparently the end of this particular wild-goose chase. By March of 1921 William Pinkerton was growing weary of these fruitless inquiries, confessing that he was beginning to believe that Logan had died after the Parachute heist.

For a brief time, Ben Kilpatrick also made it back into the news. He was released from prison in 1911, only to be arrested again for the murder of an Oliver Thornton. Concho County Sheriff Maddox escorted Kilpatrick back to Paint Rock, Texas, for trial. The charges were apparently dismissed for lack of evidence. Kilpatrick returned a free man to his brother Boone's ranch near Sheffield, Texas, where he lived with Laura Bullion. Apparently they were quite happy until Ben and another man tried robbing a train near Sanderson. They were both killed by an express messenger.

Sometime after Ben's death, Laura Bullion returned to the South, living her final years in Memphis, Tennessee, renting out rooms and doing seamstress work for local stores and drapery shops.

The last story about Harvey Logan involves no violence and takes place in Waxhaw, North Carolina. After Logan's escape from Knoxville, some thought he had crossed the mountains into the Carolinas. The story goes that a stranger, calling himself C. H. Lewis, moved to Waxhaw in the early 1900s. The man came from out "West" and was a wealthy individual. This "Harvey Logan" died in 1945.

Harvey Logan was a busy man!

Elfie Logan, Julia Landusky's daughter, made her last trip to Landusky in July of 1957 when she was seventy-eight years old. She was accompanied by one of her sisters. They introduced themselves to longtime Landusky resident Ted Duvall and, over lunch with Ted and his wife, discussed local history. They visited the graves of Pike Landusky, Johnny Logan, and Jim Winters. She spoke before the Little Rockies Historical group, saying that many lies had been told about the Logan boys. She also told them that she disliked James Horan's book, *Desperate Men,* and its portrayal of the Logans. The sisters finished their trip by going to Harlem where Lonie and Elfie had lived.

This last visit of Elfie's resonated with some Wild Bunch researchers. Among the residents whom she spoke to was Ruel Harner, who had come to the Little Rockies in 1903 and had worked as one of the last local stage drivers between Zortman and Malta. Harner related in a 1959 *Great Falls Tribune* article of Sunday, November 22, that Elfie said, "The Kid died of injuries he had received in a car accident in the state of Washington not too many years ago." Her remark was apparently made in response to a question from Harner. In a letter dated September 9, 1960, to Chicago Western historian Stacey Osgood, former lawman Phil Buckley of Harlem, Montana, stated that Harvey's Seattle death was from an automobile accident.

There is indeed a tradition in the Logan-Moran family that such an accident occurred in the 1930s. However, the senior Moran brother and his wife reportedly witnessed Elfie burn a trunkload of materials before moving to a rest home. She was overheard saying something to the effect that now nobody would ever find Harvey.

For the Logan-Moran family, it has been their belief that Logan left the outlaw life after escaping from Knoxville, surviving under a new identity. But this belief will never be confirmed without proof. Sharon Logan-Moran and her dear friend, Earl Hofeldt, thought they could put the whole matter to rest by having "J. H. Ross" dug up at Glenwood Springs to compare his DNA with Harvey's. But the cemetery's old plot records no longer exist and there have been landslides on the cemetery hill.

No one has ever successfully refuted Lowell Spence's contention that Ross was Harvey Logan, although of course the absence of important scars on the body remains an issue. Brown Waller's book about Harvey Logan concludes, "If it were not Harvey Logan who was buried in a train robber's grave on Grand River . . . the outlaw codes of the Old West certainly keep their secrets well."

No matter what you believe, Harvey "Kid Curry" Logan certainly deserved a greater role in the outlaw history of the West. However, not having been one of the Robin Hood-gentleman outlaw types, he received little attention from those researching the lives of outlaws. (Having him portrayed inaccurately by oversized actor Ted Cassidy in the 1969 classic film *Butch Cassidy and the Sundance Kid* really didn't help public perception.)

The mainstream Montana historians, such as K. Ross Toole and Joseph Kinsey Howard, have little interest in the "bump in the road" outlaw types. Toole called Logan "one of those semi-fictional outlaws that ran with the semi-fictional Hole-in-the-Wall Gang." Howard gave him a page under a chapter on the early cattle industry, calling him "one of the West's most spectacular outlaws." Howard also told the South America story of his supposed adventures. But Howard was a little more folksy-character-oriented than Toole.

Perhaps Logan would have been proud to learn that the National Criminal Investigation Bureau describes him as having had the longest criminal record ever known in the United States until 1910, and that he had accumulated rewards of forty thousand dollars for his crimes.

Now that should have gained some respect!

Bibliography

Books

Abbott, E. C., and Helena Huntington Smith. *We Pointed Them North: The Recollections of a Cowpuncher.* Norman: University of Oklahoma Press, 1971.

Adams, Andy. *The Log of the Cowboy.* New York: Airmount Publishing, 1969.

Adams, Ramon. *Burs under the Saddle.* Norman: University of Oklahoma, 1989.

Babcock, Charlotte. *Shot Down! Capital Crimes of Casper, Wyoming.* Glendo, WY: High Plains Press, 2000.

Baker, Pearl. *The Wild Bunch of Robbers Roost.* Lincoln: Bison Books, University of Nebraska Press, 1971.

Bartholmew, Ed. *Biographical Album of Western Gunfighters.* Houston, TX: The Frontier Press, 1958.

———. *Black Jack Ketchum: Last of the Hold-up Kings.* Houston, TX: The Frontier Press, 1965.

Barton, Barbara. *Den of Outlaws.* San Angelo, TX: Rangel Printing, 2000.

Branch, Douglas. *The Cowboy and His Interpreters.* New York: Cooper Square Publishers, 1976.

Brekke, Alan L. *Kid Curry, Train Robber.* Harlem, MT: Privately published, 1959.

Burroughs, John R. *Where the Old West Stayed Young.* New York: William Morrow, 1962.

Burton, Jeff. *Dynamite and Six-Shooter.* Santa Fe, NM: Palomino Press, 1970.

Charter, Anne G. *Cowboys Don't Walk! A Tale of Two.* Billings, MT: Western Organization of Rosebud Councils, 1999.

Cheney, Roberta C. *Names on the Faces of Montana.* Missoula, MT: Mountain Press Publishing, 1984.

Cheney, Truman M., and Roberta Cheney. *So Long Cowboys of the Open Range.* Helena, MT: Falcon Press, 1990.

Clay, John. *My Life on the Range.* Norman: University of Oklahoma Press, 1962.

Coburn, Walt. *Stirrup High.* Lincoln: Bison Books, University of Nebraska Books, 1957.

————. *The Story of the Circle C Ranch.* Norman: University of Oklahoma Press, 1972.

Colquhoun, James. *The History of the Clifton-Morenci Mining District:* London, 1924.

Costello, Gladys, and Dorothy Whitcomb. *Top o' the Mountain: Charley Whitcomb, Mining Man in Zortman.* Great Falls, MT: Privately published, 1976.

Crockett County Historical Society. *A History of Crockett County.* San Angelo, TX: Anchor Publishing, 1976.

Cunningham, Eugene. *Trigonometry.* Caldwell: Caxton Printers, 1971.

Cushman, Dan. *Montana: The Gold Frontier.* Great Falls, MT: Stay Away Joe Publishers, 1973.

Dalton, Emmett. *When the Daltons Rode.* Garden City, NY: Doubleday, Doran and Co., 1931.

DeArment, Robert K. *The Life and Death of a Lawman.* Norman: University of Oklahoma Press, 1992.

DeJournette, Dick, and Dawn DeJournette. *One Hundred Years of Brown's Park and Diamond Mountain.* Vernal: DeJournal Enterprises, 1996.

Didier, Hazel, ed. *The Yesteryears: History of Phillips County.* Malta, MT: Phillips County Historical Society, 1978.

Dissley, Robert L. *History of Lewistown*. Lewistown, MT: Lewistown Public Library, 2000.

Donovan, Roberta. *The First Hundred Years: A History of Lewistown, Montana*. Lewistown, MT: News-Argus, 1994.

Dorin, Patrick. *The SOO Line*. Seattle, WA: Superior Publishing, 1979.

Drago, Harry S. *Great American Cattle Trails*. New York: Bramhall Books, 1965.

Dullenty, Jim. *Harry Tracy: The Last Desperado*. Dubuque, IA: Kendall-Hunt Publishing, 1996.

Dunham, Dick, and Vivian Dunham. *The Story of Daggett County, Utah*. Denver, CO: Eastwood Printing and Publishing, 1977.

Duvall, Walter, with Helena Duvall-Arthur. *Memories of a Filly Chaser*. Privately published, 1992.

Eaton, John. *Will Carver, Outlaw*. San Antonio, TX: Anchor Publishing, 1972.

Ernst, Donna B. *Harvey Logan: Wildest of the Wild Bunch*. Kearney, NE: Morris Publishing, 2003.

———. *Sundance, My Uncle*. College Station, TX: Creative Publishing, 1992.

———. *Will Carver: A Timeline*. Privately published, 1996.

———. *Women of the Wild Bunch*. Kearney, NE: Morris Publishing, 2004.

Farlow, Edward J. *Wind River Adventures: My Life in Frontier Wyoming*. Glendo, WY: High Plains Press, 1998.

Federal Writer's Project, Works Progress Administration, American Guide Series. *Arizona*. Tucson: University of Arizona Press, 1989.

———. *Colorado*. New York: Hastings House, 1946.

———. *Montana*. New York: Hastings House, 1946.

———. *Wyoming*. Lincoln, NE: Bison Books, University of Nebraska Press, 1981.

French, William. *Some Recollections of a Western Ranchman: New Mexico, 1883–1899*. New York: Argosy-Antiquarian, 1965.

Garwood, W. R. *Catch Kid Curry.* Anne Arbor, MI: Diamond Back Westerns, Bathstreet Press, 1982.

Grosskopf, Linda, with Rick Newby. *On Flatwillow Creek: The Story of Montana's N Bar N Ranch.* Los Alamos, NM: Exception Books, 1991.

Haley, J. E. *Jeff Milton: A Good Man with a Gun.* Norman: University of Oklahoma Press, 1948.

Hardin, Floyd. *Campfires and Cowchips.* Malta, MT: Phillips County News, 1972.

Heck, Larry E. *The Adventures of Pass Patrol, Volume 5: In Search of the Outlaw Trail.* Aurora, CO: Outback Publications, 1998.

Hendricks, George. *The Badman of the West.* San Antonio, TX: The Naylor Company.

Horan, James D. *Desperate Men: The James Gang and Wild Bunch.* Rev. and enlarged edition Lincoln, NE: Bison Books, University of Nebraska Press, 1997. The Naylor Company, 1950.

———. *The Gunfighters.* New York: Crown Publishers, 1976.

———. *The Outlaws.* New York: Gramercy Books, 1994.

———. *The Pinkertons: The Detective Dynasty That Made History.* New York: Crown Publishers, 1967.

———. *The Wild Bunch.* New York: Signet, New American Library, 1958.

Horan, James D., and Paul Sann. *Pictorial History of the Wild West.* New York: Crown Publishers, 1954.

Howard, Joseph K. *Montana: High, Wide, and Handsome.* New Haven, CT: Yale University Press, 1943.

Howard, William C. *Buffalo's First Century.* Buffalo, WY: Buffalo Centennial Committee, 1984.

Hunt, Frazier. *Cap. Mossman: Last of the Great Cowman.* New York: Hastings House, 1951.

Hunter, Marvin J., and Noah H. Rose. *The Album of Gunfighters: 100 Years in Bandera.* Self-published, 1976.

Johnson, Dorothy M. *The Bloody Bozeman*. New York: McGraw-Hill, 1971.

Kalal, John, and Candy. *The Golden Era of the Little Rockies: Stories Written by Gladys Costello*. Privately published, 1990.

Kelley, Charles. *The Outlaw Trail: A History of Butch Cassidy and His Wild Bunch*. Rev. and enlarged edition. New York: Bonanza Books, 1959.

Kennedy, Michael S., ed. *Cowboys and Cattlemen*. New York: Hastings House, 1964.

Kenworth, Jesse. *Storms of Life: The Outlaw Trail and Kid Curry*. Bozeman, MT: Quarter Circle Enterprises, 1990.

Kirby, Edward M. *The Rise and Fall of the Sundance Kid*. Iola: Western Publications, 1983.

———. *The Saga of Butch Cassidy and the Wild Bunch*. Palmer Lake, CO: The Filter Press, 1977.

Lamb, F. B. *The Wild Bunch*. Edited by Alan Swallow. Denver, CO: Sage Books, 1966.

Lamb, Frank. *Kid Curry: The Life and Times of Harvey Logan and the Wild Bunch*. Boulder, CO: Johnson Books, 1991.

LeFors, Joe. *Wyoming Peace Officer: The Autobiography*. Laramie, WY: Powder River Publishers, 1953.

Lindsey, Merrill. *100 Great Guns*. New York: Walker and Company, 1967.

Lynch, Sylvia. *Harvey Logan in Knoxville*. College Station, TX: Creative Publishing, 1998.

McClure, Grace. *The Bassett Women*. Athens, OH: Swallow Press, 1987.

Meadows, Anne. *Digging Up Butch and Sundance*. Rev. ed. Lincoln: Bison Books, University of Nebraska Press, 1996.

Meany, Edmond S. *Origin of Washington Geographic Names*. Seattle: University of Washington Press, 1923.

Mokler, Alfred. *The History of Natrona County*. Chicago: R. R. Donnelly and Sons, 1923.

Monson, Mildred. *History and Organization of Blaine County*. Chinook, MT: Privately published, 1981.

Murray, Erlene. *Lest We Forget: A Short History of Early Grand Valley, Colorado, Originally Called Parachute.* Grand Junction, CO: Quahada, 1973.

O'Neal, Bill. *Encyclopedia of Western Gunfighters.* Norman: University of Oklahoma Press, 1983.

Otero, Michael A. *My Nine Years As Governor.* Albuquerque: New Mexico Press, 1940.

Paladin, Vivian A., ed. *From Buffalo Bones to Sonic Boom.* Glasgow, MT: Glasgow Jubilee Committee, 1962.

Parker, Watson P. *Deadwood the Golden Years.* Lincoln: University of Nebraska Press, 1981.

Patterson, Richard. *Butch Cassidy: A Biography.* Lincoln: Bison Books, University of Nebraska Books, 1998.

———. *Historical Atlas of the Outlaw West.* Boulder, CO: Johnson Books, 1985.

———. *The Train Robbery Era: An Encyclopedia History.* Boulder, CO: Pruett Publishing, 1991.

Peavy, Charles D. *Charles A. Siringo: A Texas Picaro.* Southwest Writers Series no. 13. Austin, TX: Stock-Vaughn, 1967.

Pointer, Larry. *In Search of Butch Cassidy.* Norman: University of Oklahoma Press, 1977.

Prassel, Frank R. *The Great American Outlaw: A Legacy of Fact and Fiction.* Norman: University of Oklahoma Press, 1993.

Redford, Robert. *The Outlaw Trail: A Journey Through Time.* New York: Grosset and Dunlap Publishers, 1978.

Rockwell, Wilson. *Memories of a Lawman: Cyrus "Doc" Shores.* Denver, CO: Sage Books, 1962.

Rollins, Phillip A. *The Cowboy: An Unconventional History of Civilization on the Old Time Cattle Range.* Albuquerque: University of New Mexico Press, 1979.

Samenow, Staton E. *Inside the Criminal Mind.* New York: Times Book Company, 1984.

Sedlacek, Signe M. *Grit, Guts and Gusto: A History of Hill County*. Havre, MT: Bear Paw Printers, 1976.

Selcer, Richard F. *The Life and Legend of a Red Light District: Hell's Half Acre*. Fort Worth: Texas Christian University Press, 1991.

Siringo. Charles A. *Cowboy Detective: A True Story of Twenty-Two Years with a World-Famous Detective Agency*. Lincoln: Bison Books, University of Nebraska Press, 1988.

———. *A Lone Star Cowboy*. Cleveland, OH: The Arthur Clark Company, 1919.

Skolin, John, and Donna McDaniel. *In Pursuit of the McCartys*. Cave Cove, OR: Reflections Publishing, 2001.

Smith, Helena H. *The War on Powder River: The History of an Insurrection*. Lincoln: Bison Books, University of Nebraska, 1966.

Smith, Henry N. *Virgin Land: The American West, Symbol and Myth*. Cambridge, MA: Harvard University Press, 1970.

Soule, Arthur. *The Tall Texan: The Story of Ben Kilpatrick*. Deer Lodge: Trail Dust Publishing, 1995.

Stanley, Francis L. C. *The Alma Story*. Pep, TX: Privately published, 1963.

———. *Desperados of New Mexico*. Denver, CO: World Press, 1953.

———. *No Tears for Black Jack*. Denver CO: World Press, 1958.

Stuart, Granville. *Pioneering in Montana: The Making of the State 1864–1918*. Lincoln, NE: Bison Books, University of Nebraska Press, 1977.

Tanner, Karen H., and John D. Tanner Jr. *Last of the Old-Time Outlaws: The George West Musgrove Story*. Norman: University of Oklahoma Press, 2002.

Unbanck, Mae. *Wyoming Place Names*. Missoula, MT: Mountain Press, 1988.

Van Pelt, Lori. *Dreamers and Schemers: Profile from Carbon County Wyoming's Past*. Glendo, WY: High Plains Press, 1991.

Viola, Harman J., and Sarah Loomis Wilson, eds. *John A. Loomis: A Texas Ranchman, a Biography*. Chadron, NE: The Fur Press, 1902.

Walker, Patsy. *The First Hundred Years: 1900–2000.* Privately published, 2000.

Walker, Tacetta. *Stories of Early Days in Wyoming: Bighorn Basin.* Casper, WY: Prairie Publishing, 1936.

Waller, Brown. *Last of the Great Train Robbers.* New York: A. S. Barnes and Company, 1968.

Wetz, Leon. *John Selman, Gunfighter.* Norman: University of Oklahoma Press, 1966.

Wilson, D. Ray. *Colorado Historical Tour Guide.* Carpentersville, IL: Crossroads Communications, 1990.

———. *Wyoming Historical Tour Guide.* Carpentersville, IL: Crossroads Communications, 1984.

Wilson, Gary A. *Outlaw Tales of Montana.* Guilford, CT: The Globe Pequot Press, 2003.

Wolle, Muriel S. *Montana Pay Dirt: A Guide to the Mining Camps of the Treasure State.* Athens, OH: Sage/Swallow Books, 1963.

Articles

Anonymous. "Kid Curry Cheated by History." *The Livingston Enterprise* (MT), n.d.

Bell, Mike. "The Killing of Lonny Logan." *The English Westerners Tally Sheet* (Spring 1990).

Ballou, M. E. "Jackson County: Its Opportunitys and Resources." *Dodson Section.* Jackson County Chamber of Commerce, 1926.

Buckley, Phil. "Curry Gang Authority." *Great Falls Tribune,* June 12, 1960.

Buck, Daniel. "Just Discovered: Sundance in Canada!" *WOLA Journal* (Winter 1997).

———. Letter to the Editor. *WOLA Journal* (Summer/Fall 1994).

———. "New Revelations about Harvey Logan Following the Parachute Train Robbery." *WOLA Journal* (Spring 1997).

Carlson, Chip. "The Tipton Robbery." *WOLA Journal* (Summer 1995).

Costello, Gladys. "Former Stagecoach Driver Recalls Little Rockies Boom." *Great Falls Tribune,* November 22, 1959.

———. "A Frontier Marshal Turns in His Star." *Great Falls Tribune,* November 4, 1954.

———. "Malta, Cattle Country." *Montana Magazine,* Spring 1997.

———. "Story of Loney Curry's Death in 1900." *Phillips County News,* March 22, 1962.

Day-Fuller, Joyce. "The Outlaws" Information collected from J. Herold Day, Buffalo, Wyoming, n.d.

Dullenty, Jim. "Central Montana: Breeding Ground of a Badman." *Lewistown-Argus,* December 3, 2003.

———. "He Saw 'Kid Curry' Rob Great Northern Train." *NOLA Quarterly* (ca. 1986).

———. "Just Found in Montana—Kid Curry's Long Lost Knoxville Manuscript." *WOLA Journal* (Spring 1994).

———. "Where Is 'Kid Curry'?" *WOLA Journal* (Fall/Winter 1995).

Dullenty, Jim, et al. "New Gold Rush in the Little Rockies." *True West,* March 1984.

Duvall, C. W. "Milk River Bill Harmon, Seventy-Five." *Great Falls Tribune,* November 17, 1935.

Dworkin, Mark. "Charlie Siringo, Letter Writer." *WOLA Journal* (Winter 2003).

Ernst, Donna B. "The Parachute Train Robbery." *Old West,* Winter 1996.

———. "Powder Springs, Outlaw Hideout." *True West,* May 1997.

———. "Secret Link with the Wild Bunch: The Dunbar Brothers of [Little Snake River Valley]." *WOLA Journal* (Fall/Winter 1996).

———. "The Sundance Kid My Uncle; Researching the Memories of [Little Snake River Valley] Residents." *Frontier Magazine,* August 1997.

———. "Unraveling Two Outlaws Named Carver." *WOLA Journal* (Fall/Winter 1997).

Flanagan, Mike. "Out West: Denver's Bawdy Holladay Street." *Denver Post Magazine,* July 27, 1986.

Fletcher, Bob. "Smoke Signals." *Montana Magazine of Western History* (April 1952).

Fowler, Gene. "There's Something in the Water." *Texas Highways,* February 1998.

Gibson, Robert. "They Know What Happened to Landusky, but Curry?" *Great Falls Tribune,* September 18, 1974.

Gorton, Michael. "Old Photos May Help Document 'Wild Bunch.'" *Livingston Enterprise,* March 24, 1992.

Graetz, Rick. "Little Rockies Country Epitomizes Wild West." *Great Falls Tribune,* December 30, 1999.

Headly, James. "Crime in Johnson County's Early Days." *Buffalo Bulletin,* July 28, 2005. Heritage edition.

Horan, James. "The Pinkertons on the Western Frontier: 1866–1911." *New York Posse Brand Book,* no. 1 (196).

Johnson, Dorothy M. "Durable Desperado Kid Curry." *Montana the Magazine of Western History* (April 1956).

Kaycee [WY] Area Chamber of Commerce. "The History of Kaycee."

Kaycee [WY] Area Chamber of Commerce and Buffalo Area Chamber of Commerce. "Buffalo and Kaycee Visitors Guide." n.d.

Kindred, Wayne. "Harvey Logan's Secret Papers." *True West,* October 1994.

———. "The Hunt for the Great Northern Train Robbers." *NOLA Quarterly* (January–March 2000).

———. "The Logan, Houk and Thornhill Letters." *WOLA Journal* (Fall 2002).

———. "The Missing Months of Harvey Logan." The Trials and Travels of Annie Rogers. *Old West* (Winter 1995).

———. "The Wilcox Train Robbery: Who Did It?" *WOLA Journal* (Spring 1999).

Logan, Bruce E. "Kid Curry, aka Harvey Logan." Free pages.genealogy .rootsweb.com/~blogan/logan3.html.

Miller, James O. "Did Butch Cassidy Plan the Wilcox Train Robbery?" n.d.

Miller, Robert. "Kid Curry, Montana Outlaw." *Montana Magazine,* Spring 1976.

Montana Album. "100 Years Ago." *Great Falls Tribune,* October 8, 2006.

———. "Retired Railway Employees Recall Curry Robbery." *Great Falls Tribune,* November 7, 1948.

Montana Parade. "Where Was Loney at the Time of Train Robbery?" *Great Falls Tribune,* November 17, 1958.

Nash, Nathanial. "Bottom Falls Out in Argentines Patagonia." *Sunday* [Portland] *Oregonian,* March 27, 1994.

North, Dick. "When the Tiger of the Wild Bunch Broke out of the Knoxville Jail." *True West,* September 1975.

Ritch, John. "Landusky-Little Rockies articles." *Great Falls Tribune,* January 20, 1935; June 21, 1936; June 28, 1936.

———. "Two Gun Gunners of the Ranges Were Real: He-Men of the Golden West." *Miles City Star,* May 24, 1934. Golden Jubilee issue.

Robinson, Gladys. "How Pike Landusky Was Killed by Kid Curry: Interviewing Tom Carter, Pioneer Little Rockies Miner." *Great Falls Tribune,* n.d.

Sheppard, Richard. "Kid Curry Captured in Tennessee" *Susquehanna Times/Magazine,* August 1998.

Smith, Helena H. "The Truth about the Hole-in-the-Wall Fight." *Montana: The Magazine of Western History* (Summer 1961).

Todd Jr, Earl. "My Uncle George Currie." *WOLA Journal* (Fall/Winter 1997).

Wilmet, Paul. "Mint [Saloon] Collection Coming to the Museum." *Great Falls Tribune,* May 14, 1989.

Wright, Alice. "Grand Valley, 1904, a Time of Outlaws, Robbery and Posses." *Daily Grand Junction Sentinel,* July 17, 1969.

Young, Edgar. "The End of Harvey Logan." *Frontier Times,* June 1927.

Gary A. Wilson's previous books are *Honky-Tonk Town: Havre, Montana's Lawless Era*, *"Long George" Francis: Gentleman Outlaw of Montana*, and *Outlaw Tales of Montana*. Biographer, historian, and publisher, Wilson has been researching the history of northern Montana and the American West since 1978. He is a founding board member of the Fort Assiniboine Preservation Association, and he is active in several local tourist and historical organizations. He lives in Havre, Montana.